£15-00

A. Caerfily   F. Ogmore
B. Cardif   G. New Castle
C. Lantriſſent   H. Neath
D. Deniſpowys   I. Llangevel
E. Cowbridge   K. Swanzey

OF BREKNOC

PART OF

MON-

MOUTH

SH:

Reſoulau

Marteria uil

Aberdare

CapGladis

Glyncorug

Eſtrydiwodak

A

Llunayneware

Lavabor

Bettus Cha

Llandouödok

C

Eglyſſylia n

Rocheſton

G

Peterſton

Caerfily

Clothyc

Lanyltidvan dray

Coche

Liſwat ne

foage

Pentearche

Bridgend

Treer

Meneche

F

Tallavant

B

Cathgarne

E

Landaf

Ogmore

Cadif

Cowbridge

Lauguian

Wyke

Lanyhangle

St Donetes

Little Nash

Lancawan

D

S. Andros

Pennarth

Llanmaie s

anveroch

ſhe F

Syly

Sylye I.

Aberthawes

Porkery

Barrye I.

Miles

1 2 3 4 5

GLAMORGAN HISTORIAN

STEWART WILLIAMS'

Glamorgan Historian

VOLUME SIX

●

COWBRIDGE - GLAMORGAN

D. BROWN AND SONS LIMITED

©

Printed in Wales by

D. BROWN AND SONS LIMITED
COWBRIDGE – GLAMORGAN
1969

INTRODUCTION

THE Investiture of H.R.H. The Prince of Wales is only of indirect interest to GLAMORGAN HISTORIAN, but as this historic occasion has been celebrated in various ways throughout the Principality I felt that a special volume, containing a larger selection than usual of plates as well as more pages of text, would not be inappropriate. The most noticeable indulgence has been the section of beautiful colour plates which, as Elis Jenkins has so rightly observed, adds distinction to the whole volume. Their publication has been made possible through the kindness of Mr. W. D. John of Newport, the celebrated authority on ceramics, who generously placed his large collection of colour blocks at my disposal.

As always, I am very grateful to the contributors and especially this time to Mr. J. B. Hilling whose lengthy and expert survey of the buildings of Cardiff must qualify for a special word of praise. I am also most appreciative of Mrs. E. Williams's kindness in offering to me her translation of the two articles which her late husband, Emeritus Professor G. J. Williams, wrote on "Wil Hopcyn and the Maid of Cefn Ydfa". By her work Mrs. Williams has given everybody an opportunity to learn the truth about the origin and development of one of Glamorgan's most popular and romantic stories. Circumstances have again prevented the publication of the articles on "Rural Rhondda" and "David Jones of Wallington", promised last time, but readers can be assured that they will definitely appear in the next volume.

Once again I am immensely grateful to my friend Mr. T. J. Hopkins, Archivist at Cardiff Central Library. He has edited Mrs. Williams's translation, and during all stages of production his guidance and knowledge have proved of inestimable value. The index is the work of another good friend, Mr. Roy Denning, to whom I extend my thanks.

The standard of production is testimony, if any be required, to the printing skill of D. Brown and Sons, Ltd. To them, and also to Cardiff Photo Engravers for great care in block making and Peter Tremewan for the excellent binding, I offer my thanks.

Finally, for allowing me to use their illustrations, I wish to thank the British Museum, National Coal Board, National Museum of Wales, Welsh School of Architecture, Royal Institution of South Wales, Glamorgan Record Office, Cardiff Public Libraries, Port Talbot Historical Society, South Wales Transport Co. Ltd., Sir David and Lady Evans Bevan, V. I. Hartshorn, T. Herridge, Elis Jenkins and Haydn Morris.

1 Crossfield Road,   STEWART WILLIAMS
Barry

CONTENTS

THE END-PAPERS *bear a reproduction of John Seller's map of Glamorgan. It is one of a series of uncoloured reprints included in his atlas* Camden's Britannia abridged *(1701), and although it has little cartographical merit, it is of interest as being one of the smallest maps of the county ever published. The original measures* $5\frac{5}{8}$ x $4\frac{1}{4}$.

In the first edition of Seller's atlas, which was published under the title Anglia Contracta *in 1697, the maps appeared in colour.*

Before the end of the eighteenth century uncoloured reprints of them were used once again to illustrate the new edition of Francis Grose's Antiquities of England and Wales, *1783-1787.*

Map reproduced by permission of Cardiff Public Libraries

ILLUSTRATIONS

Notes on New Contributors

DAVID J. FRANCIS was born in the parish of Llansannor. He was educated at Cowbridge Grammar School and University College of Wales, Aberystwyth, where he graduated with honours in Philosophy. He now teaches at Llanharry. Studying the history of the parishes of the Border Vale has long been one of his hobbies, and he hopes to complete a volume on this part of Glamorgan in the not too distant future.

J. B. HILLING, an architect and town planner, was born in Abertyswg and educated at Tredegar County Grammar School, the Welsh School of Architecture, Cardiff, and the Regent Street Polytechnic, London. After working in London, Caernarvon and Edinburgh he returned to Cardiff in 1964. He has published numerous articles on planning in Wales and Welsh buildings and is at present engaged on writing an architectural history of Wales.

PETER STEAD was born at Barry in 1943. He was educated at Barry and Gowerton Grammar Schools, and then at the University College of Swansea where he graduated with First Class Honours in History in 1964. He is now a Lecturer in Social History at Swansea, and also a Tutor in a Hall of Residence. His main research interest is the Rise of Labour in South Wales and the Nature of South Wales Society in the early twentieth century. Since 1968 he has been honorary secretary of the Glamorgan History Society.

HILARY M. THOMAS was born in Cardiff and educated at Bridgend Girls' Grammar School, and the Lewis School, Hengoed. Graduated at the University of London in 1962; then studied at Liverpool University to obtain a post-graduate Diploma in Archive Administration. She joined the staff of the Glamorgan Record Office as an assistant archivist in 1963.

W. GERWYN THOMAS is Assistant Keeper of the Department of Industry at the National Musuem of Wales. He was educated at the Amman Valley Grammar School and University College, Cardiff, where he obtained a B.Sc. degree in Mining Engineering. He is a Member of the Institute of Mining Engineers, a Chartered Engineer and an Associate Member of the British Institute of Management. From 1952-63 he lectured in mining at Birmingham University and was awarded a Ph.D. for his research on the incendivity of frictional sparks. Since his return to Wales he has been actively engaged in research into Welsh industrial history.

MARGAM ESTATE MANAGEMENT, 1765-1860

by

HILARY M. THOMAS, B.A.

IN October 1765, Hopkin Llewellyn of Brombil, Margam, son of Llewellyn Evan of Ystradyfodwg, offered his services as agent to the Margam estate[1] for a salary of £100 a year plus an allowance of £20 a year for a writing clerk. The offer was accepted, and so began an association between the Llewellyn family and the Margam estate that was to span three generations and more than a century. In fact the association was already established, as by way of a testimonial Hopkin Llewellyn referred to his eight years experience of the estate office and book-keeping, and to seven years subsequent service "of the active part in the character of an assistant", under David Rees the previous estate agent.

Such experience was an invaluable recommendation, for although land stewardship was a recognised profession by the late eighteenth century, there existed no established system of training other than an apprenticeship in an estate office. Hopkin Llewellyn's apprenticeship had been more than usually thorough. The long illness of David Rees had meant that the effective management of the Margam estate had been in his assistant's hands for almost seven years, and Hopkin's formal appointment in 1765 ensured a valuable continuity of management to an estate whose affairs were under the control of trustees. The Reverend Thomas Talbot who had inherited the Margam estate on the death of Bussy Lord Mansel in 1750, had died in 1758. His son, Thomas Mansel Talbot, would not attain his majority until 1768. The Margam estate agent who formally assumed the duties and responsibilities of management in 1765, would find himself and his activities closely scrutinised by trustees who would soon be called upon to answer for their own period of stewardship.

---

[1] Throughout this article the term "Margam estate" has been used to denote the combined Margam and Penrice estate of the Mansel Talbot family.

Hopkin Llewellyn served the Margam estate for over thirty years, being well over eighty years of age when he finally relinquished the agency in 1798. His eldest son, Hopkin Llewellyn junior, a lawyer by profession, was for several years before his death in 1797 associated with his father in the management of the estate, and it was his younger son, Griffith, also a lawyer, who was appointed to the stewardship in 1798. By a formal Deed of Appointment drawn up in July of that year Griffith Llewellyn was made steward[2] and receiver of all Thomas Mansel Talbot's Glamorgan estates, constable of Kenfig castle, and steward and court keeper of the manors. The salary for discharging these duties was fixed at £230 a year.

Lawyers were much in demand as estate agents, and when an agent had the dual qualifications of a legal training and a particular knowledge of the estate's management handed on from his father, his value to the landowner could be immense. Entries in Griffith Llewellyn's day book show him travelling from Margam to Penrice and Pyle to take instructions from Thomas Mansel Talbot, and drawing up legal instruments in matters ranging from family settlements to disputes between the Margam estate and the English Copper Company. With the increasing industrial activity in the county during the nineteenth century the next generation of estate agents were to find their legal qualifications of particular value in the effective discharge of their duties.

After Griffith Llewellyn's death in 1822 his family's connection with the Margam estate continued. Three of his sons, Thomas John, Griffith, and William, managed the estate between 1822 and 1858 for salaries ranging from £400 to £600 a year. When Griffith Llewellyn recommended his brother William to succeed him as agent in 1840 he did so "both because it would be truly painful to me to see a connexion which has so long, and I must add so agreeably, existed on the part of my family, at once severed, and because I think he's fully competent to manage your affairs". In 1857, when ill health forced William Llewellyn to resign the agency, it was his cousin William of Court Colman who was appointed to succeed him. Only with the latter's resignation in 1887 was the Llewellyn family's connection with the Margam estate office broken.

[2] The terms "steward" and "agent" were both current in the late eighteenth century, with the latter term gradually coming into general use. Hopkin Llewellyn and his successors as managers of the Margam estate usually adopted the style of "agent".

What were the duties that occupied these estate agents and how did they discharge them?

First and foremost the agent was responsible for maintaining the estate as a viable financial and economic unit. He was charged with the collection of tenants' rents, the supervision of tenancies to ensure that terms of leases were observed and farms maintained in reasonable repair, and with the oversight of all items of estate expenditure.

Each year at Ladyday the agent had to render a detailed financial statement to the landowner. On the Margam estate the annual account book was written up in the office by the clerk, with all items of income and expenditure grouped systematically under appropriate headings. The whole account was arranged on the traditional "Charge and Discharge" basis, whereby the agent was made the estate's "debtor" for all incomings and its "creditor" for all items of expenditure and for new or continued rent arrears. This double entry system of accounting was adhered to on the Margam estate until the 1840's. First came the rental, arranged by parishes and lordships, giving details of tenants' rents and arrears, and of any abatements allowed the tenants in years of economic distress. Then followed the statement of estate expenditure where, under such headings as Buildings and Repairs, Gardens and Plantations, Walling and Fencing, Salaries and Wages, Rates and Taxes, the agent accounted for his disbursements during the year. This arrangement of the account book was both traditional and functional. When books with a printed format were in use on the Margam estate Griffith Llewellyn complained to the printers that "the rent roll . . . is placed at the latter end instead of at the beginning of the book, which is nothing less than putting the cart before the horse, the receipts of the rent roll being the foundation of the account". He was also to observe, however, in another context, that the payments which he and his brothers as agents had to make for the estate required nearly as much attention and as much if not more anxiety than the receipts for which they were responsible.

A great landlord has been described[3] as the owner of estates producing at least £5,000-£6,000 a year by the end of the eighteenth century. In 1767 Hopkin Llewellyn was charged with the collection of rents in excess of £4,835; by the end of his period of stewardship rent increases had contributed to raising this total to over £7,800.

[3] G. E. Mingay, *English Landed Society in the Eighteenth Century* (1963).

In 1800 the Margam estate gross rental stood at over £8,000, and further rent increases, together with the increased industrial exploitation of the estate, had brought this total to almost £15,000 by 1820, and to almost £24,000 by the mid nineteenth century. The collection of these sums from an estate of more than 30,000 acres[4] meant that the agents had to keep not only detailed accounts but also accurate and up to date rent rolls recording the length and terms of tenants' leases.

Effective estate management involved much more than the appointing of receiving days for rent collections and the compilation of statements of rents received and arrears owing. Most great landowners and their agents adhered to the principles that a stable tenantry was beneficial to the estate, that rent arrears were preferable to the inconvenience and expense of untenanted farms, that temporary concessions to tenants in times of economic distress were better than permanent rent reductions. David Rees had expressed such views in his correspondence with the Reverend John Talbot in the 1750's and Hopkin Llewellyn and his successors followed the same general principles.

The practice of giving tenants six months grace in which to pay their rents was introduced by Thomas Mansel Talbot (1747-1813) who was an informed agriculturalist and a founder member of the Glamorganshire Agricultural Society. This period of grace enabled the tenants to sell their stock when market and fair prices were most favourable, and worked to the benefit of landlord and tenant alike. Further, the rigid half yearly or yearly accounting days appointed on many estates for rent collections were, on the Margam estate, replaced by a more flexible system whereby rents were secured monthly. The evidence of the rentals suggests that it was not only economic necessity in periods of agricultural depression that motivated the agents to allow rent arrears to run on, but an understanding of the value to the estate of a contented and stable tenantry. In 1826, when farm prices were low and tenants found difficulty in paying their rents, C. R. M. Talbot evidently suggested some revision of the system of rent collection on his estate. His agent, Griffith Llewellyn, pressed for the retention of the old system, observing that the introduction of regular half yearly receiving days would only add to the tenants' burdens.

---

[4] The "Return of owners of land, 1873" estimated C. R. M. Talbot's Glamorgan estate at 34,033 acres.

Clearly the agents exercised considerable discretion in allowing rent arrears to run on after the six months period of grace had expired, as is evident from observations made by Griffith Llewellyn to Talbot in December 1826. "Certain it is that some of the tenants take ten or twelve months to pay their rents, but we do not permit it where we think they are in circumstances to pay sooner. . . . We can if you please enforce more strictly the payment of the rents at the expiration of the six months, but we must remember that every distress occasions the ruin of a family".

The agricultural depressions of the 1820's and 1830's allowed few opportunities for rent increases. The Select Committee on the State of Agriculture reported in 1833 that landlords in every part of the United Kingdom had met the fall in prices by rent reductions. On the Margam estate rent abatements rather than outright rent reductions were favoured, and were granted from 1817 onwards. While the agents acknowledged that their accounts would be greatly simplified by a permanent rent reduction of 25% they recommended that no alteration should be made in the rents, pointing out with creditable foresight that once rents were reduced they might not be so easily raised again. When in 1837 an allowance of approximately 25% was made to most of the estate's tenants it took the form of an abatement, not an outright rent reduction.

Revisions in the terms of tenancy were rarely introduced during the lifetime of the established tenant, but changes of tenants could provide opportunities to modify terms of occupation, specify cultivation, and review rents. In 1836 Griffith Llewellyn expressed the view that C. R. M. Talbot's farms were let, generally speaking, too low, and that when tenants had changed he had gone over the properties himself to assess the possibilities of rent revisions. Landlord and agent would be particularly concerned to raise the rents of properties in which the estate had invested capital for improvements, and some of the more striking rent increases that appear in the rentals between 1800 and 1820 represent an attempt to obtain a return from investment in new and improved farm buildings. To take but two examples: the rent of Eglwys Nunydd was raised from £28 0s. 6d. to £130 a year when William Powell became the new tenant in 1818,[5]

[5] The total annual rent paid by William Powell for Eglwys Nunydd was £160, but this included £30 for additional lands in West Margam held conjointly with Eglwys Nunydd.

that of Aberbaiden from £50 to £105 before Mathew Lewis took over the tenancy in 1813. These were farms of over 400 and 200 acres respectively, but whatever the size of tenancy landlord and agent would be likely to consider the revision of terms whenever possible. The fact that for any year the rental shows few "Tenements in Hand" is evidence that the estate was successful in attracting tenants with the necessary working capital.

As a general rule on the Margam estate the tenants were responsible for repairing and maintaining their property, except in cases of accident or antiquity of building, while major improvements were financed by the estate. But in terms of practical estate management no such hard and fast rules could be followed. In 1834 Griffith Llewellyn pointed out that there were so many old and dilapidated buildings on the estate that the tenants could not be expected to repair them, but he added that those tenants who were able to do so spent considerable sums in improvements each year. The estate agent was expected to superintend repairs, and to make the necessary arrangements for the provision of materials and the recruitment of labour. In 1832 Griffith Llewellyn had anticipated that he would be relieved of some of his duties by the appointment of one William Jenkins to superintend repairs, but had been disappointed to learn of C. R. M. Talbot's disapproval of the scheme. In a letter to Talbot, that same year, the hard worked Margam agent wrote with feeling that "the receipt of the rents, the management of the accounts, and the general superintendence of the estate are ample business for your Agent and a Clerk . . . there is scarcely an hour of the day that business of yours does not come before us".

The general superintendence of the estate involved the agents in an infinite variety of duties, and called not only for many broad based interests and a wide general knowledge beyond professional legal and administrative expertise, but also for a robust constitution to cope with the many hours on horseback that such a general superintendence demanded. Requirements of comfort as much as fashion must have prompted a letter to a London saddler requesting him to pay particular attention to the shape and design of a saddle ordered by Griffith Llewellyn.

As they rode about the Margam estate the Llewellyns would have been familiar and respected figures to the bailiffs and woodwards, gamekeepers and park-keepers, and other estate employees. It was the agents' responsibility to ensure that such officials carried out their instructions and discharged their duties honestly and efficiently.   To the local bailiffs the agents delegated much responsibility for the collection of rents and the organising of receiving days, with the Penrice bailiff assuming particular importance in the scheme of management.   The formal division of the Margam estate into two distinct areas of stewardship did not occur until 1857 when William Llewellyn of Court Colman was appointed agent for Margam and the former estate clerk, John Felton, was given charge of Gower, but this division of authority had been anticipated in the 1820's.

After the building of a new house at Penrice in the 1770's and the demolition of the old house at Margam, Penrice became the Glamorgan seat of the Mansel Talbot family.   As the estate office continued to function from Margam, Hopkin Llewellyn and his son Griffith must have spent many hours travelling between Margam and Penrice to consult Thomas Mansel Talbot and Sir Christopher Cole[6] on matters affecting the estate, and to deal with local officials and tenants.   Although rent collections were arranged by the local bailiff, they were regularly supervised by the agents who were responsible for the compilation of the Margam and Penrice rentals.

Between 1826 and 1841 James George, the Gower bailiff, presented a separate annual rental and kept a general account for the Penrice section of the estate, while the annual statements of account compiled by the Llewellyns in those years related to Margam only. This development must have been precipitated both by C. R. M. Talbot's plans to build a new mansion house at Margam, plans that would entail much extra work for the Margam agency, and by the increased attention that the agents were having to pay to the industrial development of the estate.

It seems a logical and sensible decision to have transferred the oversight of a predominantly agricultural section of the estate to a well tried local bailiff, thus leaving the agents with more time to deal with the complexities of the Margam area of management.   James George remained in the position of a subordinate official.   He received payments from the Margam office to meet his financial obligations as local manager, and sent the collected rents, amounting to approximately £3,000 a year, by his son Thomas to the Llewellyns.

[6] Thomas Mansel Talbot died in 1813.   His widow, Lady Mary Talbot, married Sir Christopher Cole in 1815.

It is worth noting that during these years the Margam agents had their salaries reduced from £500 to £400 a year, presumably because the Gower portion of the estate was removed from their immediate charge.

James George was also responsible for the management of the home farm at Penrice, a task that was often given by a landlord to a locally resident estate agent.   He arranged for the sale of farm produce, supervised and paid the workmen and labourers on the farm and demesne, and provided the castle with produce.   In 1826 he valued the provisions supplied to the castle at over £420 by then current market prices.

His list included:

Sundries delivered for Sir Christopher Cole, 1825/6	Value at Market price
	£ s. d.
2453 lbs of Mutton	90 16 3½
378 lbs of Lamb	10 13 11
1003 lbs of Bacon	25 1 6
1140 lbs of Pork	28 10 0
13 roasting Pigs	3 6 0
44½ cwt of Potatoes	11 11 6
The produce of 9 Cows	60 0 0

The management of the Penrice home farm remained with James George and his son into the 1860's and beyond, long after Penrice had been supplanted by Margam as the principal residence of the Talbot family.   James George continued to compile and submit a separate Gower rental until 1842 when, following the appointment of William Llewellyn to the agency, the compilation of one composite rental was again introduced.

The maintenance and improvement of the landlord's parks and gardens, woods and plantations, was an important part of any agent's responsibilities.   Hopkin Llewellyn, in the 1770's and 1780's, would have relied as much on the capabilities of such men as George Bartlett and John Snook, gardeners at Penrice and Margam respectively, John Loveluck, gamekeeper at Margam, James George, gamekeeper at Penrice, Daniel Button, bailiff and woodward in Gower, and Thomas Cox, park-keeper at Margam, as would his son Griffith on those officials whose names and salaries are listed below:

Officials in 1818	*Yearly Salaries*
Isaac Stubbs, park-keeper and gamekeeper at Margam	£42
David Richard, bailiff and woodward at Margam	£20
James George, bailiff and gamekeeper in Gower	£40
John Snook, gardener at Margam	£42
William Gwyn, woodward at Llandough	£5

Many of these offices passed from father to son, further emphasising the continuity in the estate's management at all levels. To cite but two examples: Isaac and George Stubbs, father and son, acted as gamekeepers at Margam, while James George and his son Thomas both served as bailiffs in Gower. Each of these officials would be responsible for the various assistants employed under him, and would receive regular payments from the estate office for their wages.

The day to day administration of the estate involved the agents in almost constant dealings with estate officials and tenants.

Every year arrangements had to be made for the sale of bark and timber from the estate. Before stripping and felling took place the steward would perambulate the woods with the local woodward to mark those trees which were mature and would sell well at timber auctions. Back in the estate office he would prepare sale notices for insertion in *The Cambrian* and other newspapers.

Seldom a year passed without work having to be done on the sea wall at Aberavon and on the ditches and banks on Margam moors. In the summer of 1771 Hopkin Llewellyn rode down to Aberavon on numerous occasions to superintend the masons, labourers and carpenters who were working on the new arch and floodgates in the sea wall. Expenditure on this work was a constant and major item in the estate accounts throughout the 1770's and 1780's. It remained so well into the nineteenth century with payments recorded by the agents for such projects as the straightening of the Ffrwdwyllt river, the raising of keys and making of culverts on Margam moors.

Thomas Mansel Talbot gave personal impetus and direction to improvements in agricultural methods on his estate. Drainage and reclamation schemes were effected on low-lying land around Margam and Penrice, tenants were urged to adopt better techniques of husbandry, farm buildings were enlarged and improved at the estate's expense.

One of the recommendations of John Fox in his report to the Board of Agriculture in 1796 had been the enlargement of barns and the more frequent introduction of ox stalls as an aid to progressive farming. The Margam accounts of the late eighteenth and early nineteenth century contain many references to such improvements. A new ox stall and yard was built at Tir Pullard in 1771, a new ox stall and shed at Brombil between 1788 and 1790, while in 1849 and 1850 the Glamorganshire Agricultural Society's premium for the best fat ox was awarded to a Margam tenant, William Powell of Eglwys Nunydd. New outbuildings were constructed at Aberbaiden in 1816, Kenfig farm was provided with a new beast house in the same year. The numbers of "new erected cottages" that appear in the rentals of the 1830's and 1840's, particularly in Gower, indicate that the policy of improvement was not confined either to outbuildings or to large farms on the estate.

Often the demesne lands could be improved and cultivated more effectively. Here the agent could exercise a constant supervision and acquire technical knowledge that might be passed on to those tenants with sufficient capital and land to implement improved techniques. In 1827 Griffith Llewellyn was able to write to C. R. M. Talbot that the park at Margam was greatly improved in appearance as a result of the area recently drained having been planted with wheat, barley and oats "which are most promising crops". He was also able to report that the lawn had been marled and enclosed and the deer excluded from it. A particular incentive to agricultural improvement was offered to the Margam estate and its agricultual tenants by the proximity of an expanding industrial population associated with the local iron, copper and tinplate works.

If industrial activity on the estate stimulated agricultural production it also brought with it the problem of deforestation. From the early eighteenth century onwards a policy of large-scale planting of seeds and saplings and the protection of the plantations had done much to ensure the continuance of a well wooded estate. Walling and fencing costs on the estate in 1816 for example amounted to £151 18s. 0d.; they included payments for building a wall fence around Cwm Kenfig wood, rebuilding parts of a wall fence around an intended plantation at Cwm Maelwg, and planting trees in these and other plantations. Continued large-scale planting was urged by Thomas John and Griffith Llewellyn in the 1820's to furnish a ready supply for the Copper Company whose demands for timber were constantly increasing. By 1840 Griffith Llewellyn was reporting to C. R. M. Talbot that Glanafon wood was suffering great damage from the copper smoke, with the leaves on the trees turning brown and falling.   In the same year 12,000 spruce fir trees had been ordered for the game preserves, 13,000 scotch firs for the plantations, and large numbers of seedling larch, spruce, sycamore, ash, and white-thorn for the Margam gardens and parks.

Organisation of men and materials on the estate was an essential part of any estate agent's charge, and it was by no means unusual for a land steward to be expected to assume the additional duties of a house steward, especially when the landowner was away from home. During the long absences of Thomas Mansel Talbot and his son from Margam and Penrice their agents often exercised a close supervision of the household.   In the 1830's Griffith Llewellyn instructed the Margam servants that they were to accept no presents from visitors; when any item was required for the house they were to write it on a slip of paper and send it to him for directions.   In 1838 he investigated a complaint of misconduct against one of the Margam housemaids, found her unfit through drunkenness to carry on her duties, and dismissed her.   But Griffith Llewellyn evidently regarded such an intimate oversight of the household as no part of his normal duties, for in a letter to Talbot justifying his dismissal of the housemaid he acknowledged that he had no reason to interfere with the domestic arrangements except when requested to do so.   He did however make regular inspections of the house, stables and outbuildings, to check on the fabric of the buildings and the activities of the servants employed there.   After such inspections detailed reports often containing suggestions for the more efficient running of the establishment, were sent to Talbot.   In addition to paying wages to both estate and household servants, the agents also attended to such matters as the ordering of suits of livery for butlers, coachmen, and other household retainers, and the purchase of guns for gamekeepers and park-keepers.

Such minutiae of detail it should be remembered were attended to by men who, apart from their concern with the broad problems of estate management, were practicing lawyers, active Justices of the Peace, and considerable landowners in their own right.[7]   When in

[7] The *Return of owners of land, 1873* estimated Griffith Llewellyn of Baglan Hall's estate at over 2,846 acres with an annual rental of £2,280.

addition to the day to day routine of estate administration the agent had to assume responsibility for the oversight of extraordinary and large-scale projects on the estate his office must often have stretched his energies and capabilities to their limits.

Between 1770 and 1800 Thomas Mansel Talbot initiated schemes on his estate that included the building of a new mansion house at Penrice, an orangery and summer-house at Margam, a coaching inn at Pyle, and also encompassed the demolition of the old house at Margam.

The building of Penrice castle in the 1770's involved Hopkin Llewellyn in the oversight of a large and costly enterprise. Arrangements had to be made for the recruitment of labour from a wide area, as a whole army of labourers, masons, carpenters, blacksmiths and others would be needed. Supplies of materials had to be found and arrangements made for their transport to the site. Bricks from Bridgwater, bathstone and freestone from Bristol, alabaster from Penarth, were shipped to Oxwich and hauled from the beach to the house. Limestone, freestone, bricks and timber, provided from the estate or purchased locally, were hauled by teams of draft horses to Penrice. While David Hay, James Murray and Daniel Button supervised the labourers and workmen, and acted as clerks of works on the site, Anthony Keck the architect, and William Gubbings the master mason, directed the building operations. But much of the administrative and financial responsibility for the smooth running of the operations rested with the estate agent, and Hopkin Llewellyn evidently spent much time at Penrice checking on the progress of the work.

Similarly in the 1830's Griffith Llewellyn and his brother Thomas John found the duties of their stewardship increased by C. R. M. Talbot's plans for a new house at Margam. In 1828 the parish road from Llangynwyd to Taibach had been diverted to avoid running through Margam Park; once this project neared completion the estate agents turned their attention to arrangements for the new house. Early in 1829 they were asking Talbot for instructions— should they procure limestone for mortar, was stone to be raised and timber seasoned, should the Park be drained? Griffith Llewellyn investigated the practicability and expense of making bricks and procuring sand locally, and when work began on the house large quantities of bricks were supplied from a new kiln at Margam.

A Rent Roll of *Margam Estate* belonging to *Christopher Rice Mansel Talbot Esquire* in the several Parishes, Lordships & Divisions hereunder mentioned in the County of *Glamorgan*, Containing first a State of the *Arrears of Rent* which were returned by *Thomas John Llewellyn* and *Griffith Llewellyn* in their last *Account* with the said *Chr Rice Mansel Talbot* to be standing out the 24th day of *March 1831*. And also of the Amount of the *Year's Rent* of the said *Estate* ending at *Michaelmas 1831*. Together with the *Gross Amount of Cash* paid to the said *Thomas John Llewellyn & Griffith Llewellyn* on Account thereof And also of the Amount of so much of the said *Rent & Arrears* as were standing out in the Tenants hands the 24th day of *March 1832*, And also so much thereof as as were looked upon as *Irrecoverable & Lost*. Together with the Amount of *Temporary Abatements* in consequence of the depreciation of Farm produce made to the Tenants by Order of *Mr Talbot*:—

Parishes Lordships Divisions and Tenements Names	No	Tenants Names	Arr of Rent standing out 24th March 1831	The Years Rent ending at Michas 1831	Gross Payments to TJ&G Llewellyn	Art of Rent standing out 24th March 1832	Art of Rent found 24th March 1832 Irrecoverable	Abatement made the Tenants
Aberavon								
Baily Castell, Main faw & Cae Cnoddock	1	Mrs C. Llewellyn		9	9			
Part of late Edwd Pulleuns & 2 Crofts	2	Ditto		7 10	7 10			
Part late ditto & Caiar Merfa	3	Rice Powell	4 10	9	9	4 10		2 5
A Mess & Tenement	4	Thos Richard	20 5	13 10	27	6 15		
A House & Garden	5	Messr R. Smith & Co	8 4	5	2 18 4	2 10		
A Smith Shop	6	John Jones	10		10	1		
Ter of Sandy	7	Rees David	10 10	7	14	3 10		4 7
A Meadow & Croft lot pl No 5	8	Ditto	2 7 6	1 15	3 5		17 6	
A Dwelling House	9	Jenkin Joseph	1 4	2 8	2 8	1 4		
£			39 14 10	55 13	76 1 4	19 6 6		6 12
Bettws								
Cefn y Gelly farm	1	Richd Bradford Esqr	12 10	25	25	12 10		

Baglan Hall

By permission of Port Talbot Historical Society

Llewellyn family residences

Court Colman

Margam Castle

Photograph by Elis Jenkins

By permission of Sir David and Lady Evans Bevan

Mansel Talbot family residences

Penrice Castle

By permission of Western Mail

Per Contra _____ Creditor.

By the Amount of Cash paid for Interest & Allowance Money from the 24th day
of March 1799. exclusive to the 24th day of March 1800 inclusive as appears
51 in folio that the Margent refers to _____ 1055 __ 10

52 By ditto for Annuities paid from Ditto to Ditto as appears in folio p Margent _____ 125 14 10

By ditto for the separate and particular Use of Thomas Mansel Talbot Esquire from
54 ditto to ditto as appears in Folio p ditto _____ 6260 4

55 By ditto for Salaries & Wages from ditto to ditto as appears in Folio p ditto _____ 406 3 6

By ditto for Rates Taxes and Chief Rents from ditto to ditto as appears
57 in Folio p ditto _____ 395 0 6

58 By ditto for Walling and Fencing from ditto to ditto as appears in Folio p ditto _____ 149 13 6½

59 By ditto for Buildings & Repairs from ditto to ditto as appears in Folio p ditto _____ 9 4 8

By ditto for Casual and Promiscuous Disbursements from ditto to
71 ditto as appears in Folio p ditto _____ 691 12 4½

By ditto on Account of the Lanridian Colliery from ditto to ditto
72 as appears in Folio p ditto _____ 550

By the Amount of the Arrears of Rent and Cash Money p Contra
which became due at Michaelmas 1799 and standing in the Tenants Hands
39 the 24th day of March 1800 as by the Total thereof appears in Folio p ditto _____ 3089 13

By Ditto of the Arrears of Rent standing out the 24th day of March 1799
Irrecoverable and Lost in the preceding Year for the reasons stated in fo. 77. as
39 by the Total thereof appears in fo. p Margent _____ 159 6 1¾

By Balance due from the said Accomptant _____ 185 3 9½

£13077 5 2¼

2d October 1800
Then settled and allowed the above Accompt and agreed that the Sum
of One Hundred and Eighty five pounds three Shillings and nine pence
halfpenny, being the Balance thereof due to the said Thomas Mansel
Talbot shall be carried to the Accomptants Account for the year ending
the 24th day of March 1801 And the Vouchers to the Closing of this
Accompt to the 24th day of March 1800 inclusive were delivered to the
said Thomas Mansel Talbot.

Thos. Mansel Talbot

Griff. Llewellyn

Margam Estate summary account, 1799-1800   By permission of Glamorgan Record Office

The agents were charged with the general oversight of the building schemes while the Margam bailiff, David Richard, who assumed the immediate duties of clerk of works, received regular sums of money from the estate office to pay the labourers.   The masons and other craftsmen were paid directly by the agents.   Between 1830 and 1832 the accounts record payments of almost £8,000 for wages, materials, and freight and haulage charges, revealing the flurry of activity on the estate as ships arrived at Aberavon and Taibach with limestone from Aberthaw, lead from Gloucester, slate from Cornwall. Wagon teams hauled stone from Pyle quarry, flagstones from Havod quarry, timber from the estate's plantations.   In the estate office the agents and their clerk scrutinised the accounts, attended to the correspondence, and kept C. R. M. Talbot informed on the progress of the work.

Such extraordinary activity cast exceptional and often burdensome duties on the agents, whose responsibilities for promoting the estate's interests knew few limitations.   An agent's charge was not defined in terms of balancing an annual account and forwarding the landowner's agricultural and industrial interests.   All aspects of local events likely to affect the estate had to be observed and studied; local gossip needed careful sifting and weighing.

In 1839 Thomas John Llewellyn and his brothers were occupied with the question of tithe commutation.   On behalf of C. R. M. Talbot, the largest single tithe owner in the county, they attended local meetings, gathered information on the value of tithes, and agreed commutation figures with the tithe commissioners.   At such a time the need to communicate as speedily as possible with Talbot in London and elsewhere became imperative, and the agents' complaints about "the uncertain and defective delivery of letters" from Neath Post Office to Baglan and Briton Ferry acquired particular point.

At election times, when the agent's local knowledge could be used to further the estate's political interests, he might find himself employed as election agent and manager.[8]   C. R. M. Talbot's support of Lord James Stuart in the borough election of 1826 prompted Griffith Llewellyn to urge Stuart to provide a customary election dinner for the Kenfig burgesses before his opponent, Wyndham Lewis,

---

[8] C. R. M. Talbot represented the county in Parliament from 1830-90.   His step-father, Sir Christopher Cole, had held the county seat from 1817-18 and 1820-30.

did so "as if you defer the burgesses will perhaps say that you treated them merely because your opponent did so". Rather less foresight was shown before the election of 1829 when seventy-nine tenants and dependents of Talbot were created burgesses solely to strengthen the Margam borough interest. None of these new burgesses paid the required admission stamp of £3 as it was not anticipated that their voting rights would be questioned. An unexpected visit from a Stamp Office inspector after the election presented Griffith Llewellyn with an equally unexpected problem—an unpaid bill for £237.

Exceptional duties of a very different kind devolved upon the agents as a result of the industrial development of the estate. In 1765 Hopkin Llewellyn had spoken of the prospect of much additional trouble to the agency and profit to the Talbot family from coal and iron and from the new works at Aberavon. He himself was to see the expansion of the English Copper Company's Taibach works, the growth of the local iron industry, and the growing demands of such industries for supplies of coal and timber. Non-agricultural profits to the estate rose sharply as industrial activity increased. Income from royalties on coal, limestone and other minerals soared; sleeping rents, surface rents and wayleaves, paid by the estate's industrial tenants, assumed increasing importance in the agents' annual accounts. By the 1850's "Casual and Promiscuous" receipts which in 1800 had amounted to less than £2,000 totalled over £17,000, and were composed almost entirely of the profits of industry.

The Copper Works at Taibach and Cwmavon worked coal deposits on the Margam estate and opened collieries at Goytre and Morfa, Oakwood, Argoed, Mynydd Buchan and elsewhere, while the requirements of the Margam Tinplate Works and the Maesteg Iron Works also ensured large profits to the Margam estate. As Hopkin Llewellyn had forecast, the involvement of the estate in industrial development meant that the estate agents' duties were greatly increased. Negotiations for the terms of mineral leases, the collection of royalties, or the settlement of boundary disputes, involved the agency in copious correspondence, intricate accountancy, and frequent legal proceedings. The agents could rely on C. R. M. Talbot's own acute business sense to lay down broad lines of policy, and could call on the mineral agents and surveyors employed on the estate for specialist technical knowledge, but they themselves were expected to direct and supervise all aspects of industrial enterprise.

Closely allied to industrial expansion was the development of communications. Plans for road improvements, tramroads and railways, docks and harbours had to be considered and studied by the agents in the context of the estate's best interests. In 1826 and 1827 Griffith and William Llewellyn were involved in a long dispute with the Duffryn Llynvi Railway Company over the purchase price of land acquired by the Company from the estate. Two years later they gave local support and expression to C. R. M. Talbot's hostility to a proposed branch of the Duffryn Llynvi line through Margam to Briton Ferry, thereby furthering Talbot's own plans for the development of Aberavon harbour. As the architect of the *Aberavon Harbour Acts* of 1834 and 1836, and the largest single shareholder in the Harbour Company, C. R. M. Talbot was deeply involved in the harbour scheme. Once work began on the project it was his estate agent who made frequent visits of inspection to the site and compiled detailed progress reports. Similarly with developments in road and railroad communications, the Margam agents studied proposed routes, gave careful consideration to their likely effect on the estate, and weighed short term inconveniences against long term advantages.

As land stewards and house stewards, election agents, industrial managers, and general directors and co-ordinators of the Margam estate's diverse interests, Hopkin Llewellyn and his successors must have had frequent occasion to echo the words of that earlier agent David Rees who, as early as 1748, complained: "the Constant business that I have on my Hands . . . is Great, and the People I have Everyday to answer are many, so that often when I think to be able to do a great Deal I am prevented interrupted and hindered from doing anything, otherwise than the Present business of the Day".

ACKNOWLEDGEMENTS

The main manuscript sources used in the preparation of this article have been the Margam and Penrice estate collections, and the Llewellyn family papers. The author wishes to express her thanks to Colonel W. H. C. Llewellyn, John Lloyd Esq., and C. Methuen Campbell Esq., all of whom afforded her ready access to their estate and family papers.

Acknowledgement is also made to the custodians of the various manuscript and printed sources to which reference has been made at the National Library of Wales, the Glamorgan Record Office, and the Cardiff Central Library.

THE BUILDINGS OF CARDIFF:
AN HISTORICAL SURVEY

by

J. B. HILLING, A.R.I.B.A., A.M.T.P.I.

THE most important feature of any town, apart from the people who live and work there, is its buildings and its layout. Take away the buildings and, of course, you have no town. The buildings are something more, though, than mere piles of bricks and stones. They are in a sense frozen history, for in many buildings that still survive, history has become crystallised. The buildings themselves are, in fact, part of history—often the only tangible evidence that is left—and when a building is demolished a part of our history is swept away. Cardiff has now reached a stage in its story when some of its older buildings and landmarks are being destroyed. In the near future, when urban renewal really gets under way, still more buildings are likely to be lost. Yet in Cardiff there seems to be an unusual amount of indifference to what is of value in the city. The result is that to many people who have never visited the Welsh capital, it is still considered to be a squalid seaport surrounded by coal mines and slag tips.

The purpose of this survey is to show that even in a largely nineteenth century industrial town like Cardiff there is a rich heritage of architecture. Cardiff is a Victorian town to people who know it, but paradoxically the only buildings that are remembered are the medieval ones or those in twentieth century Cathays Park. Undoubtedly the castle is the most fascinating building in the city, both historically and architecturally, embodying as it does examples of architecture ranging from Roman times to the late nineteenth century. Cathays Park is also a unique complex of buildings. These, however, are not the only examples of architecture that there are in the capital city. Indeed, we do the nineteenth century developers and their architects a grave injustice if we forget the buildings that they left us. As we shall see, the majority of buildings mentioned in this survey date from the last century.

Nevertheless, it must be admitted that there is very little real urban feeling in the streets of Cardiff. It does not have the same visual impact as other provincial capitals like Edinburgh or Dublin. There is an historical reason for this and it is simply that whereas the other towns grew continuously over centuries, Cardiff's growth mushroomed in a matter of a few decades. There are many individual buildings of merit in Cardiff and there are some really magnificent parks—but all in between is a haphazard jumble of bits and pieces and by-law streets. The intervening areas were not built according to any consistent architectural tradition but were, it seems, left to sort themselves out, the overall result being an architectural no-man's land.

This survey deals with the period from the Norman Conquest up to the Second World War, starting with the late eleventh century because this is the real beginning of Cardiff, and finishing, more or less, in the 1930's, not because there are no good modern buildings in Cardiff, but because the more recent a building is the more difficult it is "to discount the influence of passing fashion", and being involved in the day to day business of architecture it is difficult for me to be entirely objective in my views. The more interesting of the recent buildings are, however, mentioned briefly at the end of the chapter.

The area covered is mainly the city centre and the docks together with the outlying districts of Roath and Canton. This forms an entity and has a character distinct from that of Llandaff or the more recent parts of the city. The city centre, the docks and Cathays coincide with the area included within the borough of Cardiff from Norman times up to 1875, and the addition of Roath and Canton completes the territorial limits of Cardiff up to 1922. Together these include the majority of Cardiff's pre-twentieth century buildings.

Finally, a word about the maps. The buildings of each period are shown on a series of sketch maps that depict the built-up areas of the city at different stages. This has been done partly to avoid overcrowding a single map with too many buildings, and what is more important, so that each building can be more easily related to its contemporary environment or, in other words, the street pattern of the town as it existed when the building was erected. It also enables one to see that while on the one hand Cardiff has expanded far beyond its original size, on the other hand the hub of the town, around St. John's church and the castle, has remained remarkably similar in layout to the present day.

ELEVENTH TO EIGHTEENTH CENTURY

The actual founding of Cardiff is said to have taken place in 1081 by William the Conqueror on his way through Morgannwg on a pilgrimage to Tyddewi (St. David's) in Pembrokeshire. With the overthrow of Prince Iestyn ap Gwrgan of Morgannwg by Fitzhamon some ten years later Cardiff came directly under Norman rule. Fitzhamon promptly converted the derelict Roman fort into his headquarters and castle and transformed the Welsh commote of Cibwr, formerly part of the cantref of Senghenydd, into the new Norman lordship of Cardiff. Around the castle, the low-lying lands were quickly settled by the Anglo-Normans, while the unfree groups of Welsh serfs lived in hamlets in the northern part of the lordship. Further north still, the free Welsh continued to occupy the hill-lands as independent lordships for nearly another two hundred years.

By the beginning of the twelfth century, Cardiff had become a fully constituted borough and a church (St. Mary's) was established near the present junction of St. Mary Street and Wood Street. In order to consolidate their gains numerous "motte" castles, consisting of wooden keeps on earthen mounds, were hastily built by the Normans in and around Cardiff.

The earliest and most important of these was, of course, Cardiff Castle itself. Here, within the remains of the quadrangular Roman fort[1], the Normans immediately raised a large mound and built a timber stockade keep on top of it. All was not well, though, for the Normans. The Welsh resented the advance and the expanding claims of the invaders and at every opportunity they swept down from the hills to raid and harass the Norman settlers. On a number of occasions they made vigorous attempts to oust the Normans altogether from their conquered lands. On one occasion, in 1158, Ifor ap Meurig (Ifor Bach), the Welsh lord of Senghenydd, attacked Cardiff Castle at night and, according to Giraldus Cambrensis "secretly scaled the walls and seizing the count and countess with their only son, carried them off into the woods and did not release them

---

[1] The North-gate and much of the reconstructed curtain-walls of the Castle are modelled on those of the Roman fort and in a number of places the original Roman stonework can be seen at the base of the walls.

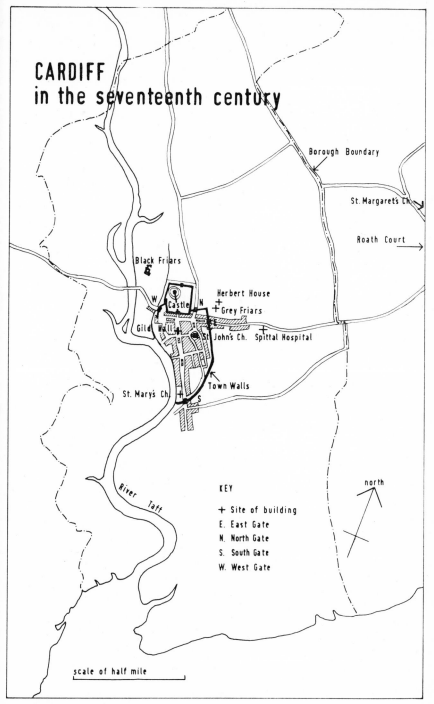

CARDIFF
in the seventeenth century

Borough Boundary

St. Margaret's Ch.

Roath Court

Black Friars

E

W

Castle

N

Herbert House

Grey Friars

Gild Hall

St. John's Ch. Spittal Hospital

Town Walls

St. Mary's Ch.

S

north

River Taff

KEY

+ Site of building
E. East Gate
N. North Gate
S. South Gate
W. West Gate

scale of half mile

Cardiff in the early seventeenth century showing places mentioned on John Speed's Map of Cardiff, 1610.

until he had recovered everything that had been unjustly taken from him".[2]   In order to counter the growing Welsh pressure, the wooden keep was, before the end of the twelfth century, rebuilt in stone.

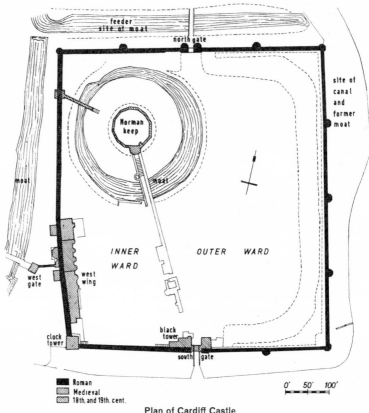

Plan of Cardiff Castle

The new keep in the form of a twelve-sided stone shell structure, with walls six feet thick, was the focal point of the castle.   Perfectly preserved and perched high up on the steep mound surrounded by a circular moat, the keep still stands as a monument to the Normans. In the thirteenth century, Gilbert de Clare added a new gatehouse tower to the keep and built the Black Tower (by the South Gate), connecting it to the keep by a massive stone wall.   In 1404 the castle

[2] Giraldus Cambrensis, *Itinerary through Wales* (Everyman edition), p. 58.

was captured by Owain Glyndŵr and the West Gate was destroyed. The existing West Gate built in 1921 is a replica of the medieval original.

From the eleventh century up until the fifteenth century the keep itself was the residence of the Lords of the Castle and their retainers. With more settled times during the fifteenth century new residential and administrative quarters were built along the west curtain wall. The first of these buildings was the Octagon Tower, erected by the Earl of Warwick about 1430, and followed by the Great Hall. In Tudor and Stuart times further additions were built, including the sixteenth century Herbert Tower. After a period of neglect and disrepair, modernisation was undertaken at the end of the eighteenth century when the first Lord Bute made considerable alterations. First, he asked Robert Adam, the greatest British architect of the eighteenth century, to prepare designs for rebuilding the west wing of the castle. Adam's proposals were on a grandiose scale which included a new central block designed in a gimmicky mixture of Gothic and Classical styles. The scheme was rejected, and in 1777 Bute gave the commission instead to "Capability" Brown and to Brown's son-in-law Henry Holland, the former being responsible for the landscaping and the latter for the structural work. Today, most of the interior work has been rebuilt but much of the external work still remains as Brown and Holland left it.

Meanwhile the borough of Cardiff continued to flourish and by the end of the thirteenth century it had grown into a moderate-sized town of about two thousand people. The town defences, consisting of a ditch and embankment, were strengthened by the addition of stone walls, running from the south-east corner of the castle to the Friary and then continuing east of the Hayes to the bottom end of St. Mary Street where the walls turned west towards the river Taff. The North or Senghenydd Gate (the foundations of which are still partly visible) stood at the south-east corner of the castle, the East or Crokerton Gate stood at the junction of The Friary and Queen Street, the South Gate or Porth Llongau stood at the end of St. Mary Street and the West Gate or Porth Miscin stood at the south-west corner of the castle.

Within the town walls a new church, St. John the Baptist, was built during these early years. The earliest recorded mention of St. John's is in the latter part of the twelfth century, during the Norman

period, although the earliest parts still visible are the early thirteenth
century arches on the south side of the chancel.   It was originally a
chapel of ease to St. Mary's, but gradually grew in importance and
eventually became the parish church after the decline of the earlier
church at the beginning of the seventeenth century. Possibly damaged
in Owain Glyndŵr's rebellion, St. John's was almost entirely rebuilt in
1453 in Perpendicular style and twenty years later the superb tower
was commissioned by Anne, the wife of Richard the Third.   In 1813
the church was restored and galleries added, but the latter were
removed in 1889 when the two outer aisles were added.   Thus today
the building consists of a nave of five bays, chancel, west tower and
twin aisles on either side of the nave.

The main entrance of St. John's is through the west porch under
the tower.   Over the porch there is a lofty stone vaulted gallery,
drenched with light from the exceptionally fine Perpendicular window
and reached by a narrow side stairway.   Above this is the tower itself,
"a magnificent, simple, soaring ashlar bastion graced by a glory of

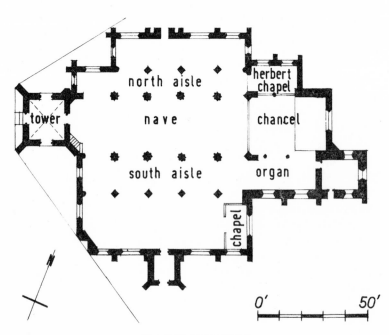

Plan of St. John's Church

pinnacles".[3]   It was designed by John Hart, who also built the famous tower of Wrexham church in North Wales.   The tower is in three stages, with two elegant ogee arches at the base and a large window over the entrance, tall unglazed windows to the upper stages, and is elaborately crowned at the top by an exquisite embattled parapet with lantern pinnacles of delicate open stonework at each of the four corners.   The nave and chancel are spanned by a single curved ceiling, now painted red, giving the central part of the church a feeling of spaciousness.   Inside, the most interesting pre-Victorian part, however, is the Herbert Chapel with its seventeenth century Jacobean monument to the Herbert brothers, separated from the chancel by a centuries old carved-oak screen.   Altogether, St. John's is a fine example of medieval church-building.   Although not a very large church, being only 140 feet long from end to end, it manages to convey an atmosphere of profound solemnity mellowed with age and enriched by colourful windows.

Outside the town walls two friaries were built in the thirteenth century. The earliest was Black Friars, erected by the Dominican Friars in 1242 on land between the castle and the river. It continued in existence for nearly three hundred years until the Dissolution of the Monasteries, after which the buildings fell into ruins, the site being occupied by a dwelling-house demolished in 1830. In 1887 the site was excavated by Lord Bute, and the plan of the church and the domestic buildings marked out later by low brick walls.   The church was about 130 feet long and comprised a short nave of four bays, north and south aisles and a choir.   To the north of the

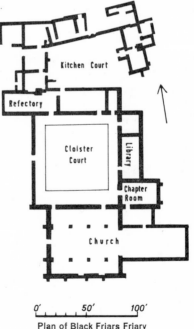

Plan of Black Friars Friary
Redrawn from Archaeologia Cambrensis
1901

[3] P. Leech, *A View of Cardiff* (1968), p. 4.

church there was a cloistered court with the chapterhouse and library on the east side and the common-room (with dormitory above) and refectory on the north side. Beyond these were the kitchens, storehouses and possibly an infirmary.

The other friary was founded in 1280 to the east of the castle by Gilbert de Clare, Lord of Glamorgan, for the Franciscan order of Grey Friars. These Cardiff Grey Friars appear to have been sympathetic and friendly towards the Welsh, and it was in their church that Llywelyn Bren, the leader of the Welsh revolt in 1316, was buried after being executed as a traitor in 1318. It was largely because of the friars' friendly attitude that the friary itself was spared by Owain Glyndŵr in the war of 1404 when much of the borough was destroyed. The friary church was the largest in Cardiff, measuring 154 feet from end to end. It comprised a nave of six bays, north and south aisles, a choir and probably a square bell tower at the north-west corner of the nave. Beyond the church, on the side away from the town, stretched the domestic quarters of the friars. During the sixteenth century the buildings fell into ruins and disappeared completely, until the site was excavated by Lord Bute and the walls marked out in 1887. These, together with the ruins of Herbert House, which is dealt with later on, remained visible until quite recently at the corner of Greyfriars Road and The Friary, but have now disappeared for ever to make way for new office development.

By the middle of the sixteenth century the medieval era was over. In Wales its close was marked by the Dissolution of the Monasteries in 1537-9. A new era was proclaimed in its stead by the Acts of Union of 1536-1542, and with the formal union of Wales and England, Cardiff emerged as a "free" borough. By the terms of the Acts of Union, Cardiff was given representation, jointly with other Glamorgan boroughs, in Parliament. The first grant of a royal charter was made by Elizabeth I in 1581 and this was renewed in 1600 and 1608.

By the terms of the Dissolution of the Monasteries the properties of the Black Friars and the Grey Friars were confiscated in 1538 and then sold to new owners who built their own town houses with stones taken from the ill-fated friaries. From the ruins of Grey Friars the Herbert family built a palatial mansion, the fragmentary remains of which stood until recently in the centre of the city alongside the friary site. After the castle the Herbert mansion was the largest house in

Cardiff and, according to John Speed's map of Cardiff (1610), was a large three-storey building with high gables, quadrangular in layout around an open court, and had a tower topped by a cupola.

Another fine medieval building was the manor house at Roath, which was later altered and enlarged. Rice Merrick, writing in 1578, referred to it saying that within the Roath lordship "stood an old Pyle, compassed with a Mote, which is called 'the Court'; but now in ruyne".

Throughout the sixteenth and seventeenth centuries Cardiff continued to grow in importance although it did not expand very much in size. Merrick described Cardiff as "beautiful with many fair houses and large streets". In 1602 George Owen wrote of Cardiff as being "the fayrest towne in Wales yett not the welthiest". A somewhat different view was expressed by another writer of the same period when he reported that it was "the general resort of pirates". Piracy was not the only form of trade, though, for by the end of the sixteenth century Cardiff was engaged in a considerable coastwise trade in foodstuffs to Bristol and other small ports in the Severn Sea, while three ships were also making a regular run with coal and cloth to La Rochelle in France.

By the early part of the seventeenth century the built-up area of the borough had begun to overflow beyond the town walls along the present lines of Queen Street and Bute Street. Within the walls the pattern of streets was remarkably similar to the street layout today, except that the course of the river Taff ran more easterly, enabling small ships to come up as far as the quay at the end of present-day Quay Street. St. Mary's church stood at the southern end of the town near the river which, according to John Speed, was "undermining her foundations and threatening her fall". At the northern end of the town was the "castell" which contained the Shire Hall. The Town House (or Gild Hall) was in the middle of High Street which then formed the main axis of the town. Nearby stood St. John's church, much as it is today.

Until the nineteenth century the borough's population remained static at just under two thousand inhabitants, and improvements to the town progressed only slowly although by the latter part of the eighteenth century there was a noticeable quickening of the pace. In 1747 the Gild Hall was rebuilt and in 1774 an Act was passed "for the better paving, cleansing and lighting of the streets of Cardiff".

Finally, just before the turmoil of the industrial era of the nineteenth century broke loose, the town was unharnessed and the town gates were taken down and removed; firstly the East and West Gates in 1781, then the North Gate in 1786, and lastly the South Gate in 1802.

EARLY AND MID-NINETEENTH CENTURY

At the end of the eighteenth century Cardiff was little more than a very small and sleepy market town—a town which had hardly changed during the three previous centuries and still retained intact its medieval street plan enclosed by the borough walls and overlooked by the castle.   During the nineteenth century the town grew at a phenomenal rate, being completely transformed to become the metropolis of Wales and the greatest coal port in the world.   The transformation took place in three distinct phases of building development, each closely related to events concerned primarily with the industrialisation of the valleys north of Cardiff.   The first phase was heralded by the opening of the Glamorganshire Canal in the last decade of the eighteenth century and lasted until about 1840. The second phase began with the opening of the first dock coupled with the building of the Taff Vale Railway.   The final phase, starting about 1870, was the direct result of the growth of coal mining and in particular its exploitation in the Rhondda Valleys.

In the first half of the nineteenth century Cardiff's main trade was exporting iron, the port being the natural outlet for iron produced some twenty-five miles up the valley at Merthyr Tydfil following the

---

Key to buildings of the early and mid-nineteenth century

1. Cemetery Chapels, Fairoak Road
2. Eglwys Dewi Sant, St. Andrew's Crescent
3. Presbyterian Chapel, Windsor Place
4. Infirmary (Old University College), Newport Road
5. St. Peter's R.C. Church, St. Peter's Street
6. Tredegarville Baptist Church, The Parade
7. National Provincial Bank, 5 High Street
8. Old Town Hall, St. Mary Street (site of)
9. Bethany Baptist Chapel, Wharton Court
10. Capel Sion, The Hayes (site of)
11. Presbyterian Chapel, Frederick Street
12. Capel Ebenezer, Ebenezer Street
13. Congregational Chapel, Charles Street
14. Taff Vale Offices, Queen Street
15. Wesleyan Central Hall, Charles Street
16. Capel Tabernacl, The Hayes.
17. Old Custom House, East Wharf
18. St. Mary's Church, Bute Street
19. Bute Warehouse, Bute East Dock
20. Congregational Chapel, Hannah Street (site of)
21. St. John the Evangelist Church, Canton
22. Methodist Chapel, Conway Road
23. Sea Lock Hotel, Butetown

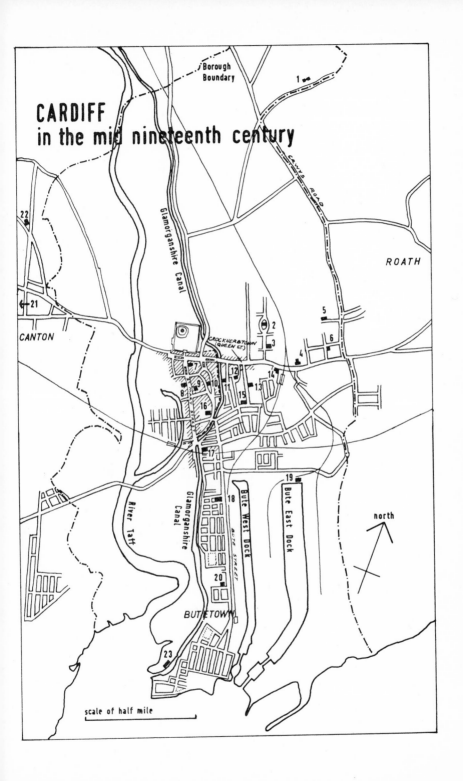

CARDIFF
in the mid nineteenth century

Borough Boundary

CAWS ROAD

ROATH

Glamorganshire Canal

22

21

CANTON

CROCKHERBTOWN
(QUEEN ST.)

2

3

5

4

6

8

9 10

12

11

13 14

15

16

17

River Taff

Glamorganshire Canal

18

Bute West Dock

Bute East Dock

BUTE STREET

19

north

20

BUTETOWN

23

scale of half mile

iron industry's rapid expansion there.   Within a few years four great
ironworks had been built at Merthyr, but their full development had
been hampered by the lack of facilities for transporting the finished
iron along the Taff valley and through the Taff gorge to the sea.   In
1790 a Bill was passed in Parliament authorising the construction of
the Glamorganshire Canal along this route and in 1794 the main part
of the canal was opened.   After passing through some fifty-odd
locks, the canal ran by the side of Cardiff Castle and followed the
line of the moat east of the old town walls as far as the river Taff
near the South Gate.   Four years later the canal was extended to the
sea-lock at the mouth of the river.

   Since the Second World War the canal has become disused.
Gone is the picturesque lock-keeper's cottage, with its thatched roof,
that once stood opposite the Law Courts.   The canal itself, instead
of reverting to a castle moat, has been thoughtlessly filled-in and
made into a car park under the very shadow of the castle walls!

   The export trade in iron that was encouraged by the opening of
the canal necessitated the establishment of a custom office to serve
the rapidly increasing port, and in 1798 the new Custom House was
built alongside the canal at the junction of what are now the East
Wharf and Customhouse Street.   The building is still in remarkably
good condition externally but it is difficult to be sure that this is the
original office.   However, the existing building has the words
"Custom House" engraved on the fascia, and it is shown on early
nineteenth century maps of the town.   It is reasonable to assume that
this is in fact the 1798 Custom House and is therefore one of the
earliest buildings of any note in Cardiff, apart from the castle and
St. John's church.   It is a modest two-storey stuccoed structure in a
rather crude Palladian design.   The upper floor is plain with tall
round-headed windows, while the ground floor has shorter rectangular
windows and rusticated stonework.   The main entrance faces East
Wharf and comprises a round-headed doorway between paired
pilasters supporting a segmental arch.   The Custom House was
extended in identical style along the Customhouse Street frontage
later on in the century.

   With the opening of the Glamorganshire Canal, Cardiff prospered and its population increased steadily from less than two
thousand in 1801 to more than ten thousand forty years later.[4]   Trade

---

[4] The combined population of the borough together with Canton and Roath in
   1841 was 11,442.

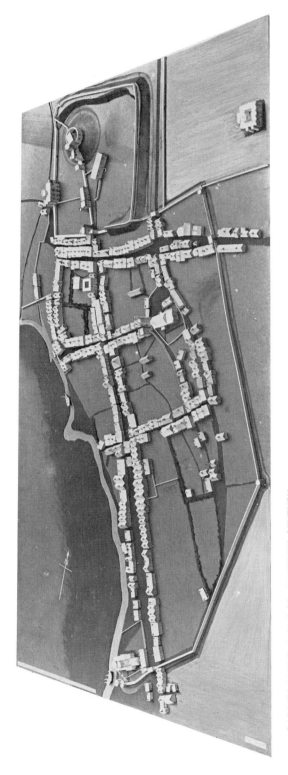

CARDIFF IN THE EARLY SEVENTEENTH CENTURY

Model based on John Speed's map of Cardiff, 1610. The Castle stands at the north end (right hand) of the town and old St. Mary's Church stands at the south end (left hand) of St. Mary Street. In the centre is St. John's Church. The river can be seen behind St. Mary Street, with the shipping quay near the junction of Quay Street and Womanby Street

By permission of the National Museum of Wales

Cardiff Castle

Left:

Reconstructed
North Gate of
Roman fort

Photograph by
T. Herridge

Right:

The Norman shell
keep on its earthen
motte

Photograph by
J. B. Hilling

Left:

St. John's Church, Perpendicular tower, 1473

Right:

St. Mary's Church, Bute Street, 1843

John Foster, architect

Photographs by T. Herridge

The old National Provincial Bank, High Street, 1835

Taff Vale Railway Offices, Queen Street, 1860

Photographs by T. Herridge

The old Custom House, East Wharf, 1798

Bute Warehouse, Bute East Dock, 1861

Photographs by T. Herridge

W. S. Clark, engineer

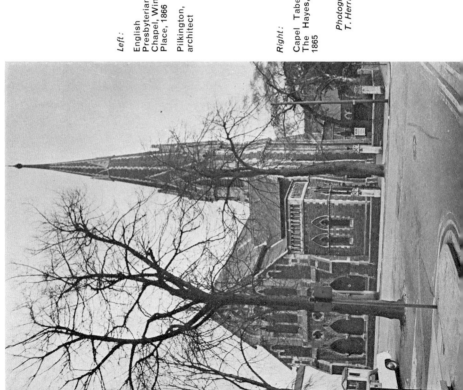

Left:

English
Presbyterian
Chapel, Windsor
Place, 1866

Pilkington,
architect

Right:

Capel Tabernacl,
The Hayes, rebuilt
1865

*Photographs by
T. Herridge*

Congregational
Chapel, Hannah
Street, 1867 (now
demolished)

Interior and Exterior
views

Habershon and Pite,
architects

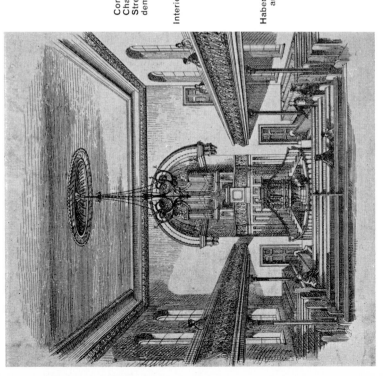

By permission of Cardiff Public Libraries

Congregational Chapel, Wood Street, 1864
By permission of the Welsh School of Architecture

Cemetery Chapels, Fairoak Road, 1859   Thomas and Waring, architects
Photograph by T. Herridge

between Cardiff and Bristol flourished and in 1833 the first steamboat service between the two towns was started. Building development does not appear, at first glance, to have kept pace with the dramatic increase in population during these early years of the nineteenth century. Indeed, apart from some ribbon development along Crockherbtown (Queen Street) and to the south near the canal, expansion beyond the town walls had scarcely started.

First appearances are, however, deceptive. In fact the old town was rapidly being built-up to much higher densities than ever before and spacious town gardens became narrow courts tightly packed with terraces of mean houses. As in so many other towns which became victims (albeit willing victims) of the industrial revolution, the sudden population explosion changed the whole character of building. One result was a decline in the standards of craftsmanship. Up until the end of the eighteenth century a house-owner might still embellish the entrance to his house with a handsome portico expertly carved in wood, such as the one in Roman Doric style which once adorned a dwelling in Working Street and is now in the Welsh Folk Museum, or on a more elaborate scale, like the semi-circular porch fronting the rebuilt Georgian mansion at Roath Court. In the nineteenth century only the very rich could afford such decoration and even then the workmanship was usually of an inferior quality although not as poor as it was to become in the twentieth century. By the time that building development really got going in Cardiff the leisurely days of Georgian classicism were almost gone.

The increase in population also changed the type of buildings that were required. The new requirements were for mass housing, factories and warehouses, offices, hospitals, schools and, significantly, for churches and chapels. Few public buildings, apart from chapels, were built during the earliest phase, though, and fewer have survived in their original form. The earliest nineteenth century public buildings were two Baptist chapels—Bethany English Baptist built in 1806 and Tabernacl Welsh Baptist, the home for a time of the famous preacher Christmas Evans, built in 1821. The earliest nonconformist chapel in Cardiff, however, was Trinity Congregational in Womanby Street which was originally erected in 1696 and was rebuilt in 1847 after a fire. Two other Welsh "capeli" soon followed; Capel Sion (Calvinistic Methodist) built on the site of the Central Library between 1820 and 1830, and Capel Ebenezer (Congregationalist) built in 1828 and enlarged in 1854.   A theatre was built in 1827 on the site of the Park Hotel and lasted until 1877 when it was burnt down.   The most imposing building was the Infirmary, erected in 1834 on land donated by Lord Bute in Newport Road.   It was a large building with a pedimented centre-bay and a Doric porch.   In 1866 it was enlarged and in 1883 it became the home of the first University College before it was finally demolished after the Second World War.[5]   One other building that probably dates from this early period is the Old Sea Lock Hotel at the entrance to the Glamorganshire Canal.   It is now empty but still stands, forlorn and tawdry, at the side of the filled-in canal in Butetown.

With the implementation of the *Municipal Corporation Act* in 1835, the last relics of the medieval borough were discarded and Cardiff started to develop as a modern town complete with an elected council.   The changed status reflected the growing importance of the borough.   As if to confirm this situation the National Provincial Bank set up a branch at 5 High Street in 1835.   It was not Cardiff's first bank; a bank had previously been established as far back as 1792 on the opposite side of High Street (on the site of the present Lloyd's Bank) and was followed later by others in Duke Street and near the Quay.   The National Provincial Bank was, however, the first of the national banks in Cardiff and is also the earliest bank building that still survives, although it is now a shop (Cresta Silks Ltd.) and has undergone some alteration as a consequence of the ground floor being extended forward in the early twentieth century. The upper floor is set back now and is thus hardly noticed by the busy shoppers in the street below.   Yet, with its finely proportioned façade of ashlared stone and its tall narrow windows and Ionic columns and pediment, it is a delightful example of restrained late Georgian or, more precisely, Neo-Greek architecture.   The ground floor arcade of round-headed arches has unfortunately gone.

For some time after the opening of the Glamorganshire Canal iron remained the chief export, but soon coal exports began to compete with the iron traffic and eventually overhauled it, even though as late as the end of the eighteenth century a Cardiff customs official had written that no coal was ever likely to be exported from the port "as it would be too expensive to bring it down here from the internal

[5] The Old University College building was demolished in 1961 to make way for a new Engineering Department.

country".[6] A far-reaching impetus was given to the export of coal by the opening of docks at the port. For some time in fact the Marquess of Bute had considered the possibility of building a dock, and in 1830 he decided on the construction of the Bute West Dock in the marsh lands south of the town. "Its construction cost him some £350,000 and he risked his whole fortune in the enterprise. It was, possibly, the first venture on so large a scale to be undertaken anywhere in the world by one man at his own expense".[7] The dock was opened for shipping in 1839 and with it the second phase of the nineteenth century development of Cardiff started.

With the increased demand for coal for steam power and the opening of new collieries in the Aberdare district the coal industry became well established. The dock already built proved to be insufficient to deal with the expanding coal exports and it soon became necessary to build a second dock. This, the Bute East Dock, was constructed parallel to the earlier dock between 1855 and 1859 by Sir John Rennie in association with W. S. Clark, the resident dock engineer.

The port did not deal entirely in exports of iron and coal, however, but had a general merchandise import trade as well, and following the opening of the second Bute Dock a number of warehouses were erected to deal with these imports. Though warehouses were never built at Cardiff in the same profusion as at other major seaports, nevertheless those which were erected were constructed in the same solid utilitarian manner as elsewhere. The largest warehouses are those along the eastern wharf of the Bute East Dock, but apart from their size, which range from four, five and six storeys to a stone tower block eight floors high, they are not particularly interesting. The most remarkable building by far of these is the Bute Warehouse alongside the north wharf of the Bute East Dock. It is also the earliest of the warehouses, being built in 1861 to the designs of the engineer, W. S. Clark. An outstanding product of the industrial era, it derives its simple qualities from the straightforward use of the materials of the new age. The result is an architectonic expression of strength, boldness and functional integrity. Seen from the outside the warehouse is a neat four-storey rectangular block faced entirely in brick punctuated by rows of small round-headed windows.

[6] D. Williams, *History of Modern Wales* (1950), p. 189.
[7] Ibid., p. 217.

The most notable feature, however, is its internal construction which consists of an iron framework of beams and round cast-iron columns, six bays long by three bays wide.   The floors are each carried on brick vaulting which span between the grid of iron beams.   Both the floor vaulting and the rows of stout quasi-Doric columns can be seen on the ground floor which opens directly on to the wharf side.

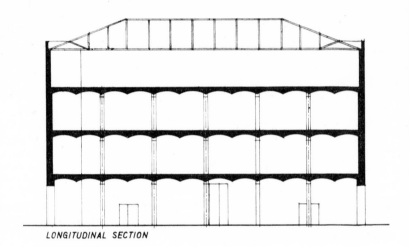

LONGITUDINAL SECTION

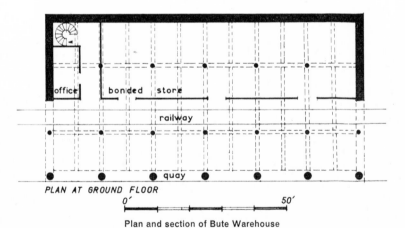

PLAN AT GROUND FLOOR

0'   50'

Plan and section of Bute Warehouse

Based on measured drawing by D. Hamley and M. Iles, by permission of the Welsh School of Architecture

During the years between the construction of the two Bute docks Cardiff began to expand rapidly southwards. Development was restricted to a narrow chunk of land lying between the docks on the east and the Glamorganshire Canal on the west. Down the centre of this area ran Bute Street in a straight line from the Hayes Bridge to the Pier Head and alongside it blocks of dwellings were quickly thrown up so that the workers could be as near to the docks as possible.

Since old St. Mary's church had been largely washed away by the river Taff in the seventeenth century there had been no church to serve the southern part of the town, but with the continually growing numbers of people a parish church was now sorely needed. To this end William Wordsworth was induced in 1842 to write a sonnet to help in fund-raising for a new church to take the place of the original foundation. Wordsworth beseeched the builders to

> "Let the new Church be worthy of its aim
> That in its beauty Cardiff may rejoice".

John Foster, a Liverpool architect, replied with a vigorous design for a church in quasi-Romanesque style. The new St. Mary's, sited at the upper end of Bute Street and built with the aid of a parliamentary grant at a cost of £5,724, was opened in 1843. John Ballinger, writing his guide to the city at the beginning of the twentieth century, blithely recorded that this church "has no architectural interest".[8] How wrong he was. St. Mary's was, in fact, an *avant-garde* building for its time and is something more than just a rectangular hall to seat 1,800 people. The nave with its two aisles is divided into five bays by massive round columns with Byzantine capitals supporting bold and semi-circular arched arcades which in turn support a plain flat ceiling. At the west end tall square towers with pyramidical stone roofs occupy the corners and in between these Foster squeezed a dark, rib-vaulted apse. Originally a great three-decker pulpit stood in the apse, but like the unsightly side-galleries this was later removed. Unfortunately the interior still suffers from too many superfluous bits and pieces and could do with a tactful spring-clean. The exterior is more rewarding and in spite of the arcade of sham windows in front of the apse it shows a restrained handling of details which gives the building an agreeably austere character.

[8] John Ballinger, *Guide to Cardiff* (1908), p. 75.

Within fifteen years Butetown was virtually completed and had become the main business area of Cardiff, while Bute Street itself had become a fashionable shopping centre. The residential development was laid out on a grid-iron plan and varied considerably in quality from rude cottage terraces to the genteel-rustic terrace of Windsor Esplanade (built about 1850) looking smugly out across the harbour entrance to Penarth Head opposite. In between were two and three-storey blocks of dwellings, some of which, with their cast-iron balconies, must have once looked quite elegant.

By the time that the first Bute dock was opened the Glamorganshire Canal had already become inadequate to meet the colossal requirements for transporting coal and iron down the valley and for carrying iron-ore back up the valley to Merthyr. The only way of fulfilling the requirements was by constructing railways. As far back as 1834 Isambard Brunel, the great railway engineer, "had been asked to report on the practicability of a railway to convey iron from Merthyr to the seaboard".[9] Brunel proposed a single narrow gauge track with six passing places, at an estimated cost of just over a hundred and ninety thousand pounds. His scheme was eventually carried out and in 1840 the Taff Vale Railway, as it was known, was opened from Cardiff to Abercynon, being extended in the following year to Merthyr Tydfil. This was the first important railway in Wales. The original Taff Vale Station (now Queen Street Station) was a ramshackle affair clad in weatherboarding. Later it was rebuilt. In 1860 new offices for the railway company were built near the station, facing Queen Street. According to one writer "this mid-Victorian building, neither Gothic nor Albertine, is complete in itself and has something of the severe charm of a toy Horse Guards".[10] It is all in light yellow brick trimmed with stone, now dingy with age and smoke from the trains that crossed the bridge nearby, and it has a miniature clock tower over the central bay of the building.

In 1850 the South Wales Railway was opened, thus joining Cardiff directly with Swansea and Chepstow at first and later with Gloucester and London. Brunel was again the engineer for the railway but this time he insisted on the track being broad gauge to match the system that he had advocated for the Great Western Railway with which it was linked. In order to make available a site

[9] E. L. Chappell, *History of the Port of Cardiff* (1939), p. 83.
[10] P. Leech, *A View of Cardiff* (1968), p. 21

for the General Station it was necessary first to divert the course of the river Taff. This work was started in 1849 and provided, in addition, the extra benefits of stemming the floods that used to occur periodically and of reclaiming land for development.

On the land reclaimed by the diversion Temperance Town was laid out and completed by 1864. The first building to be erected there was the Temperance Hall.[11] No public houses were allowed to be built, hence the name given to the district. Entertainment was later provided by a permanent circus which was built behind the Temperance Hall near the present General Post Office.

About the middle of the century changes were also taking place in the heart of the old town. The old Gild Hall, which stood in the middle of High Street, had now outlived its usefulness and was replaced in 1853 by a new Town Hall and Corn Exchange on the opposite side of the street on the site now occupied by the former Co-operative Society Building. This was Cardiff's third Town Hall and was a rather graceless two-storey edifice with a Palladian front incorporating some ponderous Ionic columns. It was extended in 1876 by James Seward and Thomas and survived up to the beginning of the twentieth century until it, too, became inadequate to meet the town's needs and was replaced by the City Hall in Cathays Park.

Communications, this time by road, were improved with the rebuilding of Cardiff Bridge in 1859 to replace an eighteenth century bridge, the abutments of which can still be seen just to the north of the present bridge. The new bridge enabled further expansion to take place on the west side of the Taff, one early result of this being the partial laying-out of Cathedral Road in the sixties.

About the same time Windsor Place was laid out. This, together with adjoining St. Andrew's Crescent and St. Andrew's Place, is something to value, for it is now the only street in the city centre which has any unity and architectural character of its own. Planned in the classical manner on an axis it begins as a narrow gap on the northern side of Queen Street and then suddenly widens out into a broad *piazza* lined with trees leading towards Eglwys Dewi Sant, the focal point of the whole design. Long three-storey red brick terraces

[11] It was not a success, however, and the Hall was converted into a music hall and circus. Later it was purchased to be used as a place of worship and as the Wood Street Congregational chapel it became one of the largest chapels in the country, seating 3,000 people.

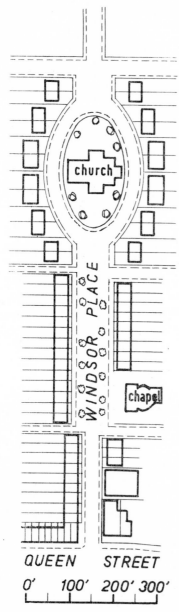

QUEEN   STREET

0'   100'   200' 300'

Plan of Windsor Place and St. Andrew's
Crescent as originally built

with round-headed doorways and wrought iron balconies give the street a Georgian flavour. Unfortunately, the charm of this setting has been largely spoilt in the last few years by office buildings, advertisements, car parking and, worst of all, decapitation of the top end by the introduction of a main traffic route across it.

The cruciform church of Dewi Sant sits solidly on the island of St. Andrew's Crescent and effectively terminates the vista down Windsor Place, although not as well as it might have done had the church been built with a central tower or spire.   In fact John Prichard of Llandaff, the architect of the church, had intended both a tower and spire.   His ideas were too expensive and by the time the building reached the eaves, funds ran out and the work was stopped. Colonel Roose was then called in to complete the roof and chancel in a less elaborate manner and the church was consecrated in 1863 as St. Andrew's.[12] In 1885 the building was enlarged by the addition of side-chapels, the architect this time being William Butterfield. Externally, the church appears   as   a   straightforward

[12] It was not until after the Second World War that the church was reconsecrated as Dewi Sant, taking the place of the Welsh Church in Howard Gardens which had been destroyed in an airraid in 1941.

design in Early English Gothic. Internally, its once attractive interior, with mural paintings done on the spot by C. F. A. Voysey (1888), has now been somewhat truncated by internal re-planning.

At the other end of Windsor Place is the English Presbyterian chapel, built in 1866, a few years later than Dewi Sant, in the short time of eight months. This building, with its delightfully ornate spire, was designed by Pilkington in a richly embellished version of Early English, and as a result is perhaps too romantically Gothic for its soberly classical environment. The intrusion was emphasized by enlarging the front of the church in 1893, so that it now projects forward of the other buildings in the street. The church was gutted by fire in 1910 and was renovated by Colonel Bruce Vaughan without any variation in design.

The architectural character of both Dewi Sant and the Presbyterian chapel was the result of the Gothic Revival movement. The movement to revive the Gothic style had started in England as far back as the late eighteenth century. It came to a head during the 1820's when Gothic became accepted as a recognised style for the flood of "economical" churches built under the *Church Building Act* of 1818. The movement was also a reflection of the religious revivals of the early nineteenth century. Side by side with the new religious fervour large numbers of churches and chapels were built everywhere to cater for an ever-growing population. Most of these buildings were designed in some form of Gothic style. Even the Nonconformist chapels were, as often as not, Gothic or at least had pointed arches, although elsewhere in Wales the general basis of chapel design continued to be Classical in opposition to the Established Church.

St. Mary's, Bute Street, was a portent. It was a historicist revival of Romanesque, one of the earliest periods of English architecture, but it was not Gothic. One of the earliest of the Gothic Revival churches[13] in Cardiff was the Wesleyan Methodist Central Hall[14] in Charles Street. Built in 1850, it has a fine late Perpendicular east front by James Wilson. The Congregational chapel,[15] also in

---

[13] The earliest was St. David's Roman Catholic church on the corner of David Street and Bute Terrace which was built in 1842. As a building it is architecturally uninteresting.
[14] The Central Hall is now the headquarters of the Welsh National Opera Company.
[15] Architect: R. G. Thomas of Newport.

Charles Street, was built a little later in 1855 in Decorated Gothic and stands high above a lower hall and is braced externally by wide, arched, buttresses. This was followed in 1866 by Frederick Street Presbyterian chapel, again in Decorated Gothic but of a rather flat and uninspired kind.

Further afield, in Canton, John Prichard designed the church of St. John the Evangelist. Like Prichard's Dewi Sant this church is sited on an elliptical island in the middle of a pleasant street of good three-storey houses. St. John's also had a similarly protracted history of building, though on this occasion the tower and spire were eventually built. When construction started in 1854 Canton was still a small hamlet, though not for long, for land in the area had already been sold (1840) in lots of ten to twenty acres to building syndicates, so that long before the church was finished Canton had become a densely built-up suburb of 10,000 or more people. In 1855 the Decorated Gothic church was consecrated with only the nave completed. Two aisles were added in 1859 and the broach spire with its attendant corner spirelets was built in 1870. In the following year the chancel was added, but it was not until 1902 that the church was finally completed by enlarging the nave to provide an extra 150 seats.

In the newly built-up area immediately east of the old town two new churches were built within a short distance of each other in 1861. The better of the two, St. Peter's Roman Catholic church in St. Peter's Street, is a large shapely structure with a fine late Decorated tower. It was designed by Charles Hansom of Bristol, the brother of the inventor of the famous "hansom cab". Inside, it has a lofty nave, with an open trussed timber roof and spacious aisles. The stained glass windows are superb, particularly those to the apsidal east end, which were made by Mayer and Co. of Munich, Germany. Tredegarville Baptist chapel in the Parade is a more showy Decorated Gothic building with stonework picked out in grey and white.

Not all the chapels, however, were Gothic. Some of the older ones were now too small to serve the multiplying population and had to be enlarged. Bethany Baptist chapel in Wharton Court, for instance, was completely rebuilt in 1864 with a Classical façade incorporating round-headed windows and the usual pediment. Inside, two-tier cast-iron columns supported an arcade of semi-circular arches and clerestory which in turn carried the roof. In 1965 the building became incorporated in extensions to James Howell's store, the façade being retained as a setting for the new pedestrian court and as an entrance to the shop. Capel Tabernacl also proved to be too small and was enlarged in 1842. In 1865 the chapel was rebuilt at a cost of £3,000 in the record time of six months. Apart from some renovations and the addition of an organ chamber in 1905, it still stands as it was built—an austere, rather forbidding, interpretation of the Classical formula in need of some paint. Hannah Street Congregational chapel[16] in Butetown was a more stylistically authentic version of Classical design. It was built in 1867 and had an impressive neo-Greek façade with Corinthian columns and was approached by a steep flight of steps. Unfortunately this, one of the best-looking chapels in Cardiff, had a short life. Because of dwindling congregations it was sold in 1917 to become a warehouse and was demolished a few years ago to make room for redevelopment in the area.

A characteristic feature common to many of the earlier nonconformist chapels throughout urban Wales is the way in which the chapel proper is built above a lower school hall. Presumably this was done for two reasons; to economise on land and also to give extra height to the building in order to make it as prominent as possible. Many of the Cardiff chapels, particularly the Welsh ones, adopted this principle of planning, but the one that demonstrates it most strikingly is Conway Road Methodist in Canton. Built in 1869, it towers impressively above its triangular site and is one of Cardiff's largest chapels. With its long external staircase sweeping up in the grand manner to a large polygonal entrance porch it has a Baroque atmosphere about it although the architectural style generally is only vaguely Classical. The interior of the chapel appears very spacious, an effect heightened by a deep horseshoe shaped balcony and a wide curving ceiling.

Just as there was an urgent need everywhere for new places of worship for the living, so also more burial places were needed for the dead. Until the middle of the century the only burial grounds had been small ones attached to St. John the Baptist church and to Bethany, Ebenezer, Sion and Tabernacl chapels. In 1847 a small cemetery near the prison in Adamsdown was added, but this too became inadequate and further land was needed. So urgent was the need that the Corporation held a competition in 1857 for the design of twin Cemetery Chapels (Episcopal and Dissenters), Lodge and

[16] Architects: W. G. Habershon and A. R. Pite.

Reception Room before they had decided where the new cemetery itself should be sited. The competition, which carried an award of twenty guineas, was won by R. G. Thomas of Newport and T. Waring of Cardiff who had entered a Decorated Gothic scheme under the pseudonym "Excelsior". Eventually the Burial Board acquired a site on the Wedal Farm off Whitchurch Road and the two chapels and lodge etc. were built to the competition design for the sum of £5,200, in time for the opening of the cemetery in 1859. In 1858 the Board also asked the architects to design a separate Roman Catholic chapel on the other side of the cemetery and this was consecrated together with the others. Thomas and Waring's design for the main complex was both novel and functional. A triple gateway of pointed arches leads into a wide forecourt and beyond this can be seen the three buildings grouped together. In the centre is the Reception Room, forming the lowest floor of a three-storey octagonal tower surmounted by a spire and this is linked to the chapels on either side by high pointed arches. The whole group has a refreshingly vigorous look about it, largely because instead of emphasizing the individual chapels in the way which one might have expected, the chapels have been used instead as secondary elements to focus attention on the central tower. In its uninhibited use of earlier forms and decoration in an original way the building anticipates something of the ostentatious virility of later Victorian architecture that was soon to follow.

LATE NINETEENTH CENTURY

From about 1870 onwards the population and coal exports of Cardiff soared upwards, largely as a result of the spectacular expansion of mining in the Rhondda valleys. In 1871 the borough's population was 39,536[17] and coal exports were just under two million tons per year. Within a generation the population had quadrupled to 164,333 (in 1901) and coal exports from Cardiff had risen to nearly eight million tons annually. The borough was enlarged in 1875 to include Roath and Canton and thus for the first time it became the largest town in Wales. The town continued to expand at a tremendous rate. Nearby villages such as Roath and Canton were swallowed up by the rapidly spreading development and outlying farms

[17] The combined population of Cardiff, Canton and Roath in 1871 was 57,363.

such as the Grange, Splott, Pengam, Adamsdown, Pen-y-lan and Maendy gave their names to new suburbs.

The sudden concentration of a large population in Cardiff resulting from the exploitation of iron and coal in the nearby valleys, caused an explosion in the town's urban growth. The inevitable consequence of this was overcrowded houses in a morass of mean streets without adequate water or sewerage systems culminating in squalor and early death. The sudden growth also accounted for the erection of numerous public buildings during the latter part of the nineteenth century, many of them designed by renowned architects.

For many people the biggest changes in this period were not so much technical as intellectual and spiritual ones. "Culture and enlightenment . . . meant art schools, concert halls, public libraries and institutes, church schools, gaols, workhouses, orphanages and, above all, new churches".[18]

In Cardiff, as in so many other towns and cities, this was the era of High Victorian architecture, the period of vigorous, extrovert and original design. In Cardiff the architecture of the time was also caught up in the "battle of the styles", a battle which in other towns had already been largely fought. Up until the sixties the architectural style of a building had been easily decided—ecclesiastical buildings (other than Nonconformist chapels) were Romanesque or austere Gothic to suggest piety, and public buildings were pompous Classical to symbolise civic pride. In the latter part of the century the range of buildings was far wider and the question was more difficult to decide. During this period most of Cardiff's commercial buildings were erected; and who could rule whether an office block should be Venetian Gothic or Palladian, or whether a hotel should be French Gothic or French Renaissance?

For one architect the question was never in any doubt. This was William Burges, the architect appointed by the third Marquess of Bute in 1865 to advise on the condition of Cardiff Castle and to restore it. The choice of architect was most fortunate, for Burges was a convinced medievalist and for him a medieval castle could only be restored in a medieval manner. His idea of medieval architecture was, however, a very personal and romantic one. Throughout his life, Burges was busy measuring Gothic buildings, studying Gothic ornament and reading Gothic manuscripts. His sketch-books were

[18] Robert Furneaux Jordan, *Victorian Architecture* (1966), p. 40.

of vellum, he owned a complete medieval outfit of clothes and his own house in London had a working portcullis.

Five buildings in or near Cardiff owe their authorship to Burges. Of these the restored castle is the most outstanding and most famous. "By the time Burges had finished with it, the Castle, with its fantastically rich interiors, had become one of the most gorgeous houses of its time".[19] Burges's restoration of the west wing was virtually a rebuilding, adding, as he did, completely new buildings alongside the other work.

The chief features of his exotic "restoration" were the sumptuous rooms full of heavy carving and decorated with scenes illustrating themes from Classical and Moorish mythology and murals depicting medieval life.   There are massive fireplaces; one carved out of a single block of stone, another in the form of a castle gateway and a superb white marble chimney-piece inset with lapis lazuli.   Windows are filled with stained glass and walls are inlaid with precious stones. There are splendid coffered ceilings covered with gold leaf decoration, vaulted roofs and a dome covered with mirrors.   Indeed the very names of the rooms themselves are redolent with the atmosphere

[19] Ibid., p. 102.

Key to buildings of the late nineteenth century

1. Convent of the Good Shepherd Chapel, Ty Gwyn Road (site of)
2. Nazareth House, North Road
3. St. Teilo's Church, Woodville Road
4. Roath Park Methodist Chapel, Albany Road
5. Roath Park Presbyterian Chapel, Marlborough Road
6. St. Margaret's Church, Waterloo Road
7. Synagogue, Cathedral Road
8. Castle Mews
9. Cardiff Castle
10. Park House, Park Place
11. Park Hotel, Park Place
12. Queen's Chambers, Queen Street
13. Central Library
14. St. David's R.C. Cathedral, Charles Street
15. Taff Vale Station (Queen Street)
16. Capel Pembroke Terrace, Churchill Way
17. General Post Office, Westgate Street
18. Royal Hotel, St. Mary Street
19. Prince of Wales Theatre, Wood Street
20. Great Western Hotel, St. Mary Street
21. Unitarian Church, West Grove
22. Cardiff High School for Girls, The Parade
23. 28 The Parade
24. St. James' Church, Newport Road
25. Royal Infirmary, Newport Road
26. St. Anne's Church, Snipe Street
27. Trinity Chapel, Four Elms Road
28. St. German's Church, Star Street
29. St. Saviour's Church, Splott Road
30. Cardiff Malting House, Lewis Road
31. St. Paul's Church, Paget Street
32. Imperial Buildings, Mount Stuart Square
33. Stock Exchange, Mount Stuart Square
34. St. Stephen's Church, West Bute Street
35. Pascoe House, Bute Street
36. Custom House, Bute Street
37. Corys' Buildings, Bute Street
38. Board of Trade Offices, Bute Place
39. Midland Bank Chambers, Bute Street
40. Pierhead Chambers, Bute Street
41. Merchants' Exchange, Bute Street
42. Pierhead Building (Docks Office), Bute West Dock
43. Scandinavian Church, Bute West Dock

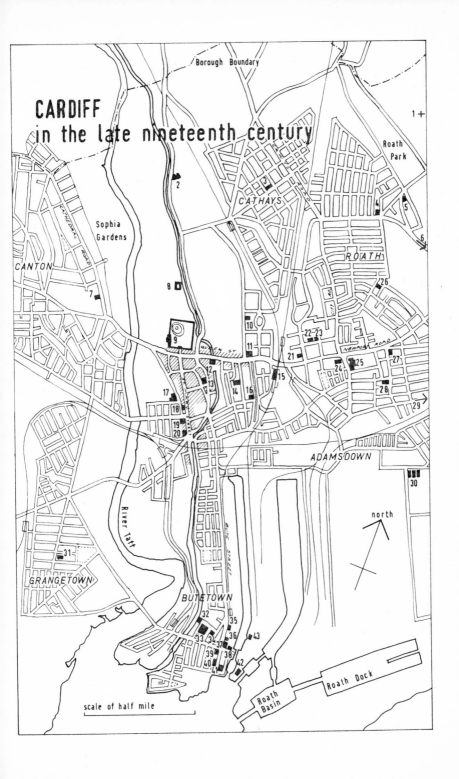

of the Middle Ages at its most romantic; for instance, the Chaucer Room, with its paintings illustrating the literature of the fourteenth century poet, and the Arab Room designed to represent a harem.

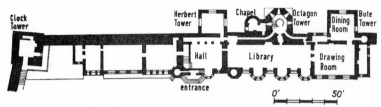

Cardiff Castle: ground floor plan of west wing

The rebuilding of the castle by Burges started in 1867 with the building of the 150 feet high Clock Tower at the south-western corner. Work was started next on the Bute Tower followed by alterations to the Beauchamp Tower, the Herbert Tower and the medieval Octagon Tower. The medieval Great Hall was divided vertically to form a Banqueting Hall and a Library. Before the restoration had been finished, Burges died at the age of 54. The work was carried on, however, to drawings previously sketched by the master medievalist and the rebuilding was finally completed in 1890. Meanwhile the Black Tower, i.e. the one to the west of the South Gate, was restored by John Prichard.

To the north of the castle, Burges built the stables (otherwise known as Castle Mews) for Lord Bute. These were built in two stages, starting with the north and east wings in 1869 and extended by the addition of the south and west wings in 1875. The completed building is a very sober affair, being little more than a straightforward two-storey quadrangular block built in rubble-stone with ashlared edging to the openings. But even with this building Burges was able to create some interest by providing a gabled entrance with pointed arches in the centre of the main façades and by adding a timber balcony at first floor level to the internal court.

Altogether different is Park House,[20] Burges's other building in central Cardiff. Although comparatively small and compact it is one of his best works and according to Professor H. R. Hitchcock "prepared the way for Burges's fine collegiate work in America".[21] It

[20] Now the offices of Cardiff Rural District Council.
[21] H. R. Hitchcock, *Nineteenth and Twentieth Century Architecture* (1958), p. 188.

Cardiff Castle, west wing.   Restored and built by Wm. Burges, 1867-90   *Photograph by T. Herridge*

Cardiff Castle, Banqueting Hall.   Restored by Wm. Burges, 1873-4

Photograph by W. D. Dighton, 1889   *By permission of Cardiff Public Libraries*

Private Houses

Left:

Park House, Park Place, 1874

William Burges, architect

Right:

28 The Parade

Photographs by T. Herridge

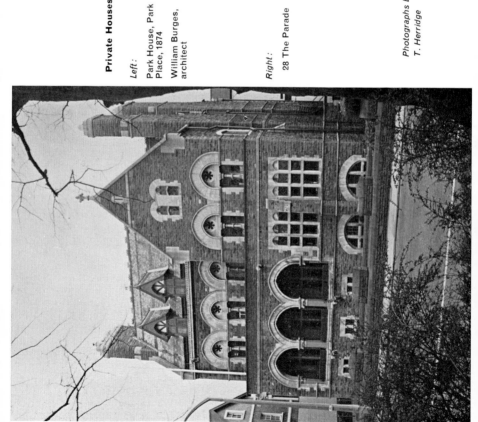

Left:

Central Library, The
Hayes, south
front added 1896

Edwin Seward,
architect

Right:

Queen's Chambers
Queen Street,
c. 1870-80

*Photographs by
T. Herridge*

Great Western Hotel, St. Mary Street, *c.* 1875-79

Park Hotel, Queen Street, 1885

Photographs by T. Herridge

Habershon and Fawckner, architects

Royal Infirmary, Newport Road, 1883   Seward and Thomas, architects

By permission of the National Museum of Wales

Proposed Town Hall in Temperance Town   J. K. Collett, architect

By permission of Western Mail

Left:

Capel Pembroke
Terrace, Churchill
Way, 1877

Henry C. Harris,
architect

Right:

Roath Park
Presbyterian
Chapel,
Marlborough Road,
1897

Habershon and
Fawckner,
architects

*Photographs by
T. Herridge*

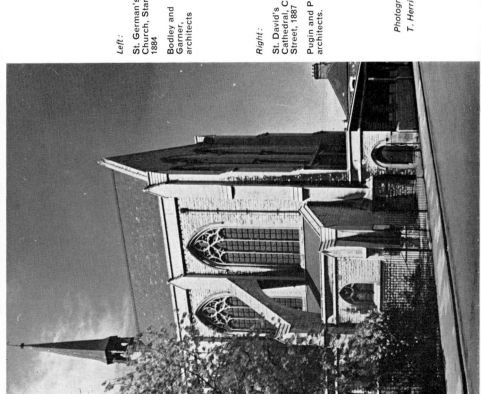

Left:

St. German's Church, Star Street, 1884.

Bodley and Garner, architects

Right:

St. David's Cathedral, Charles Street, 1887

Pugin and Pugin, architects.

Photographs by T. Herridge

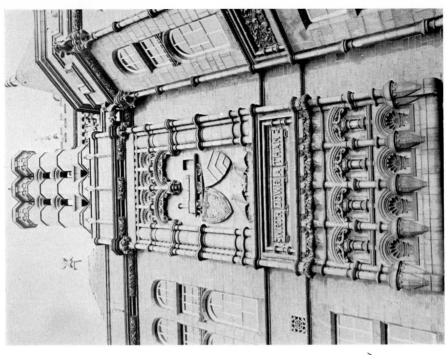

Left.:

Pier Head
Building, Bute
Docks, 1896

William Frame,
architect

Right:

Detail of decorated
panel

*Photographs by
T. Herridge*

was built in 1874 for Mr. McConnochie, Lord Bute's engineer for the Cardiff Docks. The design of the building is in a rich Neo-Gothic style with a French bias, excellently detailed in stone though not as exuberant as the restorations to the castle. Asymetrically planned, it has an arcade of three tall pointed arches supported on red marble columns to the front of the house and a similar loggia leading to the main entrance on the north side. Above the entrance there is a lofty stair hall with wide timber

Ground floor plan of Park House

Based on measured drawing by J. E. Davies, M. Robertson and R. T. Tranter, by permission of the Welsh School of Architecture

staircase beautifully designed with elaborately carved balustrades. At the landing there is a large Gothic window in three bays and high above this is a panelled and vaulted ceiling which together succeed in making this one of the most impressive and exciting interior spaces of any building in Cardiff.

Burges's other Cardiff building, apart from Castell Coch, appears to have been a chapel at the Convent of the Good Shepherd, Ty Gwyn Road, Pen-y-lan. Information on the subject is scarce, but Hunter Blair records Lord Bute as writing: "I am about starting a convent of 'Sisters of the Good Shepherd', about a mile from this town (Cardiff) . . . Burges is to do the Chapel, wherein I propose to erect a large gothic baldequin. The building is now an old barn".[22] There is also a terse note in Burges's diary for 1870, viz: "Cardiff Chapel (Barn)"[23] but nothing else relating to this building. The Convent itself was erected in 1872 at Lord Bute's expense. It has recently been demolished to make way for the Eastern Avenue by-pass.

[22] Sir David Oswald Hunter-Blair, *John Patrick, Third Marquis of Bute, K. T. A Memoir* (1912), p. 93.
[23] Quoted by Charles Handley-Read in a letter to the author.

The latter part of the nineteenth century saw a revival of commercial and shopping interests in the historic centre of the town along St. Mary Street and Queen Street. New hotels reflected, on one hand, the town's growing wealth and prosperity and, on the other, the variety of architectural styles which were becoming readily available as archaeological knowledge became more widespread. The Royal Hotel, St. Mary Street, was one of the first of Cardiff's modern hotels. Designed by C. E. Bernard and built in 1866 (though not formally opened until later), it was a five-storey version of an Italian Renaissance palace; in fact, a far distant relative of the Palazzo Farnese in Rome. Since then the entrance has been altered, the bracketted balconies have been removed and the building itself has been dwarfed by a southward extension (1896), so that the original hotel has now lost much of its former character.

The *pièce de résistance* amongst the hotels is undoubtedly the Great Western at the southern tip of St. Mary Street. It is a superb example of High Victorian architecture, yet strangely it has been forgotten and nothing seems to be known of either its designer or the date when it was built. It was certainly in existence by 1879 (according to the first 25 inch ordnance survey map) and it was probably built a few years earlier to cater for the growing number of railway passengers. The curved façade of the Great Western Hotel is a gorgeous piece of romanticism with a French medieval bias, ornamented by a multitude of Gothic windows and steep gables together with oriel turrets complete with conical spires; altogether a jewel amongst Cardiff's street architecture.

In Queen Street the most impressive building is the Park Hotel, built in 1885 and designed by W. G. Habershon in partnership with Fawckner. French Renaissance in style, it looks something like a watered-down version of the Louvre. Indeed it is one of the few older buildings in the town centre that has the scale and quality one would expect to find as normal in a capital city.

Also in Queen Street is the Queen's Chambers which was formerly a hotel and is another interesting example of Victorian romanticism. Built above the entrance to the Queen Street Arcade in the 1870's, it has an appropriately Venetian Gothic façade, directly inspired by Ruskin's book, *The Stones of Venice*. The old Glamorganshire Canal at one time passed alongside the Queen's Chambers, but whether the design was prompted by the close proximity of the building to the canal or because the style happened to be fashionable at the time is an open question. It is of interest to note here that the Llandaff architects, Prichard and Seddon, were great admirers of John Ruskin and it is they no doubt who were responsible, more than anyone else, for encouraging the introduction of the Venetian style into the Cardiff area. Another example of a building inspired by Ruskin's adoration of Venice is the Prince of Wales Theatre, Wood Street. This was built, as the Theatre Royal, in 1878 and was extended in the early twentieth century when the Classical front to the St. Mary Street entrance was added.

There was also a burst of activity in the field of public building during the last two decades of the nineteenth century. Within a few short years in the 1880's the Central Library and a new Infirmary were built, the University College of South Wales was opened in the old Infirmary buildings in Newport Road, the Taff Vale Station was rebuilt and the Market Hall was enlarged.

The Central Library, built in 1882, has the benefit of a fine site between St. John's church and the Hayes. Its design, by James Seward and Thomas, together with the addition by Edwin Seward,[24] is, however, somewhat disappointing for such an important public building, for though the structure is bold and compact its architectural detailing suffers from an unimaginative and heavy-handed use of classical idioms. The ground floor with its tall simple windows is straightforward enough. The first floor containing the Reference Library is less restrained and forms a heavy *piano nobile* expressed externally by a row of Doric columns on the south front and by projecting bays on the east and west sides. At roof level all restraint appears to have been abandoned—the result being a continuous deep frieze extended upwards on the south front with a top-heavy parapet, decorated with a recessed panel containing figures representing Literature, Calligraphy and Printing and surmounted by a sculptured bust of Minerva, the goddess of thought and invention.

Seward and Thomas were also the architects for the Royal Infirmary, which was built, at a cost of £28,000, in 1883 on a new site obtained through the generosity of Lord Bute, at the junction of Glossop Road and Newport Road. This collection of buildings, which was extended in 1892 and 1908, was designed in a generally Jacobean style with a large Gothic tower at the rear.

[24] The southern half of the building was added by Edwin Seward in 1896.

In 1887 the Taff Vale Station in Queen Street was completely rebuilt at a cost of £20,000. While not in any way exceptional, it is a good straightforward example of building from the Railway Age, the architect being Wallace of Westminster. "The style adopted for the station by the architect is mixed Gothic".[25]

Cardiff was now becoming an important communications centre for the postal and telephone services as well as for railways and shipping. Indeed, it was at Cardiff that the initial venture of the Post Office in the telephone business took place with the opening of the first trunk line in Great Britain between Cardiff and Newport in 1881. At this time the head post office was situated in St. Mary Street in a building opened in 1868. The present General Post Office in Westgate Street was erected in 1896, at a cost of £68,000. It was expected to meet all requirements for fifty years but was in fact soon extended on the south side to meet the needs of the expanding telephone section. The buildings were designed by Henry Tanner in Neo-Classical style, incorporating a Corinthian entrance portico, heavily detailed portland-stone façades and an unusual sky-line which, with its steeply pitched roofs, pediments, round-headed windows, baroque gables and octagonal corner lantern supporting a truncated spire, seems more in the spirit of Gothic than Classical architecture.

Until the foundation of the School Board in 1875, Cardiff had been poorly provided with educational facilities. The only schools serving the town were St. John's (in what is now The Friary), an infants school established in 1840, and a few schools founded by various religious societies. The first Board school was built in 1878 and after that there was a continual increase in the number of schools so that by 1908 there were some 36 elementary schools as well as schools for the deaf and for the blind, and in addition two municipal secondary schools and two intermediate schools. Few had any architectural pretensions. The only one of any interest is the Cardiff High School for Girls (formerly the Intermediate School for Girls) in the Parade, a four-storey building built in 1898 with a Classical front and an Ionic entrance portico and a quasi-medieval assembly hall. More interesting is 28 The Parade which stands alongside and which was the original home of the school when it was founded in 1895. It was built as a three-storey private house in the sixties or seventies for

[25] *Engineering*, 16 September 1887.

the Billups family whose monograms, JEB and SCB, appear on the twin bays. Designed in a mixture of styles incorporating a Doric portico, Dutch gables, tall Tudor type brick chimneys and a large octagonal cupola over the staircase hall, it is nevertheless one of the finest houses in central Cardiff.

Housing and street architecture, though, was generally at a low ebb during late Victorian times. In the main it consisted of standardised by-law planned streets. Occasionally, in the higher-income areas, attempts were made to create a more distinguished architectural environment by embellishing the houses with decorative porches and by tree planting. Some of the more memorable examples are Cathedral Road, Plasturton Avenue, Richmond Terrace and the Taff Embankment, all built in the eighties. The most successful of these is Cathedral Road, though it has now been somewhat marred by unsympathetic office block development. Tree-lined and spacious, it runs for almost a mile towards Llandaff and has just sufficient a curve to close the vista at each end and make it complete in itself. There are a few large detached houses dating from the sixties and seventies at the lower end but mostly it consists of three-storey semi-detached and terraced houses built in the eighties with steep gables and a variety of Gothic and Classical arches over the doorways, including narrow pointed, four-centred, ogee, semi-circular and pedimented.

In the field of church architecture there was also great activity and it was during these last decades of the nineteenth century that most of Cardiff's churches and chapels were built. This was the Golden Age for ecclesiastical architects, though not all made the best of their opportunities. John Prichard, as the Diocesan architect, appears to have had the more important jobs. In addition to restoring St. John the Baptist in the town centre and enlarging it in 1887 by the addition of two outer aisles, Prichard was also responsible for designing the new parish church of St. Margaret's at Roath.

Old St. Margaret's, which had stood since the late twelfth century, was a "church of simple proportions, white-washed and with but a single bell turret".[26] It was demolished in 1869 to make way for the new church which was opened in 1873. The new St. Margaret's is a squat, cruciform building in early Decorated style with an uncompleted central tower. Externally, it is not one of Prichard's best works; the interior, however, is a different kettle of fish altogether.

[26] W. Rees, *Cardiff : A History of the City* (1962), p. 64.

Dark and gloomy, it has a mellow, age-old atmosphere enriched by bold detailing. Windows are few, but the stained glass "is fine, both in design and quality, being all the work of one firm, Messrs. Burleson and Grylls, and, it is presumed, from designs by the late G. F. Bodley".[27] The walls are in light-coloured brick enlivened by black and red diaper work, with piers of cream and pink sandstone bands alternating with marble. In the north-east angle, between the chancel and the north transept, Lord Bute had a mortuary chapel built in 1883 as a mausoleum for members of his family. The chapel is more ornate than the rest of the church, having a rib-vaulted ceiling and a mosaic floor and is separated from the chancel by an elegant wrought-iron screen.

Prichard was also responsible for designing Nazareth House in North Road. Built in 1874 and extended in 1908 it comprises a not very exciting group of buildings all in a vaguely Early English Gothic style and a chapel raised high above a lower hall complete with a small side turret and tall chimneys.

Although most of the ecclesiastical designers were local architects there were some notable exceptions. The most notable was the distinguished church architect, G. F. Bodley, who with T. Garner built two churches in the Adamsdown area during the eighties. Of these, St. German's church, Star Street, built in 1884 in Decorated Gothic, is one of the finest nineteenth century churches in Wales. Its superb interior has a graceful simplicity and soaring spaciousness that gives it a cathedral-like atmosphere emphasised by clusters of tall slender columns supporting a panelled wagon-vault roof. The chancel is large and has a flight of steps leading up to the high altar behind which there is a rather garish reredos and a splendid trio of tall lancet windows with stained glass installed in 1900. Wrought-iron screens separate the chancel from chapels on either side; on the north a small chapel dedicated to St. Agnes, and on the south the Lady Chapel, with new windows designed by Hugh Easton in 1953. Over both chapels there is graceful ribbed stone vaulting. The exterior of the church is not as impressive as the interior, mainly because there is no tower or spire to catch the eye, but there are some interesting features such as flying buttresses over the side-chapels, a slate covered fléche (or spirelet) over the chancel roof and a handsome, spiky, wrought-iron Calvary sculpture by Frank Roper near the west

[27] J. Ballinger, *Guide to Cardiff* (1908), p. 75.

entrance. St. German's was narrowly missed by bombing in 1941 (although some damage was done), but the parish hall alongside was destroyed and a new one has since been built on the same site.

Bodley and Garner's other church is St. Saviour's, Carlisle Street, built in 1888. As at St. German's, the site of St. Saviour's was given by Lord Tredegar. The design of the church was closely modelled on that of the fifteenth century church of St. Mary's, Tenby, and like that it also consists of a nave, two aisles, chancel and two side chapels all roughly equal in width and height. Whereas the Tenby church has a fine tower and spire, St. Saviour's unfortunately does not, its outward appearance suffering from this omission. The interior has a panelled wagon-vault roof and stained glass windows designed by Bodley in Perpendicular style, while along the aisle walls there are the Fourteen Stations of the Cross sculpted in aluminium by Frank Roper in 1963. The high altar at the east end of the chancel is again similar to the Tenby church in that it is approached by an impressive flight of marble steps.

One of Cardiff's most imposing churches, when seen from the outside, is St. James's, Newport Road. It is a gaunt-looking building erected in 1894 with the aid of voluntary subscriptions at a cost of £10,000 to the designs of Colonel Bruce Vaughan. The emphasis throughout is on height; a lofty tower and slim broach spire as a focal point and tall lancet windows but low side aisles to emphasise the comparative height of the nave. Inside, the walls are all in ashlared stone and, despite an interesting semi-circular apse at the east end, the overall effect is rather cold.

Other Anglican churches erected during this period were St.Paul's, Grangetown, built in 1890 to designs by John Pollard Seddon and John Coates Carter,[28] St. Stephen's, Butetown, by Colonel Bruce Vaughan (1894-1900), and the still uncompleted churches of St.Teilo, Cathays, by G. E. Halliday (1895-1913) and St. Anne, Roath, by J. A. Reeves (1887).

The only important Roman Catholic church constructed during this period was St. David's Cathedral in Charles Street. Undistinguished externally, except by its bulk and by a stumpy tower and spire at one corner, it is of interest mainly because it was designed by

[28] J. P. Seddon was in practice at Llandaff with John Prichard from 1852-62 and succeeded Prichard as Diocesan Architect there. After moving to London Seddon was in practice with J. C. Carter from 1885-1904.

the firm of Pugin and Pugin, in the "Second Pointed" or Decorated Gothic style advocated by Augustus Welby Northmore Pugin, the fanatical early nineteenth century Gothicist and Catholic architect, and founder of the firm.   It was built in 1887 as an ordinary church and only became a cathedral and the seat of the Roman Catholic archbishop of Wales in 1916.   The plan of the church is simple and comprises a large nave, chancel, and a gallery at the rear supported on squat round columns.   The high altar is in a recess at the west end and is surmounted by a tall, conical canopy, behind which there is a circular window with hexagonal tracery.   At the east end there is a large and very colourful stained glass window behind the gallery. The cathedral was gutted by incendiary bombs in 1941 and was restored by the architects, F. R. Bates and Son, who also installed the hammer-beam roof trusses which support the timber ceiling of the nave.

The Dissenters were not to be outdone by the Established Church but continued to erect a large number of chapels throughout the town, some of which were quite splendid buildings, vying with the episcopal churches in architectural pretentiousness. They are lasting reminders of the considerable part played by Nonconformists in the life of Cardiff in Victorian times.

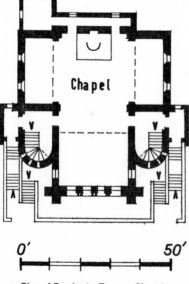

One of the most interesting of these buildings is Capel Pembroke Terrace (Calvinistic Methodist) in Churchill Way.   It was built in 1877 as the successor to the old Capel Sion,[29] the architect being Henry C. Harris of Staines, who two years previously had won a competition for new schools at Penarth.   Outwardly, the chapel was designed in Harris's own version of French Gothic.   The tall main façade has lancet windows and deeply recessed

0'   50'

Plan of Pembroke Terrace Chapel   [29] See page 41

traceried windows and is flanked by octagonal side turrets. On either side of the chapel semi-cylindrical staircase towers with steeply pointed roofs rise up out of the depths, the bases of the towers being half-hidden by suspended footbridges. The arrangement of the building marks a change in emphasis in chapel design. The chapel itself was still built over a lower hall but in its layout it was planned as a compact figure T, so that all members of the congregation would be within a reasonable distance of the speaker, and the entrance lobbies and stair towers were slotted into the corner angles. The interior, with its red brick walls and cream and black diaper work, is another departure from nonconformist tradition although decoration of this type had already been used in St. Margaret's church, Roath, and St. Augustine's church, Penarth.

Other chapels aspired to look even more like medieval churches and sometimes their designers copied directly from ancient prototypes. Three chapels in the Roath area are particularly worthy of notice. The best of these three is Roath Park Presbyterian, Marlborough Road, a very handsome building designed by Habershon and Fawckner and erected in 1897. The design is a well-blended mixture of Early English and Decorated Gothic. The entrance façade is particularly fine, but this is hardly surprising for the doorway, with its traceried arch and decorated panels, is a copy of the thirteenth century west door of Tintern Abbey and the great window above is a copy of one of the transept windows in Melrose Abbey, Scotland. At the side there is a good tower with a tall spire (150 feet high) complete with corner spirelets.

Nearby Roath Park Methodist, Albany Road, is another ecclesiastical building which, from the outside at least,is indistinguishable from an episcopalian church. Built in 1898, to designs by Jones, Richards and Budgen, it is a large cruciform edifice in Perpendicular style with a tall tower terminated by crocketted pinnacles at the corners. The hall, together with the other secondary rooms, are grouped together at the rear and illustrate the complete break from Welsh chapel tradition in this building.

Trinity Methodist, Four Elms Road, was erected in 1897 and is a more bizarre example of the uninhibited use of medieval forms. In this chapel the architect, A. V. Ingalls of Birmingham, has used a mixture of Early English, Decorated and Perpendicular Gothic and the result is somewhat vulgar.   On the main front, for instance, there is a large rose window above the entrance, flanked by a turret with crocketted pinnacles on one side and a tower complete with broach spire and spirelets on the other side.   Evidently the chapel members thought they were having a bargain with this bumper bundle!

Other religious buildings dating from this period are the Unitarian Free Christian Church in West Grove, a hideous red-brick building with an Italian Renaissance campanile, erected in 1886 to the designs of E. H. Bruton, the be-domed Jewish Synagogue built ten years later in Cathedral Road, and the Scandinavian iron-church at the side of the Bute East Dock.

At the Docks end of the town the most imposing buildings were of an entirely different nature.   This area was still the commercial heart of Cardiff and in order to handle the continually growing imports of iron ore and the ever-expanding exports of coal two new docks were constructed; the Roath Basin in 1874 followed by the Roath Dock in 1887.   Alongside these a large number of ship-repair yards and engineering works were established.   Amongst the motley collection of buildings in the docks is the Cardiff Malting House, Lewis Road, comprising a group of three similar blocks erected in 1886 and 1897.   The five-storey buildings with their tall arcades of round-headed arches and the adjoining malt-kilns with their flat-capped pyramidical roofs, are good though hardly beautiful examples of the functionalism of the industrial tradition in building.

Following the development of the docks, commercial office blocks were erected in rapid profusion and in a multitude of different designs along Bute Street and around Mount Stuart Square.   They range from the simple toll-house classicism of the Bute Road Station to the exuberant medievalism of the Pier Head Building.

After the Station the earliest building and next-in-line along Bute Street is Pascoe House, a three-storey block of offices built in 1875 for the Powell Duffryn Steam Coal Co. Ltd.   Designed in the style of an Italian *palazzo*, it has a generally Classical façade, heavily decorated with mouldings and finished with an elaborately carved cornice at the top, but, surprisingly, an entrance in the centre with a Gothic arch.

Further along stands the Custom House, a cold, correct Neo-Classical building, erected in 1898 following a petition by the Corporation in 1891 "for the Custom House to be removed to the

Docks".[30] It is completely dwarfed by the vulgarly pompous Corys' Buildings alongside, which were built a few years earlier in 1889 and are again basically Classical in style if not in spirit.

Around the corner in Bute Place is a more sophisticated building —the Board of Trade Offices, designed by E. G. Rivers and built in 1881 as the Mercantile Marine and Telegraph Office. Three-storeys high, it has an ashlar stone base with Doric columns and a Doric porch, red-brick upper floors with a row of pedimented windows and a balustraded parapet at the top. Though archaeologically correct in its details, the overall effect is nevertheless somewhat flat and dull.

The Merchant's Exchange, at the end of Bute Street, was built about the same time or shortly before the Board of Trade Offices. A bulky, three-storey, red-brick building, with high curving gables in Flemish style it is now known as Powell Duffryn House. The Pier Head Chambers, on the opposite side of Bute Street, is another building erected in the eighties, only this time in Ruskin's beloved Venetian Gothic. Further along there is the Midland Bank Chambers, a bold Baroque-looking structure built about 1890 and extended in 1903 and 1915.

In Mount Stuart Square the most important building is the Stock Exchange. Built in 1884 to handle the rapidly growing prosperity of the town, the Exchange has been altered and added to several times and now presents a very mixed appearance though still essentially Classical in style. The original south front, planned in a grandiose manner with a large central forecourt and projecting side wings, has been disastrously obscured by the addition in 1900 of a two-storey restaurant and office block designed by Edwin Seward. Now only the four-storey east façade with its centre pediment and elaborate windows displays any impression of grandeur. Inside, the spacious Coal and Shipping Hall, reconstructed entirely in wood by Seward in 1911, is a gorgeous period piece. It has a sunken floor, two tiers of balconies all around, a sloping glazed roof supported on semi-circular arches, numerous Corinthian columns and endless panelling. The overall effect is very rich, though somewhat heavy.

"Around the Exchange are splendid examples of Victorian romanticising: Gloucester Chambers is content with Renaissance cartouches as decoration; Baltic House juxtaposes galleon and steamboat stone carvings; but Crichton House, as well as flaunting an

[30] J. H. Matthews, *Cardiff Records* (1898-1911), vol. V., p. 154.

ancient galleon, wreathes pit-head gear with swathes of leaves, scrolls and fruit in an attempt to glamorise a colliery top".[31] Mount Stuart Square has a melancholy air about it now and the buildings look uncared for and dejected; their heyday has gone, probably never to return again.   Saddest of all is the once palatial Imperial Buildings; five-storeys of white glazed stone with a colonnade of massive Ionic columns, all now derelict, dirty and decrepit.

The finest building in Butetown, however, is the Pier Head Building, a French Gothic landmark standing in splendid isolation at the entrance to the docks.   It was built in 1896 as the offices of the Bute Docks Company and in some of its details seems to reveal the influence of William Burges.   This is not surprising for the architect was William Frame who, after being assistant to John Prichard, became Burges's local assistant and was largely responsible for super-vising the restoration of Castell Coch both before and after the death of Burges.   Frame was a Royal Academy Gold Medallist and, like Burges, spent much time in measuring and drawing ancient castles.

From the outside the most striking feature of this ornate terra-cotta brick building is its fine skyline produced by an exotic array of clustered hexagonal chimneys, pinnacled turrets and gargoyles cul-minating in a fine castellated clock tower over the entrance on the south front.   The west front of the Pier Head Building is ornamented by a large panel decorated with figures of ships and a locomotive between the arms of the old borough and the arms of the Bute family with, underneath, the motto "Trwy Ddwr a Thân".[32]   The interior is, for an office building, unusually lavish in decoration.   On the ground floor the entrance hall with its brightly coloured wall tiles and mosaic floor leads into a large church-like hall divided by two arcades of large semi-circular arches.   On the first floor the most ornate part is the manager's office which is a fine room with a coffered ceiling, an elaborate canopied chimney-piece and a corner-nook, all reminiscent of Burges's restored castles.

All these buildings, whether hotels, churches or offices, were, however, more or less isolated examples in the monotonous urban sprawl of by-law housing that appeared to spread irresistibly across the lowland marshes of Cardiff throughout the second half of the nineteenth century.   In happy contrast was the series of fine

[31] P. Leech, *A View of Cardiff* (1968), p. 12.
[32] "Through Water and Fire".

parks that were established during the same period. The earliest of these was Sophia Gardens, given by the Bute estate to the townspeople in 1853. This was followed in the last decade of the century by the development of Roath Park with its beautiful lake, Victoria Park and Llandaff Fields, to form the foundations of the superb public open system that Cardiff now possesses.

Gradually other improvements were made to the town. Thus in 1866 a new reservoir was built at Lisvane, in 1874 the gas system was improved and extended throughout the built-up area, in 1890 the Clarence Bridge[33] with its swing-bridge centre section was opened and in 1891 an electricity supply system was introduced enabling the first electric tram service to be started in 1902. Further reservoirs were built, this time in the Brecon Beacons to supply the town with water, and a sewerage system was constructed. Blocks of houses were even demolished in order to widen roads! Meanwhile the town council was negotiating for the purchase of Cathays Park as a place to erect public buildings symbolising the town's growing importance.[34] Thus, expanding, wealthy and prosperous, Cardiff entered the twentieth century.

EARLY TWENTIETH CENTURY

The meteoric growth of Cardiff in the nineteenth century established it as the largest and most important town in Wales. In the twentieth century its status was officially recognised, first as a city, and then, fifty years later, as the capital of Wales. For a few years life continued much the same as in the latter part of the previous century. The basic trade was still in iron and coal, and the population continued to increase at the same rate as previously. Thus, by the outbreak of the First World War, the population had risen to about 190,000 people. Coal exports alone from Cardiff had grown to a peak of ten and a half million tons a year, and in order to cater for the still expanding traffic a new 52 acre dock, the Queen Alexandra, was opened in 1907.

Early realisation of the growing civic responsibilities of the town resulted in the purchase of a large area of land at Cathays Park for

[33] Designed by William Harpur, Borough Engineer.
[34] A proposal for building a grandiose Town Hall, designed by J. K. Collett in Temperance Town, had already been considered in 1897, but fortunately this was rejected in favour of Cathays Park.

development as a civic centre. Unfortunately, while planning in the grand manner was being carried out in Cathays Park, there was little evidence of organised urban design elsewhere in the town. Thus, in the early part of the century, Cardiff, like so many other victims of the industrial revolution was, in the words of Dylan Thomas about another South Wales town, for the most part "an ugly, lovely town, crawling, sprawling, slummed, unplanned, jerry-villa'd and smug-suburbed".[35]

After the First World War, coal exports slumped sharply and continued to fall away, so that by 1951 exports were less than they had been a hundred years before in 1851, and only a fraction of the 1913 peak. The city's population continued to rise for a few years, but soon that too levelled off and remained more or less stable until after the Second World War, although Ely, Llandaff and Llanishen had all been incorporated within the city boundary in 1922. In 1938 the boundary was further extended to include Rumney, on the other side of the River Rhymney and in the county of Monmouthshire.

Although during the inter-war period the importance of coal exports had declined rapidly, the iron and steel industry had been given a major boost. In 1930, due to the trade depression and the cost of transporting iron-ore up the valleys, the large ironworks at Dowlais were transferred to the works at Cardiff (originally started in 1889) and became known as the Dowlais-Cardiff steelworks. In 1936 the works were largely rebuilt as a modern integrated steelworks.

Apart from those comprising the Civic Centre, there were few notable buildings erected during the early years of this century. They are soon described. The earliest building that should be mentioned is the Carnegie Library on Whitchurch Road. This was built in 1906 to the designs of Speir and Beavan, with money given by Andrew Carnegie, the Scottish-American philanthropist. It is a fairly small but bold building, consisting of two identical stone wings set at an angle to each other and linked by a low entrance hall topped by a spirelet. Each wing contains a lofty hall well-lighted by tall church-like windows.

The era of church building was almost over, although a few were still being built here and there. The most notable are St. Mary's Roman Catholic church, Canton, a Romanesque building erected in

[35] Dylan Thomas, *Quite early one morning* (1954), p.1.

1907 and designed by F. A. Walters, and Cathedral Road Presbyterian chapel, a solid building with battered buttresses and a squat Perpendicular tower designed by Edgar Down and built in 1903. In Butetown a red brick Greek Orthodox church with a traditional Byzantine dome was built in 1915.

One of the most important buildings to be erected after the First World War was the Welsh National School of Medicine, an architectural residue from the nineteenth century "battle of the styles", and as such the last Gothic building to be built in Cardiff. The college was originally intended to be in the form of a group of buildings, between Newport Road and the Parade, enclosing a large quadrangle. Funds ran out and in the event only two small parts were built; the Physiological Department facing Newport Road, erected in 1918 to designs by Colonel Bruce Vaughan, and the School of Preventive Medicine facing the Parade, designed by J. B. Fletcher and built in 1926. Although by different architects, both blocks are almost identical in form, being basically four-storey Bath-stone structures with brick infill panels in medieval collegiate style. A large Decorated Gothic tower, at the end of the Newport Road section, forms the chief feature of the group.

Although the Gothic style had made its last appearance as far as Cardiff's architecture was concerned, the Classical style lingered on in Cathays Park and elsewhere. The banks in particular still clung to their ostentatious Classical ways as a sign of their financial stability. The most impressive of these is the National Provincial Bank, built in 1924 in the heart of Butetown's old commercial centre. It is a monumental five-storey Neo-Greek building designed by F. C. Palmer and W. F. C. Holden. Identical façades to Bute West and Bute East Streets are each embellished with seven bays of massive two-storey high Ionic columns supporting a deep overhanging cornice. The upper three floors are plain and something of an anti-climax. Inside, great fluted Doric columns support a curved ceiling over the palatial ground-floor banking hall.

The most outstanding phenomenon of the early twentieth century and one of the most noteworthy features of Cardiff's evolution over the centuries is the justifiably famous Civic Centre in Cathays Park. Indeed, its creation and subsequent expansion to include some of the nation's principal buildings is a singular reflection of the growing importance of Cardiff and to a large extent validates the city's now recognised claim to be the capital.   The civic centre was begun more than sixty years ago and has continually developed so that today it is almost complete.

For centuries Cathays remained as open agricultural land.   The earliest form of its name, "Cate Hayes", recorded in 1682, is thought to refer to land allotments held outside the old borough.   Up until 1766 much of the land was in the possession of the Herbert family who built the house at Greyfriars nearby.   It later passed by sale to Lord John Mountstuart (afterwards Lord Bute) and in 1803 other parts were transferred from the Corporation to the Marquess.   By 1815 the whole of the land which afterwards became known as Cathays Park had been acquired by the Bute family.   A large mansion known as Cathays House was built in the north-west corner of the Park by the first Marquess of Bute, but was subsequently demolished by his grandson, the second Marquess, who renovated Cardiff Castle and used it as his residence.   The Park was enclosed between Park Place and North Road and an avenue drive was constructed through the centre on the present line of King Edward VII Avenue.

By the middle of the nineteenth century the population of Cardiff was increasing rapidly, and because of this approaches were made by the Corporation in 1859 to buy Cathays Park as a public open space, but nothing came of the negotiations.   In 1873 and 1887 the project was revived and new approaches were made to Lord Bute, but without any positive result.   In 1892 the Corporation again wrote to Lord Bute suggesting the use of Cathays Park for public purposes including a new Town Hall, Assize Court, Municipal Offices, Technical Schools and a University College so that "we could make Cardiff one of the most beautiful towns in the country".   The idea appealed to Lord Bute and he offered to sell 38 acres for £120,000. The price evidently frightened the Council, for it was not until 1898 after much further discussion of other prospective sites at Cardiff Arms Park and near the General Station, that the city acquired almost the whole 60 acre Park for £161,000.

The layout of the roads was largely determined by the conditions laid down by Lord Bute.   A detailed plan for the development of Cathays Park was then worked out by W. Harpur, the Borough Engineer.   In 1904 the main approaches from Kingsway and Park Place were completed.   Museum Avenue was opened in 1906 and this was followed by King Edward VII Avenue in 1907 and College

Left:

Tower of the University College of South Wales, Department of Engineering (originally the Institute of Physiology), Newport Road, 1918

Col. Bruce Vaughan, architect

Right:

National Provincial Bank, Bute Street, 1924,

Palmer and Holden, architects

Photographs by T. Herridge

City Hall, 1904

Lanchester, Stewart and Rickards, architects

National Museum of Wales, 1927-32

Smith and Brewer, architects

Photographs by T. Herridge

Law Courts, 1904   Lanchester, Stewart and Rickards, architects

University of Wales Institute of Science and Technology (formerly the Technical College), 1916-27
Sir Percy Thomas, architect

Photographs by T. Herridge

Left:

Glamorgan County
Hall, 1912

Harris and Moodie,
architects

Sculpture by
Albert Hodge

Right:

Detail of Welsh
National War
Memorial

Sculpture by
A. B. Pegram

*Photographs by
T. Herridge*

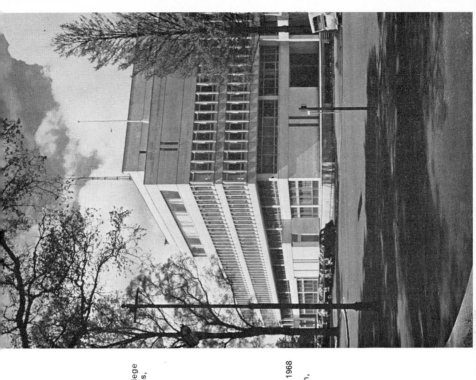

Left:

University College
of South Wales,
1909-12

W. D. Caroe,
architect

Right:

Police
Headquarters, 1968

John Dryburgh,
architect

Photographs by T. Herridge

Welsh National War Memorial, 1928

J. E. Comper, architect

University of Wales Registry, 1904

Wills and Anderson, architects

Photographs by T. Herridge

Welsh National Temple of Peace and Health, 1938   Sir Percy Thomas, architect

Welsh Office, 1938   P. K. Hanton, architect

Photographs by T. Herridge

Drawing by permission of the architects

Left:

Wales Gas Board
Bute Terrace, 1963

Alex Gordon and
Partners,
architects

Right:

Pearl Assurance
House, 1969

Sir John Burnet,
Tait and Partners,
architects

Photograph by T. Herridge

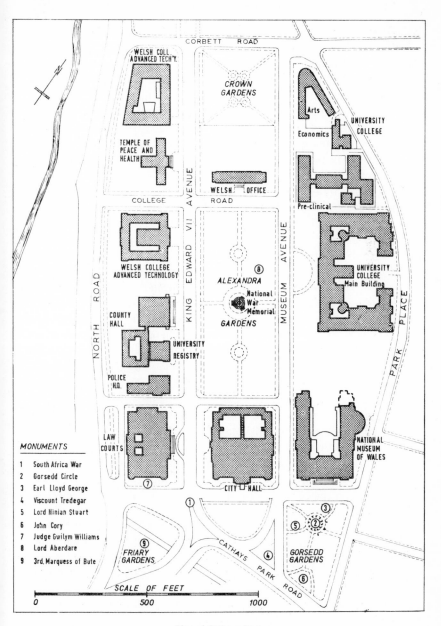

Plan of Cathays Park

Road in 1909. During this early phase Alexandra Gardens, Friary Gardens and Gorsedd Gardens were also laid out.

As soon as the provisional purchase agreement to buy Cathays Park had been signed the Corporation decided to hold a competition for the design of a new Town Hall and Law Courts. In December 1897 the first prize was won by E. A. Rickards of Lanchester, Stewart and Rickards of London. The formal ceremony of laying foundation stones took place in October 1901 and the buildings were completed in 1904. In 1906 the City Hall was officially opened by the Marquess of Bute.

The City Hall occupies a dominating position in the centre of the most southerly group of buildings in the Park. Its design is a rich and highly individual version of Renaissance architecture. It comprises a large two-storey Portland stone building, square on plan, with tall round-headed windows at the lower level and rectangular windows above. On the south façade the main entrance projects forward in a *porte cochère*. Above and behind this is the Council Chamber covered by a high dome which in turn is surmounted by a decorated pinnacle and topped by a superbly realistic dragon with rearing head and snarling tongue. At each of the four corners of the building there are square pavilions projecting above the general roof-line. In the centre of the west façade facing Edward VII Avenue is another entrance and above this is the Clock Tower, 200 feet high. As the most outstanding part of the composition, it forms a dramatic landmark. The lower part of the tower is severely plain, while the upper part is, in contrast, richly modelled.

Within the City Hall most of the main public rooms are on the first floor. Twin staircases lead to the impressive Marble Hall, with its rows of paired Sienna marble columns, which connects the Assembly Hall in the centre of the building to the Council Chamber at the front. The Assembly Hall has a richly decorated semi-circular ceiling suspended from which are elaborate pendant light fittings.

The City Hall has a large collection of statuary and paintings, the most interesting of which are a series of eleven historical statues flanking the staircases on either side of the Marble Hall. They were a gift to the City by Lord Rhondda and represent Welsh and Celtic heroes ranging from Buddug (Boadicea) and Dewi Sant to Bishop Morgan and William Williams, Pantycelyn.

The Law Courts lie to the west of the City Hall and were designed in a similar but more restrained style.   Again the building is a large rectangular two-storey one with square pavilions at each corner projecting above the normal roof line.   The main front is on the east side (to King Edward VII Avenue) facing the Clock Tower of the City Hall and contains a wide double loggia main entrance, above which are two elegant cupolas.   The west front is lower in height so that the main part of the building appears as a series of receding planes behind it.   Internally the Assize Courts and the Assembly Hall have been treated more austerely than the public rooms in the City Hall. A new Court, on stilts, was built between two original courts in 1964.

To the east of the City Hall is the National Museum of Wales, one of the finest buildings in the Park.   Although only opened to the public forty years ago, its collections have become internationally important.   In carrying out its primary purpose, *I ddysgu'r byd am Gymru, a dysgu'r Cymry am wlad eu tadau* (To teach the world about Wales and the Welsh people about their own fatherland), it has become the National History Museum, the Science Museum and the National Gallery of the Principality all in one.

The idea of a National Museum had its beginnings in a movement initiated at the 1873 National Eisteddfod.   The subject of a National Museum and National Library was later debated a number of times in Parliament, but the location of these institutions was hotly contested.   Eventually the matter was settled in 1904 by arbitration and the Museum was awarded to Cardiff while the Library went to Aberystwyth.   In 1907 the Royal Charter was granted and the first Director appointed a year later.   In 1910, an architectural competition was held for the new building; the winners, Smith and Brewer, being appointed the architects.   Four acres of land in Cathays Park had been given by the Corporation, as well as the collections of the Corporation Museum (originally founded in a small room in St. Mary Street in 1863), and in 1911 building work started.   Completion of it was postponed, however, by the First World War so that it was not until 1927 that the first part of the National Museum was officially opened.   The eastern wing and lecture theatre were opened in 1932, but no further building took place until after the Second World War.   Now the Museum has been further extended by the western wing, built in 1967 in similar style to the rest of the building to designs by T. Alwyn Lloyd and Gordon.   The northern wing, which has still to be built, will complete the building.

The National Museum is an imposing building, classical in design and nobly proportioned. On the south front, a double flight of steps leads up to the main entrance which is behind a stately Doric colonnade of tall coupled columns. On either side of the colonnade and along the east and west fronts there are projecting bays with inset columns and above each bay are sculptured groups representing various historical and artistic subjects. A continuous cornice and architrave runs around the building, above which the central dome can be seen raised behind recessed walls.

From the main entrance a vestibule leads directly into the magnificently spacious but overcrowded Main Hall, its marble columns and floors glowing in the pink light from the dome ninety feet above. At either end of the Main Hall marble stairs lead to the various galleries in the east and west wings. The semi-circular Reardon Smith Lecture Theatre attached to the side of the east wing is entered separately from Park Place.

Behind the City Hall is Alexandra Gardens, a small park, forming the heart of the civic centre. The Welsh National War Memorial stands in the middle of the Gardens. Originally it was intended that the memorial should be on the green in front of the City Hall, but this was objected to by the City Council and the Museum authorities and its present position was chosen instead. A number of architects were invited to submit designs and in 1924 the one by J. E. Comper was selected. The Memorial was unveiled in 1928 by Edward, Prince of Wales, in memory of the Welsh men and women who fell in the First World War (1914-1918). A plaque dedicated to the memory of the fallen of the Second World War (1939-1945) was added in 1949. The Memorial is in the shape of a circular colonnade with Corinthian columns. Three porches lead into a sunken court within the colonnade and at the centre is a feature incorporating fountains and sculptured figures of a soldier, a sailor and an airman, and on the top a sculpture of the winged Messenger of Victory.

Surrounding Alexandra Gardens are the rest of the buildings, all built in white portland stone, forming the civic centre. On the right hand side, behind the National Museum, stands the University College of South Wales.

The University College of South Wales and Monmouthshire had been established as far back as 1883 and was incorporated by Royal Charter a year later. The first building to be used for the College was the old Cardiff Infirmary in Newport Road. These premises soon became inadequate and in 1903 it was decided to build a new college in Cathays Park. An architectural competition was held, the winner being W. D. Caroe. The first section, including the Administrative and Arts Departments and the Library, was opened in 1909. This was followed by the Viriamu Jones Research Laboratory in 1912, the Tatem Laboratories for Chemistry and Physics in 1930 and further extensions on the Park Place side in 1954 and 1962.

The design is in an early English Renaissance style in the form of a large hollow rectangle enclosing a quadrangle. The main front facing Museum Avenue is elaborately detailed and, compared with other buildings in Cathays Park, tends to be too fussy. The central part of the main façade projects forward, containing an arcaded entrance with rusticated columns at the lower level, Ionic columns at first floor level, and above, a deep cornice surmounted by a pediment. On either side, square pavilions are extended upwards an extra floor. Behind the entrance hall at first floor level is the Draper's Library which is the principal room in the building. The Library is in the form of a large galleried hall with a lofty semi-circular ceiling pierced by side windows. The north and south façades of the College are more restrained than the front. The east façade to Park Place is in two parts, one on either side of the rear entrance, each ending in a three-storey pavilion. Unfortunately, the centre portion of the east side, which was to have contained the Great Hall, was never carried out and the internal quad has become another car park.

To the north of the main building are three post-war buildings, all designed by Sir Percy Thomas and Son. The earliest, at the northern tip of the site, is the unprepossessing Arts Building. Next to this is the Faculty of Economics building, a thirteen-storey slab tower with fine views across the park from the top. Nearest the Main College is the massive Pre-Clinical building consisting of a central wing for the Department of Physiology and two side wings for the Departments of Biochemistry and Anatomy; all built over a raised podium with car parking underneath.

Opposite the University College, on the far side of Alexandra Gardens, are a series of smaller buildings. Going north from the Law Courts the first building is the recently opened (1968) Police Headquarters. Designed by John Dryburgh, the city architect, it is the most successful of the post-war buildings in the Park. Good proportions and careful modelling of windows allows it to fit in amongst its neighbours without resort to classical detail and decoration.

Next comes the University of Wales Registry, a small building somewhat overshadowed by the buildings alongside. It is the administrative headquarters of the University of Wales. Following the founding of the University, there was much discussion as to which town should have the headquarters. Eventually it was decided in favour of Cardiff and the University Registry was erected in 1904. A pleasant, unpretentious two-storey building with a small internal court, it was desiged by Wills and Anderson in Renaissance style with Ionic columns fronting the entrance.

The County Hall is probably the most outstanding classical composition of all the buildings in the Park. It stands mid-way along King Edward VII Avenue and was built in 1912 to the designs of the architects, Vincent Harris and T. A. Moodie, who won a competition for the building. A broad flight of steps leads up from the Avenue to the very graceful main front, which comprises a wide portico with pairs of tall Corinthian columns carrying a deep cornice and balustraded parapet, flanked by corner pavilions with pilasters. On either side of the steps are large sculptural groups by Albert Hodge symbolising Navigation and Mining. The west front, facing North Road, is treated more simply and has as its chief features a bold balcony supported on massive curved stone brackets and a carving in the centre by Arthur Broadbent.

An extension to the County Hall was built at the rear in 1932. It is a well proportioned but unexciting four-storey building designed by Sir Percy Thomas in the Italian Renaissance style to blend with the rear of the main building. The extension is in the form of a square placed around a central courtyard and linked to the earlier building by an enclosed bridge.

The next building, after the County Hall, is the University of Wales Institute of Science and Technology, formerly known merely as the Technical College. The earliest beginnings of the Technical College were the Science and Art classes which commenced in 1865 in the old Free Library in St. Mary Street. In 1894 a Technical School was opened in Dumfries Place. This soon became inadequate and before the First World War an architectural competition was held for a new Technical College in Cathays Park, on the west side of

King Edward VII Avenue.   The winners of the competition were Ivor Jones and Percy Thomas.   Thomas (later Sir Percy Thomas) was then in his early twenties and this was his first major building. Later he designed many of the public buildings in Cardiff and elsewhere in Wales and twice became president of the Royal Institute of British Architects.

The Technical College was planned in the form of a hollow rectangle with an assembly hall occupying a large part of the internal court.   Only three sides of the building had been completed when it was opened in 1916; the fourth wing, facing North Road, being added in 1927.   The design of the building is austere Neo-Greek, most of the elevations being plain areas of ashlar stone punctuated by rows of tall windows.   The main façade, however, is given extra emphasis by a large portico with a colonnade of Doric columns in front of the main entrance.   A new building, again in the form of a three-storey hollow rectangle, was built at the end of King Edward VII Avenue as an annexe to the Institute and was opened in 1960.   The design is by Sir Percy Thomas and Son and has been handled in a very simple, straightforward manner, with rows of narrow windows, but with no ornament except for a relief sculpture over the entrance.

Sited between the two buildings of the University Institute is the Welsh National Temple of Peace and Health.   The Temple of Peace, as it is called, is a monument to the visionary illusion of the League of Nations and to the ideals of Henry Richard, the Welsh "Apostle of Peace".   Ironically, a short while after the Temple was opened in 1938 by one of the war-bereaved mothers of the First World War, the Second World War started.   Although unfortunate in its timing and in its cold architectural style, the building is a symbol of the devotion of the people of Wales to the humanitarian causes of Peace and Health, which is the purpose for which it was erected as a gift by Lord Davies of Llandinam.

The building, designed by Sir Percy Thomas, stands near the northern end of King Edward VII Avenue.   T-shaped in plan it was conceived as a modern version of the classical style.   The central feature is the Temple itself, forming the leg of the "T".   In front of the Temple there is a tall entrance hall which is approached through a bold portico with four square columns, behind which are three tall windows decorated with figures representing Health, Peace and Justice.   From the marble-lined walls and floor of the entrance hall, a short flight of steps leads up into the Temple. Here, eight great square columns faced in black and gold marble divide the hall into nave and aisles. Between the columns, large glass light fittings hang suspended from a coffered ceiling.

Under the Temple there is a small crypt, housing the Welsh National Book of Remembrance in which are written the names of 35,000 Welsh men and women who lost their lives in the First World War. Each day at eleven o'clock one of the 1,100 vellum pages of the book is turned as a perpetual memorial.

Finally, at the northern end of the Park and facing Alexandra Gardens, there is the Welsh Office. It was started as a government building as long ago as 1914 but was abandoned at the foundation stage owing to the First World War. It was not until twenty years later that plans were prepared for another building, and this was eventually opened in 1938.

The Crown Building, as the Welsh Office is otherwise known, was designed by P. K. Hanton and is again in a modern version of the classical style, which harmonises well with the rest of the buildings. It has four floors over a basement and consists of a single long block with the entrance in the centre. Tall windows extend vertically across the three lower floors and are separated by flat pilaster piers. A projecting cornice is carried around the building and above this is the top floor. Heraldic shields bearing the arms of each Welsh county and county borough have been arranged on the bronze window panels at the fronts and ends, while above the main entrance is a stone carving of the royal coat of arms. Internally, a domed vestibule leads to the main hall and staircase, which in turn leads to the conference room on the first floor.

Apart from an anticipated government building behind the Welsh Office, the scheme for the development of Cathays Park proper is complete. The Civic Centre has been frequently criticised because the buildings are generally too low to give a true urban feeling and also because there are no vistas from the town into Cathays Park. These are two failings which cannot be denied. Nevertheless, the combination of white buildings and parkland is very attractive and abundant trees help to integrate the various styles of buildings so that with all its failings the Civic Centre is still a magnificent reminder of the vision of its creators.

With the return of peace after the Second World War came a return to prosperity. Since the war, Cardiff has become a major commercial centre and the home of many national institutions and organisations. There has been a considerable change in the city's employment structure, so that while port traffic has receded into the background, this has been offset by an increase in manufacturing industry and commerce. Thus Cardiff has become the commercial and cultural capital of Wales, and in 1955, in the face of challenges from Aberystwyth, Caernarvon and Llandrindod, it became officially recognised by royal decree as the Capital of Wales.

In the field of building there has also been considerable activity. Significantly, this is most evident in the large number of offices and collegiate buildings that have been erected. Architecturally the most rewarding buildings are probably the post-war churches and chapels. None of these, however, are in the central area.[36] In the central area the most important post-war buildings, apart from those in Cathays Park, are the offices of the Wales Gas Board by Alex Gordon and Partners (1963) in Bute Terrace, a striking eight-storey glass tower supported on concrete columns over a lower three-storey block; the yellow-brick College of Art by the City Architect, John Dryburgh (1966), in Howard Gardens; and the Empire Pool, Wood Street, by the City Engineer, E. C. Roberts (1958), in collaboration with Sir Percy Thomas.

What of the future Cardiff? As an administrative centre, both commercially and as a result of possible future government devolution, the city is certain to benefit and become more and more important as the capital of Wales. Architecturally, the city is also likely to make considerable gains, with projects already in the pipeline for important buildings such as the National Theatre, the National Recreation Centre in Sophia Gardens, a new City Library, a Design Centre, a Concert Hall, possibly a National Gallery and perhaps one day a Welsh Parliament.

It is in the field of planning, however, that we can expect to see the greatest physical changes. More and more land will be required for housing, industry, shopping, offices, car parking, roads and public open space. While the present population of Cardiff and Penarth is

[36] The new Islamic Mosque in Butetown should perhaps be mentioned in this context. Opened in February 1969, it comprises a tall, white cylinder covered by a shallow dome and a single storey wing with triangular windows.

about 300,000 it is likely that this will increase to between 400,000 and 500,000 by the year 2000.

Already the general lines for planning the city centre have been laid down in the Probe Study Report prepared by Professor Colin Buchanan and Partners in 1966. The premise on which this report was based is that Cardiff has two main functions. One is its national function as capital of Wales, the other is its regional function as the main centre of the South Wales industrial complex. In order to carry out these functions which cater for a wide range of administrative, commercial and cultural needs, a high standard of accessibility is essential. This will mean the construction of many new motorways through the city, designed to fit in between existing environmental areas so that communities are disturbed as little as possible and the central parks system is safeguarded.

In the city centre the main changes are likely to be the development of a large new shopping precinct between Queen Street and Bute Terrace and the continued development of the Cathays Park area as the official and cultural heart of the capital. There is also the distant possibility of major development of the dock system.

Thus we may expect that the city, though much magnified and changed beyond recognition, will, as Camden described Cardiff nearly four hundred years ago,[37] still be in the years to come "a propper fine towne and a very commodious haven".

[37] W. Camden, *Britain* . . . . . *newly translated into English by Philemon Holland* (1610).

BIBLIOGRAPHICAL NOTE

Much of the background information for the above article has been drawn from: John Hobson Matthews, *Cardiff Records* (6 vols., Cardiff, 1898-1911), John Ballinger, *Guide to Cardiff* (Cardiff, 1908), Edgar L. Chappell, *History of the Port of Cardiff* (Cardiff, 1939) and William Rees, *Cardiff: A History of the City* (Cardiff, 1962). Information regarding specific buildings has also been gleaned from various issues of *The Builder* and *Archaeologia Cambrensis*. Published sources other than those mentioned above have been cited in the footnotes. In addition, many people, too numerous to mention individually,have helped me, and have often gone to considerable trouble to do so, with information regarding particular buildings. Personal mention should be made, however, of Terence Herridge who has spent much time in taking the photographs specially for this article.

VERNON HARTSHORN:
MINERS' AGENT AND CABINET MINISTER
by
PETER STEAD, B.A.

O N E of the most formative developments in the making of present-day South Wales was the "Rise of Labour". This term is used to describe those vast changes which, at the end of the last century and in the early decades of the present century, completely transformed the social and political position of the working-classes. In particular this transformation was seen in the greatly increased importance of working-class industrial and political organisations. The system of collective bargaining allowed the development of powerful trade unions, and in politics the Labour Party gradually grew stronger.

These developments brought into being in South Wales a new class of Labour leaders. These men, unlike the working-class leaders of the nineteenth century, did not lead small sectional organisations, but emerged as the most powerful and influential men in the whole community. Just as in the early nineteenth century South Wales had been led by its ironmasters, and in the late nineteenth century had been led by Liberal Nonconformists, now in the early twentieth century South Wales was to be led by the leaders of organised labour. In this modern period many of South Wales's greatest sons were to be trade union leaders or Labour politicians.

The first generation of these new Labour leaders emerged in the years from 1900 down to the 1920's. Their experience was a complex one. It was made up of Socialist idealism; of an awareness of the evils of industrial society; of an awareness of the power of the organisations they led, and of an awareness of their own ability to assume increased responsibilities within a supposedly democratic community. This common experience, however, did not produce an homogeneous leadership. Some of these early Labour leaders, like Charles Stanton of Aberdare, became wild irresponsible demagogues; whilst others, like Noah Ablett of Maerdy, became highly theoretical Marxists. Opposed to men of the Stanton and Ablett type were the older leaders—men like "Mabon" and William Brace, who often seemed afraid of the new power they themselves had helped to create. This diversity of leadership, though, can be misleading, for there were central themes in the "Rise of Labour", and there were Labour leaders at this time whose careers seem to illustrate these themes. In other words, there were men whose experiences seem so central to what was happening in South Wales at that time. Such a man was Vernon Hartshorn.

*   *   *

Vernon Hartshorn was a remarkable man, and a man whose name should be better known in his native South Wales. He was amongst the first of the new Labour leaders who emerged in South Wales at the start of this century. He was exceptional inasmuch as he went much further than most, and he ended his career as a national politician. He served in the first two Labour Cabinets of 1924 and 1929, and thus became the first Welsh miner to attain Cabinet status. He also played a valuable role on the famous Simon Commission on India which was set up in 1927. When he died in 1931 he was a prominent man, and he merited a full obituary in *The Times* in which fulsome tributes were paid by Ramsay MacDonald, Arthur Henderson, Clement Attlee and Sir John Simon. Equally remarkable, though, was Hartshorn's early career, and here we shall be concerned with the way in which in the years from 1905 to 1924 Hartshorn's experience was so central to what was happening in South Wales. His early career illustrates all the tensions and bitterness experienced by early Labour leaders, whilst at the same time it shows the changing status of Labour leaders within the community.

Hartshorn was born in 1872 at Pontywaun, near Risca in Monmouthshire. As a boy and as a young man he worked for ten years in the Abercarn and Risca collieries before ill-health forced him to take on first a surface job and subsequently an office job at Cardiff docks. He returned to work in the colliery at Risca and soon began to emerge as a prominent figure in that area of Monmouthshire. He was an early convert to the Independent Labour Party (the I.L.P.) and through the organisation secured election to the Risca Urban District Council. In 1901 he was elected check-weigher at the Risca colliery, and so started his long career in industrial relations. The first major turning-point in his career came, however, in 1905 when, at the age of thirty-three, he was elected Miners' Agent for the Maesteg District of the South Wales Miners Federation (the S.W.M.F.). Hartshorn now moved to Maesteg, the town with which he was to be associated for the rest of his career.

In a sense, Hartshorn was already an important man. The Miners' Agent in any area rapidly became one of the most influential men in local social and industrial life. Now, as the leader of five thousand miners in the Maesteg District, Hartshorn would play a vital part in determining the whole tone of life in that community. In addition, as a Miners' Agent he now sat on the Executive of the S.W.M.F. and so became one of the twenty or so men responsible for determining the nature of industrial relations in the great South Wales coal industry as a whole. In 1905, then, Hartshorn had a clear power base both in Maesteg and in South Wales generally, and in the following years he greatly increased his power and influence in both these areas.

In Maesteg, Hartshorn's firm but responsible leadership of the miners not only made the Maesteg District one of the best organised districts in the S.W.M.F. but also turned it into one of the small handful of districts (the others were the Rhondda No. 1 District and the Aberdare District) to which the rest of the coalfield looked for leadership. He also resumed his political activities, and was soon a member of the Maesteg U.D.C. In 1908 he was elected as chairman of that body, and was referred to as "the most talked-of man in Maesteg". Hartshorn's position as the outstanding leader of Labour in one town in Glamorgan was firmly established within a few years of his arrival in Maesteg. Within the next few years his name was to be widely known throughout the coalfield. His fame was to come both in the spheres of industrial relations and of politics.

As far as industrial relations were concerned, Hartshorn's fame came through his actions on the S.W.M.F. Executive. This body was in 1905 still dominated by "Mabon" and his cautious tactics, but right from the start Hartshorn joined with two Monmouthshire miners' agents, George Barker and James Winstone, in forwarding less cautious proposals. Gradually in the years after 1905 Hartshorn was emerging as one of the key men on the Executive. He often took the lead in discussions on wage and working conditions, and his new prominence was borne out by the way in which his comments were always quoted at length in both the local and national press. The peak of his influence came in 1912 when, after firmly criticising the sectional tactics of the new militant leaders produced by the Cambrian Combine dispute of 1910-1911, his advocacy of national action by the miners resulted in the *Minimum Wage Act*.

In 1912 there can be no doubt that Hartshorn was the most significant miners' leader in South Wales. In 1911 he was returned at the top of the poll in the South Wales miners' ballot for representatives on the national executive of the Miners Federation of Great Britain (the M.F.G.B.), triumphing over most of the other prominent miners' leaders in South Wales. In that same year, D. A. Thomas, the great South Wales coalowner, singled out Hartshorn as the man who really mattered in the S.W.M.F. He pointed out that he had always regarded Hartshorn "as a man of great capacity, and of intellectual ability far above any of the older leaders". By 1912 he was widely known nationally, and *The Times* described him as "the most powerful personality in the present miners movement" as well as "its guiding spirit". Hartshorn's position in these years before the First World War was due in part to his ability and his articulation, but also in part to the way in which he represented the views of so many miners. On the one hand, he never gave up criticising the caution of "Mabon" and the older leaders, for they were "too conciliatory" and their policy was a "policy of drift". On the other hand, he had no time for the new so-called Syndicalist policy born in mid-Rhondda in 1910. From the start he criticised the tactics and policy outlined in *The Miner's Next Step* of 1912. In the Cambrian dispute he pointed out that the miners had used "a steam-hammer to crack a nut", and whilst many of the so-called Syndicalists co-operated with Hartshorn in the Minimum Wage campaign, they were always kept aware that he was not one of their number. In these years Hartshorn was militant but never extreme. Journalists were always surprised when meeting him to find that he was not the firebrand they expected. To the *Labour Leader* he was "not the wild impetuous brand" of trade unionist. The *Evening Express* found that he had "an individuality of his own". . .; he was "kindly, courteous, modest and suave in his demeanour, and business-like in his methods". Coming as he did, then, between

"Mabon" and the Syndicalists, Hartshorn clearly represented the state of South Wales mining opinion in these years. In its combination of toughness and conciliation; of criticism and constructive suggestion; of socialist idealism and realism, his policy was the policy for the day.

Hartshorn's role in industrial relations before 1914 gives him a firm place in the "Rise of Labour" in South Wales. It was in the political sphere, however, that perhaps his most controversial contribution was made. Certainly his political career affords valuable insights into the nature of South Wales politics and of South Wales society in the first decades of the century. His contribution to the political sphere of the "Rise of Labour" came through his early and consistent attachment to the principle of independent Labour representation. From the end of the nineteenth century Hartshorn was a member of the I.L.P. and an advocate of the Labour Party, but when in 1905 he joined the Executive of the S.W.M.F. he did so at a time when the M.F.G.B. was still not affiliated to the Labour Party, and when many of the more influential miners' leaders were clearly opposed to any attempts at affiliation. Soon Hartshorn was prominent in urging affiliation, and when in 1906 and 1908 ballots were held on this issue, he became caught up in widely-reported squabbles with some of the older leaders. In the event the 1908 ballot was a success for the I.L.P.-ers like Hartshorn, and the process of integrating the miners' parliamentary scheme into the Labour Party structure began.

Hartshorn's main political battle in these years was fought, however, at a local rather than at a national level. It was a battle nevertheless of great significance and one which brought him yet further national publicity. He had moved to Maesteg in December 1905—a matter of a few weeks before the General Election in early 1906. This election is usually spoken of as having seen the great triumph of Liberalism in South Wales. It is perhaps better understood as having seen the triumph of "Progressivism". Progressivism was Liberalism modified so as to allow fairly full working-class participation. It allowed the Liberals to court working-class support, and it allowed trade unionists to enter politics without feeling the need for an independent working-class political party. As far as South Wales was concerned, it allowed the miners to stay outside the Labour Party, and in 1906 it allowed "Mabon" and the other miners' M.P.s to be returned as "Lib-Labs". The triumph of

Progressivism in 1906 was a heavy blow to the small but growing number of I.L.P. branches in South Wales, and Keir Hardie remained the only genuine Labour M.P. in Wales.

The General Election of 1906 had a big impact on Hartshorn. Not only was he angered by the Progressive pose of the miners' leaders, but also at the S.W.M.F. general reluctance to oppose Progressive Liberals. Above all, perhaps, he was angered by events in his own constituency. At that time Maesteg was part of the mid-Glamorgan constituency, which since 1890 had been represented by S. T. Evans. Evans had all the qualifications for a good South Wales Liberal politician—he was born at Skewen, had studied at Aberystwyth and London Universities, he was a K.C., and one of the nation's leading barristers. He could also claim to be a good Progressive, for he was a keen Welshman and, as a barrister, he had done a greal deal of work for the S.W.M.F. Such were his qualifications that in December 1905 the S.W.M.F. resolved not to oppose him in mid-Glamorgan. The result was that in the General Election of 1906 he was returned unopposed.

This decision of the S.W.M.F. was soon the subject of a great deal of adverse criticism by many miners in the mid-Glamorgan constituency, and especially by the Maesteg miners. The immediate result was that within a few months these miners had taken the initiative in the formation of a mid-Glamorgan Labour Party. This organisation, which represented the several miners districts in the constituency, as well as other trade unionists, I.L.P. and Co-operative branches, was one of the first really effective independent Labour organisations to be set up in any South Wales constituency. Throughout the early stages of its formation, Hartshorn chaired most of the vital meetings, and in May he was elected its first president. He went out of his way to make clear the position of the new body. He stated that he was not going to "waste time on a mongrel association. It was to be a Labour organisation or nothing. If the Liberals chose to contest the division against Labour, then let them fight it out". His position was unambiguous—he was a Labour man and not a Progressive.

Hartshorn was soon adopted as the Labour candidate in mid-Glamorgan, and everyone now looked forward to the electoral contest between him and S. T. Evans. This election was expected to be an important indication of what was happening in South Wales

Rt. Hon. Vernon Hartshorn, P.C., O.B.E., M.P., J.P.

10, Downing Street,
Whitehall.

15 March 1931

My Dear Mrs. Blackthorn

I can only just send my
saddest sympathies to you & your
family. This blow is too heavy &
too sudden to write about. How
hidden is destiny & death. I know
from bowed down in heart & body you
are, & I can just offer you my
hand in helpfulness. You know what
I felt for him, & how long we had
been companions together in the
great work to which we had devoted
our lives. He had his joy of success,
& that will be some consolation to you.

He has gone in the midst of a time of great weariness & difficulty & is at rest. His memory will remain a fragrance to all of us. May you & your family find some consolation in knowing how valuable his life was & how much he is esteemed.

Believe me to be

Yours always sincerely

J. Ramsay MacDonald

A letter of condolence from the Prime Minister, James Ramsay MacDonald, to Mrs. Vernon Hartshorn

Vernon Hartshorn can be seen standing second from the right, middle row, in this photograph of the first Labour Cabinet, 1924'

Photographs and letter reproduced by kind permission of Mr. V. I. Hartshorn.

as a whole.   The *Christian World* said the election would afford "a
practical test of the value of the Independent pledge in Wales", and
that a defeat for Hartshorn would mean that "Mr. Keir Hardie's
supremacy in Welsh Labour politics will be proved to be very largely
nominal".   The opportunity for such an election came sooner than
was expected, and was also to be repeated within a few years.   In
September 1906 and in February 1908, there were to be by-elections
in mid-Glamorgan.   Both were occasioned by the appointment of
S. T. Evans to various legal positions, and on both occasions he
offered himself for re-election.   These were followed in January 1910
by the General Election in which again S. T. Evans (he was now
Solicitor-General and therefore Sir Samuel Evans) offered himself
for re-election.   On these three occasions the Mid-Glamorgan
Labour Party was ready to run Hartshorn as a Labour candidate,
but on each occasion the S.W.M.F. Executive prevented a contest.

This thrice-repeated failure of the S.W.M.F. to allow a
Hartshorn candidature obviously led to a great deal of bitterness and
became something of a *cause célébre*.   The relationships between
Hartshorn and his Progressive colleagues on the Executive grew very
tense.   There were complex reasons for the S.W.M.F. decision not
to oppose Evans, but it was obvious to all that the miners' leaders
were still attempting to preserve the Progressive position of 1906.
After the first by-election one Maesteg miner said that the policy of
the S.W.M.F. Executive seemed to be one of making "soft seats for
big guns".   The *Labour Leader* accused the S.W.M.F. of "publicly
handing over a Parliamentary seat to the capitalists".

Hartshorn was fated never to oppose Evans, for in 1910, just
after the General Election, the latter was elevated to the bench.
Electoral excitement did not now end in mid-Glamorgan, however,
as there was a by-election in March as well as a further General
Election in December.   In both these elections the Liberals were
opposed by Hartshorn running as an independent Labour candidate.
In both elections, however, Hartshorn was decisively beaten by the
Liberal candidate.   The Liberal candidate in the by-election (who
was put forward almost entirely as a result of local initiative) was
F. W. Gibbins—a Quaker tinplate manufacturer from Neath.   In
the General Election the candidate was an ambitious Liberal
journalist from Aberystwyth, J. Hugh Edwards.   The results
were :

By-Election	*General Election*
F. W. Gibbins—8,920	J. H. Edwards—7,624
V. Hartshorn—6,210	V. Hartshorn—6,102

These results are of the greatest significance to any historian interested in the "Rise of Labour". They show that in a constituency with an overwhelming working-class electorate, it was still very difficult for Labour candidates to defeat well-chosen Liberals. Hartshorn was one of the best known public figures in mid-Glamorgan and he had been before the electorate for four years, and yet he still could not overcome the attachment to Liberalism.

Both defeats were to be followed by long post-mortems amongst Labour supporters, and it became clear that they were far from happy with the way in which the Liberals had fought the campaigns. The Liberal candidates adopted the normal Progressive tactic of posing as men of the community—men whose standards and values were those of the community as a whole. It followed that Hartshorn had to be depicted as a danger to those standards and values, and this danger was to be found in three of his characteristics. In the first place his Welshness was questioned. This was a favourite Liberal trick, and it forced Hartshorn to pledge his loyalty to Wales. In March 1910 he commented that "anyone would think to hear some people talk that I have been brought up amongst the Hottentots". The second line of attack was Hartshorn's extremism. Many Liberals argued that a more moderate Labour leader might well have been allowed an unopposed return in mid-Glamorgan. Hartshorn, however, was different—he was a Socialist and not a Progressive.

It was the third line of attack adopted by the Liberals which really made the two contests of 1910 so bitter. The Liberals once again made use of religion, and made a strong appeal to the Nonconformists. This was accompanied by whispering campaigns which questioned Hartshorn's adherence to Nonconformist beliefs. Hartshorn himself had been brought up as a Primitive Methodist, and at one time had been a lay-preacher, but in 1910 he was not known for his active Nonconformity. In any case all Labour supporters resented this kind of campaigning and saw it as Liberal electioneering at its worst. Hartshorn pointed out that the whole by-election had been conducted in terms of Christianity against Socialism. His conclusion was that "a more sordid or unscrupulous contest has never been waged in the history of the country". Later in the year, after his second defeat, he analysed the situation in the following terms: "The Labour Party in Mid-Glamorgan is faced with the dead-weight of generations of Liberal tradition and prejudice. We have to overcome the active hostility of a couple of hundred Nonconformist ministers, but we shall go on".

Such was the triple-attack on Hartshorn in 1910, and it affords a classic example of the ways in which Liberalism and Progressivism countered the offensive of independent Labour representation. It was always referred to as Socialism, and because of its alien, extremist and secular aspects, always depicted as a threat to the values and standards of the South Wales community. In spite of these attacks and in spite of the disappointment amongst Hartshorn's supporters, there was still a great deal of pride in what he had achieved. For years he had advocated independent Labour contests, and now in 1910 he had come to the electors as a Labour man. It was clearly understood that his candidature was qualitatively different from that of any of the other miners' candidates. Throughout his campaign the emphasis had been on "independence" rather than on the Progressive concensus. To "Argus", writing in the Social Democratic Federation Journal *Justice*, the miners of South Wales "would live to hail Hartshorn as the man who opened out to them a new vista in politics".

In the years after 1910 Hartshorn remained the Labour candidate in mid-Glamorgan, but now, as described above, it was industrial relations which took up most of his time. This was to be the pattern of his life down to 1914. In these years before the First World War he continued in politics and in industrial relations to be at the centre of events in the "Rise of Labour".

* * *

The First World War was undoubtedly the major turning point in modern Welsh history. South Wales in 1918 and subsequent years was to be very different from the South Wales of 1914. These vast changes were to be fully reflected in the career of Vernon Hartshorn, and as in the earlier years of the century, his experiences can tell us so much of what was happening in South Wales.

In politics the war years had a major impact on Hartshorn's career. In 1910 he had been twice defeated in mid-Glamorgan.

There was in 1918 no longer a mid-Glamorgan constituency, but in that year he was elected unopposed for the new Ogmore division. His candidature was widely supported by the commercial and professional classes in Maesteg, and in November 1918 the local Liberal organisation unanimously decided not to oppose him.

The "extremist" of 1910 had in 1918 become the obvious man to represent Ogmore. This surprising development was in part caused by the changed nature of South Wales society. The old shibboleths of Welsh Nationalism and of Nonconformity had become irrelevant. It was also caused in part by the changed nature of Vernon Hartshorn. Before the 1918 election one Maesteg tradesman pointed out that "they were prepared to forget 'Saul' to deal with 'Paul' ". The new "Paul" had been created because Hartshorn like many other trade unionists, had been presented during the war years with every opportunity to emerge as a responsible political figure. Throughout these years he had stressed the need for productivity (he served on the Coal Controllers Advisory Committee and the Coal Trade Organisation Committee); he had done nothing to hold up recruiting; he had served on innumerable prices and relief committees, and he had sat on the Commission of Inquiry into Industrial Unrest in 1917. For his wartime services he was awarded the O.B.E. The same Maesteg tradesman quoted above summed up this record by saying that "Mr. Hartshorn's actions and conduct for the last four years convinced us that he possessed all the qualities necessary for an ideal Parliamentary representative".

To some extremists Hartshorn had moved to the right, but most people accepted his new position as a natural development. He, as much as anyone, was aware of his new position. In October 1918 he argued that "The Labour Party had broadened its basis of welcome to all in a broad combination. Its appeal was to all that will render useful service to the community".

In industrial relations, as in politics, Hartshorn found himself in a new position as a result of the war years. Here his new position was of increased difficulty, for the new extremist elements which first appeared in 1910 had greatly increased their strength during the war years, and after 1918 continued to make things embarrassing for some of the older miners' leaders. Many of these left-wing leaders now clearly saw Hartshorn as an establishment figure, but notwithstanding these growing difficulties he was to remain on the

S.W.M.F. Executive and on the M.F.G.B. Executive. These were turbulent years though, and in November 1920 Hartshorn resigned his position on the M.F.G.B. Executive as a protest against the activities of extremist elements in South Wales. In particular, he was protesting against the undermining of his position as a national negotiator. After his resignation he openly denounced the militants and singled out the leaders of the Unofficial Reform Committee. Hartshorn's view was that "a stand has to be taken against the demoralisation with which the S.W.M.F. is threatened". The threat came from men with "reckless minds and muddled views". He went on to describe one militant leader, A. J. Cook, as "the biggest fool in the coalfield", and the other extremists he termed "feather-brains". His final warning was that "We live in a real world, we must face reality". The effect of the resignation was only temporary, for in 1922 Hartshorn returned to the M.F.G.B. Executive. In that year also, following the death of James Winstone, he was elected to the presidency of the S.W.M.F. and so he remained at the centre of mining trade unionism. Increasingly, though, it was clear that the day was being carried by more militant voices. These turbulent years had brought forward new men, and it must have been with some relief that Hartshorn ceased to be a national negotiator for the miners in 1924. From this point on his main concern was to be national politics in the wider sense, although as a miners' M.P. he was still deeply concerned with the miners' struggle.

Hartshorn was only 58 when he died in March 1931, but in his lifetime he had seen great changes, both in his own circumstances and in the nature of South Wales society. His early career reveals all the excitement, all the optimism, and yet all the bitterness of the early Labour years. To many people in the years before 1914, he seemed a man of the future: to many in the years after 1920, he seemed a leader of the past. But at every moment in the years from 1900 to the 1920's, his experiences belonged in the mainstream of the "Rise of Labour". Above all, Hartshorn's career indicated the changing status of working-class leaders. He shows the way in which Labour became respectable. It became respectable not by going back on its principles, but by proving itself in terms of service to the community. In particular, it was the I.L.P. leaders who understood that Labour would be fulfilled not by destroying society but by serving it.

Hartshorn was ideally suited to this task of serving the community. Throughout his career he was described as a "Socialist of the I.L.P. type". He was never a great theoretician and never a great emotional orator. His talents were more limited, but perhaps more practical. He had a clear mind, and what William Graham described as "the gift of lucid attractive exposition". He was at his best in detailed negotiations, and in making intelligible and detailed statistics relating to coal mining. Indeed, after 1918 it was Hartshorn's detailed knowledge of mining which brought him to the attention of national Labour leaders. Both in giving evidence to the famous Sankey Commission in 1919 and in grilling Lloyd-George's ministers in Parliament, he showed his utter professionalism as a trade unionist. This was the miners' agent of some fifteen years standing, showing his ability at a national level. It was this ability which took him on to his national political career in the shape of the Cabinet and the Simon Commission.

These practical talents of Hartshorn did not make him a great man, but they made him an able and an important Labour leader. They certainly made him into the type of Labour leader that most people in South Wales were prepared to accept. More than anything else, though, Hartshorn was a man of his time. The checkweigher had become a miners' agent; the miners' agent had become a cabinet minister. The man who had entered Maesteg in 1905 as a little known trade unionist, was buried in Maesteg in 1931 as a privy counsellor. He had been the most important man in Maesteg for as long as some people could remember. In many ways that was what the "Rise of Labour" was all about.

BIBLIOGRAPHICAL NOTE

The essential books for this period are: K. O. Morgan's *Wales in British Politics, 1868-1922* (1963), and R. Page Arnot's *South Wales Miners* (1967). Mid-Glamorgan politics are discussed in Roy Gregory's *The Miners and British Politics, 1906-1914* (1968). There are entries on Hartshorn in the *Dictionary of Welsh Biography* (1959) and in Volume II of *The Encyclopaedia of the Labour Movement* (edited by H. B. Lees-Smith). His obituary was printed in *The Times* on 14 March 1931. The most useful information on Hartshorn's career is to be found in the files of the following newpapers: *South Wales Daily News, Glamorgan Gazette, Llais Llafur, Western Mail, Labour Leader* and *Justice*.

ACKNOWLEDGEMENT

I am extremely grateful to Vernon Hartshorn's son, Mr. V. I. Hartshorn, for his very kind assistance in several matters, and also for his permission to reproduce the photographs and letter which accompany this article.

EDWARD LHUYD AND GLAMORGAN

by

MOELWYN I. WILLIAMS, M.A., PH.D.

EDWARD LHUYD was born in the year 1660. He was the son of Edward Lloyd of Llanforda, near Oswestry, and Bridget Pryse of Glan-ffraid, near Tal-y-bont, in Cardiganshire. From an early age he became deeply interested in the antiquities, more especially in genealogy and heraldry. He also became a keen student of chemistry, botany, geology, anatomy and philology. His achievements in these fields of study eventually made him one of the foremost scholars of his day.

In 1682 Lhuyd registered as a student in Jesus College, Oxford, where he soon became an assistant to his mentor, Dr. Robert Plot, a Professor of Chemistry and the first Keeper of the Ashmoleum Museum—a post to which Lhuyd himself was appointed in 1691 as successor to Dr. Plot.

The opportunities that came his way in the year 1693 were of signal importance in Lhuyd's career. In that year Swalle and Churchill, two London booksellers, undertook the publication of a new edition of Camden's *Britannia*, and Edward Gibson, a friend of Lhuyd's, accepted the editorship of that work. It is not surprising, therefore, that Lhuyd, in turn, was invited to supply notes on the section of *Britannia* dealing with the North Wales counties. He readily agreed to "doe something for two or three counties", namely, Denbighshire, Merionethshire and Montgomeryshire, with which he was already well acquainted. Other scholars were invited to undertake the remaining counties of Wales, but we are told that later, "imagining some difficulty in it . . . altered their thoughts". In view of this change of heart by the would-be contributors, Lhuyd was then asked to undertake on his own the whole section on Wales. After settling some personal differences with the publishers, he finally agreed to their request. Thus, in the middle of August 1693, he set out from Oxford to South Wales on what was described as a "speedy journey". Writing from Oxford on 10 October following, Lhuyd referred to this journey in these words:[1] "I have been about 7 weeks of late in South Wales . . . The reason for my journey thither, was because I have been persuaded to undertake not only ye three counties I at first designed; but also all Wales, Monmouthshire included. Mr. Swall (*sic.*) and Mr. Churchill (who are my task-masters) did not require I should put myself to ye trouble and expences of a journey into Wales; for they care not how little is done for that country . . .". But Lhuyd probably had other reasons for undertaking the "seven weeks' tour" in 1693. "I thought it necessary", he declared "to take a journey into South Wales because I had few acquaintance there, from whom I might receive information". Again, more significantly, he wrote: "If what we doe now will prove worth acceptance, something more material may be attempted hereafter, especially if some of our more judicious and learned Gentm. shall be disposed to favour it". These remarks may have adumbrated the "more material" and far-reaching project which was later to be undertaken in the form of his "Parochial Queries in order to a geographical dictionary etc. of Wales" (1696), and the first volume of *Archaeologia Britannica* (1707). As far as one can establish, Lhuyd visited Glamorgan for the first time in 1693, and succeeded in making acquaintances which were later to serve him in good stead.

Lhuyd's antiquarian interest in his native Wales was undoubtedly stimulated and sustained at Oxford by the works of Dr. Robert Plot, and particularly his *History of Staffordshire*. In 1694 the Principal of Jesus College "talks much of a 'History of Wales' and offers his interest to dispose ye gentry to give me ye like encouragement y^t Dr. Plot met with in Staffordshire". Lhuyd's response to the Principal's "interest" is expressed in one of his letters thus: "I answer'd y^t in two or three years time, I hoped to capacitate my self for it, and y^t I should then be very glad of such an employment". Without a doubt, Lhuyd had succeeded, in no small measure, in enlisting the interest and practical support of the gentlemen of Glamorgan in his several projects. By 1695 Lhuyd was able to report in another letter that "some Gentlemen in

---

[1] Extracts from Lhuyd's correspondence which are quoted in this article have been taken from *Early science in Oxford*, vol. XIV—Life and letters of Edward Lhuyd, by R. T. Gunther (Oxford, 1945).

Glamorganshire have invited me to undertake a *Natural History of Wales* with an offer of an annual pension from their County of about ten pounds for the space of seaven years; to enable me to travail etc: but I know not how the gentry of other country's (*sic*) stand affected". It would seem, therefore, that it was the gentry of Glamorgan who first suggested the *Natural History of Wales* to Lhuyd. They certainly supported his endeavours, as is amply demonstrated in the pages of the *Glossography* volume of *Archaeologia Britannica* published in 1707. Among the "Subscribers towards the Author's Travels" in connection with that work, "as also those who were pleased to contribute without subscribing", were listed no fewer than twenty members of the Glamorgan gentry, including Sir John Aubrey, Sir Edward Stradling of St. Donat's, Richard Seys, Esquire, of Boverton, Thomas Button of Cottrel (descendant of Rice Merrick), and Sir Thomas Mansel of Margam, to whom Lhuyd actually dedicated the first volume of *Archaeologia Britannica*. In his dedicatory note, Lhuyd wrote:

> Sir,
> Having so long since receiv'd the Honour of your Commands; I dread like a bad Steward the tendring You so Inconsiderable a part of my charge . . . But whatever Fate attends it, I have a Great while long'd for so Publick an Occasion of expressing my due Sense of your Generosity and manifesting Your Laudable Aim at the promoting of Learning in General . . ."

By 1696 Lhuyd had prepared and printed his *Parochial Queries*. He had framed 31 questions about the geography, natural history, and the antiquities of Wales for which he hoped to receive answers in respect of every parish in Wales, and it was principally through the personal contacts he had established during his earlier visit to Wales that he planned to have his queries distributed.

It is not always easy to follow the course of Lhuyd's journeys into Wales, but from his published letters we find that towards the end of April 1697, ". . . the carrier took into Monmouthshire" what Thomas Tanner called Lhuyd's moving Library which included "Magnifying glasses and other instruments, books of reference and MSS. for collation". By the following August he and his assistants had reached Cowbridge in Glamorgan. Lhuyd explains the purpose of his excursion into Glamorganshire in 1697 thus: "It would be most to my interest to goe to Cornwall . . . but having promis'd ye Gentry of Glamorganshire and Carmarthenshire (where I have the greatest number of subscribers)[2] to survey those countreys with all convenient speed I find myself obliged to make my first businesse".

It is quite probable that before reaching Cowbridge, Lhuyd had made a detour into other parts of Glamorgan, such as Caerphilly where he spoke to the local inhabitants who showed him "an inscription (as they supposed) on one of the steps of the Tower" of the castle. It seems that he had visited Gelligaer during his previous tour in 1693 where he had met with a British inscription "on a stone pillar about 3 yards high on the tip of a mountain call'd Cefn Gelli Gaer in Glamorganshire".

Lhuyd remained in Cowbridge for about two months copying a manuscript. He explained these circumstances in a letter, dated 22 September 1697, to Mr. William Williams of the Ashmolean Museum, Oxford: ". . . I intended to have been in Carmarthenshire about a month since; but have been detained by Mr. Wilkins[3] of Lhan Vair in this neighbourhood these 2 months: for so long a time the copying of an old Welsh MS took up: which had he been willing to restore to ye owner we might have bought for twenty shillings". The MS. referred to by Lhuyd was, in fact, the famous Red Book of Hergest (*Llyfr Coch Hergest*) which was later presented to the Library of Jesus College, Oxford, by Thomas Wilkins's son.

During their stay in the Cowbridge area, Lhuyd and his assistants visited the old parish of Llandyfodwg in the "mountainous parts of this County, in order to copy out a large Welsh MS. which the owner was not willing to spare above two or three days, and that in his neighbourhood". Lhuyd, referring to the manuscript in question, stated that it "was writ on vellom, about 300 years since". Lhuyd also visited the neighbouring parish of Ystradyfodwg where "In a steep rock called Craig-y-park and others" he recorded "we observed divers veins of coal exposed to sight as naked as the rock . . .". When Lhuyd made this observation in 1697, the population of the parish was only about 550, but with the exploitation

---

[2] It is worth noting that up to October, 1696, the gentry of Glamorganshire had "subscribed as much as a third part of all Wales".

[3] This was the Thomas Wilkins to whom Edmund Gamage, Rector of Coychurch, referred in one of his replies to Lhuyd's *Queries:* "We have not many skilled in ye Welsh. I suppose ye best is ye R^{d.} Thomas Wilkins rector of St. Mary Church & Llanmaes".

of the "veins of coal" in a later century the population increased phenomenally, and in 1871 it stood at 16,925, and in 1921 it had reached a total of 162,717.

It is fairly clear that Lhuyd acquired a vast amount of first-hand knowledge of extensive tracts of Glamorgan. In addition to his journeys into parts of the *Blaenau*, he visited many areas in the lower regions of the Vale. For instance, on 18 July 1697, he was at St. George's, near Cardiff, and on 22 July he went to St.Nicholas. He also visited Barry and its neighbourhood where he observed an abundance of *Entrochi*—"one whereof I saw in a rock at the Isle of Barry, about 15 inches in length: and an other about 10 inches long, but as thick as a cane". Some time was spent examining these specimens, for he recorded that "We took their figures and dimensions, but could not get off the stones without breaking". Later Lhuyd had probably journeyed to Ogmore, in the western limits of the Vale, for in a letter dated 25 September 1697, and addressed (while he was still staying in Cowbridge) to the Rev. Thomas Tanner, he enclosed ". . . an old Crosse on ye bank of ye River Ogwr at Merthyr Mawr a small village of this County".

As far as we can establish, Lhuyd and his assistants left Cowbridge for Swansea via Margam in the autumn of 1697. His progress thither is somewhat clouded in obscurity, but it is fairly certain that he had made many friendly contacts *en route*, and had observed closely the natural features of the countryside. It is fairly evident, too, that Lhuyd's preparations for his journey into Glamorgan had been well planned, and his intentions communicated to several of his friends there. For instance, a letter from Isaac Hamon on 23 July 1697 was addressed thus: "For Mr. Edward Lhuyd at the house of Mr. David Jones in Swanzey. Deliver this as soone as he comes to town".[4] Hamon obviously knew of Lhuyd's visitation.

In passing, it is worth noting how important private correspondence was as a medium of communicating information from one investigator to another during a period when there were few opportunities for published "monographs" or articles in periodicals. Lhuyd lived and laboured at a time when new discoveries and conclusions were often transmitted through private correspondence

---

[4] F. V. Emery: "Edward Lhuyd and some of his Glamorgan correspondents". *Trans. Cymmrodorion Society*, 1965, p. 77, n. 38.

between scholars of like interest. We know very little about the close links that were maintained between scholars through the letters they wrote to each other. Lhuyd's parochial queries were, in fact, only an extension of this method of communication and represented a forerunner of the questionnaire method which is, even today, practised widely in many branches of sociological research.

Returning to our main topic, it is probably true to say that Lhuyd's contribution to the history of Glamorgan in the late seventeenth century may, perhaps, be measured not only in terms of his own personal achievements, but also by the work he inspired others to undertake on his behalf. This has been clearly demonstrated by Mr. Frank Emery in his "Edward Lhuyd and some of his Glamorgan correspondents. . ."[5] where he shows, in some detail, the considerable help given to Lhuyd by the Ven. John Williams (1649-1701) of Swansea, and Isaac Hamon of Bishopston in amassing a vast amount of historical material relating more particularly to the Gower.   The degree of co-operation he enjoyed varied from county to county.   For instance, in referring to the *Queries* he had sent out, Lhuyd wrote in December 1697 saying that they were answered by "not above 20 parishes in Monmouthshire, about 50 or 60 in Glamorganshire . . .".   The number of replies to the *Queries* which were received throughout the Welsh counties generally has already been examined in an interesting article by Mr. Frank Emery.[6]   We shall now move on to examine very briefly the replies to the Queries which applied to Glamorgan.

Although the *Queries* consisted of 31 sets of questions, they were seldom answered *in toto*.   Nevertheless, many of the replies submitted are of immense interest and importance to the local historian of today.   Space does not permit of a detailed analysis of the contents of all the Glamorgan replies, but we shall take a few random examples from *Parochialia* in order to illustrate their scope.

In the replies to the *Queries* supplied by Mr. Anthony Thomas for the parish of Baglan[7] we are given an interesting insight into early industrialism in this area. The "lower parcell" had at least

---

[5]   *Ibid.*, pp. 59-114.

[6]   "A map of Edward Lhuyd's Parochial Queries . . .".   *Trans. Cymmrodorion Society*, 1958, pp. 41-52.

[7]   *Parochialia*, being a summary of answers to "Parochial Queries" issued by Ed. Lhuyd. Ed. by R. H. Morris (London, Cambrian Archaeological Association), Part II, 1911, pp. 27-35.

forty veins of coal in which "from time to time there hath beene a world of coale dig'd . . .". There was, in the neighbourhood of the Baglan sea coast "one remarkable pit" which ran "upon an horizontall line from West to East upwards of 700 fathoms, and in a perpendicular from the top of the highest hill under wch the vein runs, judg'd to be at least 200 fathoms deep . . .".

The hazards of mining the coal by candle-light in one of the veins "notable for its feiry and dampish quality", are clearly exposed in the following account: "Some 50 yeares a gon it took fire and sing'd and smother'd to death one of the workmen and soe 'twas given over. But of late years 'twas attempted againe with good successe at first. Where the coale was good and hard, there was no difficulty, nor danger in working it, only they wanted light, because their candles would not burn for want of Aire. But in other places . . . their candles would burn and blare so fierce that it fired the pit four severall times within this 12 months, and some sindg'd everytime but not to endanger their lives".

The social consequences of the seventeenth century industrial activities in the Baglan area are reflected in the fact that of the eighty houses that stood in the parish in 1696 "most of them (were) cottages for poor colliers". The total number of inhabitants, men, women, and children, was given as 350, which meant that the average size of each household was approximately 4.1, a figure which corresponded closely to the national average and one which is used in computing local population totals for the seventeenth century.

Despite the encroachment of industrialism in the neighbourhood, Welsh continued to be spoken "w^thout any alteration . . . notwithstanding the continuall trade there is and hath been there for severall ages by English men for coale and heardly . . . understand any English such is their love to the Brittish language".

The influences of the local climate, especially on the immigrant section of the population, is worth noting. In answer to question 19 of the *Queries*, we find that "This parish in lower parts as all the neighbourhood (especially to newcommers) is subject to agues, feavers and scurvies, and of late to gripeing, and fluxes. There is not at present but few ancient men in the parish and but one exceeding 70, but severall women". The men of this age, we are told "are much inferior in strength and stature to those of the very last age as some now liveing aver".

Moving from Baglan to Sully in the south-eastern part of the Glamorgan coastal region, we are again given a glimpse of the commercial activities of the county as conducted from its small creeks. Lhuyd's correspondent in Sully[8] stated that "Here is a very good Harbour for trade, especially from Swanbury (i.e. Swanbridge) to Uphill, Bristoll, and elsewhere with cattle, sheep and Hoggs". In fact, the official records of this trade show that the small ships that sailed from Sully, many of them owned by local farmers, sometimes carried as many as 120 sheep or 30 head of cattle on board. There were in the parish of Sully at that time about 40 houses and 100 inhabitants, including "Severall ancient persons w[h] age of 60 and 70 years". The air was "temperate, sweet and wholesome", which fact Lhuyd probably correlated with the longevity of many of the inhabitants.

Edmund Gamage, Rector of Coychurch,[9] supplied many interesting observations in his replies to Lhuyd's *Queries*. For example, Coychurch was an "indifferent good place for health", but many lived to a ripe age. The inhabitants were "middle sized active and ingenious and fair of complection". There was plenty of freestone and tiles in the neighbourhood, as well as "cole enough and if wrought, lead enough, and limestone for lime" which was used in large quantities on the land. The language spoken in the parish was "p'tly English p'tly Welsh", which was attributed to the "tradeing being for y[e] most parte with Summer (Somerset) and Devonshires w[ch] spoiles our Welsh".

The answers to Lhuyd's *Queries* relating to the parish of Llancarvan[10] are also worth noting here. They provide us, for instance, with useful figures regarding the number of houses and their inhabitants in each of the eight villages which comprise the parish of Llancarvan. For convenience, the figures given have been tabulated thus:

Village		Houses	Inhabitants
Llancarvan	.....	38	115
Llanbethery	.....	20	58
Llancadle	.....	26	96
Tregoffe	.....	16	58
Liege Castle	.....	12	56
Walterston	.....	14	63
Moulton	.....	20	91
Penon	.....	11	42

[8] *Ibid.*, p. 45.
[9] *Ibid.*, pp. 14-15.
[10] *Ibid.*, pp. 21-23.

In short, we may say that the total population of Llancarvan in 1696 was 579, and the number of houses was 157. The average household would accordingly have been approximately 3.7 persons. These figures, however, must be treated with caution.

The inhabitants were said to have been of middle stature, and their complexion was "somewhat fair". Regarding their diet, Lhuyd's correspondent stated that "Antipathy to any manner of meat and drink I find in none but of good digestion considering their slothfulness". Moreover, the inhabitants of Llancarvan were "very subject to toothaches and rheumes especially in the bottome near the river sides by reason of thick misty foggy aere" and consequently "very few nowadayes attain the yeares of 80".

The soil was well suited for wheat and oats "but the lands by the sides of the several rivers" were of deep mould "and very fertile soile casting some yeares 7 or 8 load of hay upon acre w^h", notes the correspondent, "you may well believe by ye length of the Knotgrasse growing on Lanbethery morse w^h is 9 or 10 foot long" and which "certainly fattens the swine y^t feeds thereon".

Llantrisant, which is nowadays identified with the Royal Mint, was referred to in *Parochialia*[11] as a market town with three fairs a year and "ye market day always on Fryday". The inhabitants were reputed to be very healthy, and there were "divers persons of above a 100 years old". The town was well watered "with numerous fountains and very fine springs". One of these springs, called Ffynnon-y-Graig, was known "to cure the King's Evil". Indeed, we are told that a Mr. Lougher, "the late vicar's man was cured thereof". On the common land "above the town" all freemen had "liberty of grazing". There were several coal works at nearby Castellau, Rhiw-Saeson, "and in divers parts of the Traen, one of the Hamletts of Llantrisent". There were also iron mines under the town at Pont-y-Felin-newydd, not to mention quarries "of fine paved stone and tyle", as well as limestones.

Sufficient has now been said for our present purpose to demonstrate the wealth of information which Lhuyd succeeded in extracting from his Glamorgan correspondents. Unfortunately, only twelve parishes are accounted for in *Parochialia*, but as we have already pointed out, many of the replies he received are missing.[12]

[11] *Ibid.*, pp. 8-10.
[12] *see* supra, p. .100

Nevertheless, what little has hitherto come to light reveals the colossal amount of work Lhuyd was able to accomplish during his relatively short lifetime, and historians investigating the social scene in seventeenth century Glamorgan, and indeed in Wales generally, will always be heavily indebted to him and his "Queries". He not only pioneered in the technique of using the questionnaire method of historical investigation, but he also demonstrated the importance of "field-work" as a complementary exercise in local historical research.

It is fitting that a scholar of Lhuyd's stature who, in his day, was so widely supported by the gentry of Glamorgan and who spent so much of his own time in acquainting himself with the county, should be remembered by readers of the *Glamorgan Historian*.

One question, however, still remains unanswered, namely, to what extent were the Glamorgan gentry, by virtue of their interest in the "natural" history of the county, responsible for introducing a change in the emphasis of Lhuyd's enquiries in Glamorgan? For instance, readers will have noted the absence of any reference in Lhuyd's published letters to the great megalithic monuments at St. Nicholas, such as the chambered tomb at Tinkinswood, although he appears to have visited the parish in person. Again, why did Lhuyd fail to visit Llancarvan and Llantwit Major, ancient centres associated respectively with St. Cadoc and St. Illtud, and so obviously rich in antiquarian interest?[13] Yet, during his stay in Cowbridge he found time to visit the parishes of Llandyfodwg and Ystradyfodwg where he observed "divers veins of coal". Could it have been that the Glamorgan gentry, men like the Mansels of Margam, were employing Lhuyd with an eye to finding out more about the mineral potential of certain areas of Glamorgan at a time when "industrialism" and "commercialism" were attracting the attention and capital of local entrepreneurs? These are interesting questions deserving further consideration.

---

[13] I am grateful to Professor E. G. Bowen for his comments on this subject.

SWANSEA'S PARKS AND PUBLIC LIBRARIES

by

TOM RIDD, M.A.

NOTHING is more remarkable in the history of municipal administration than the growth of civic pride which occurred in the late nineteenth century. It expressed itself as a desire on the part of town councils to make available to their urban populations recreational and cultural amenities such as parks and public libraries in addition to those essential environmental services such as scavenging, water supply, and main-drainage which they had provided or which they were struggling valiantly to provide. At a time when these basic environmental services were far from adequate and by no means comprehensive: on the contrary, when their growing complexity and urgency alone were sufficient to tax the resources and consume the energies of the most enterprising and conscientious local authorities, a number of municipal authorities by the early 1870's had heeded the advice of John Bright, the famous co-founder of the Anti-Corn Law League, and expended more money "on those things which are found to be essential to the health, comfort and improvement of our people". In short, they had added a new dimension to the scope of municipal administration and had started to make provision for the recreational and cultural well-being of the inhabitants of their local government areas.

That John Bright was hardly abreast of the more progressive elements in local administration, if ahead of the more conservative, was due in no small part to the breakdown of the monopoly exercised by the middle-class over municipal administration since the date of its inception under the provisions of the *Municipal Corporations Act* of 1835. The widening of the municipal franchise which followed from the passing of this act—as indeed the widening of the parliamentary franchise following the passing of the *Reform Act* of 1832—resulted not only in a potential increase in the influence of public opinion on municipal authorities but also produced a change in the attitude and character of those who sought election to the councils and, consequently, a change in the composition of the councils themselves.   Thus, the Swansea alderman who, in 1870, solemnly announced that he had spent some hundreds of pounds in his efforts to win a seat on the council and that his object in doing so was to keep the rates as low as possible, must have found himself increasingly out of place in, and out of touch with, a council which since 1866 had spent nearly £700 on the publication of a sumptuous edition of George Grant Francis' *Swansea Charters*.

Enlightened municipal administration, however, needed not only men with new, progressive ideas and attitudes to its scope and purpose but money and, more importantly in municipal affairs, a willingness to spend money.   The middle-class economists who had dominated municipal government in the first half of the nineteenth century had repeatedly made "lack of funds" the main excuse for their discouragement and parsimonious curtailment of municipal enterprise and activity.   In the early 1870's this excuse could be promulgated no longer.   Money was then available.   The years 1867 to 1873 were truly golden ones.   The business community, in the words of Benjamin Disraeli, experienced "a convulsion of prosperity" which warmed its heart and, in its private capacity as ratepayers, loosened its purse strings to such an extent that when subsequently the industrial and commercial skies darkened, the new trends in municipal government which this short period of prosperity had encouraged could not be reversed.   Municipal government had taken an enormous step forward away from the essentially pragmatic philosophy of the early nineteenth century with its concentration on basic environmental services to the more enlightened, idealistic philosophy of the early twentieth century with its concentration on a more elaborate, variegated and comprehensive range of community services.

While Swansea can certainly claim to have been in the vanguard of the municipal assault on the problems associated with public health administration—it had municipalised its water-supply in 1852 and had enjoyed the services of a properly qualified Medical Officer of Health since 1866—it had failed to keep abreast with developments in other branches of municipal administration; in particular, it had not grasped the nettle of providing recreational and cultural amenities such as parks and public libraries.   Swansea, perhaps, was more fortunate than many industrial towns in that it was a seaside town situated on the shore of a truly majestic, glorious bay—a natural open space or urban lung—the sands of which at low water afforded "an ample field for wholesome exercise". Yet the very existence of this natural lung along with the bland assumption that the poorer classes needed but little relaxation ensured that in terms of public services, parks and recreational facilities would be the cinderella of Swansea's municipal services.

The earliest conscious move to provide public parks in Swansea was made in connection with the building of the Brynmill and Cwmdonkin reservoirs. In 1849 the former was described as standing "in the midst of grassland with its margin laid out in walks and planted with evergreen shrubs". When, therefore, the Town Council acquired the property of the Swansea Waterworks Company in 1852, the first of the town's parks had already commenced its long career. In 1854 the Council, in its capacity as the Local Board of Health, spent £100 on laying out the grounds around the Cwmdonkin reservoir. Contemporary opinion was not entirely in favour of such extravagance and one disgruntled wit "supposed the Board intended planting birches there so that they would always have rods in pickle for the backs of the ratepayers". Unfortunately, both of these parks were situated in the midst of what was then a sparsely populated area and did little, if anything, to serve the needs of the mass of the townspeople in terms of open spaces. It was not until the 1870's that a real attempt was made to cope with this particular social problem.

"The Open Spaces Movement" as this campaign to acquire recreational facilities for the mass of the population was known in Swansea, will be ever associated with the name of William Thomas whose persistency and indefatigable exertions in this cause earned him the title "The Welsh Pioneer of Open Spaces". Born on 23 January 1816, William Thomas first entered public life at the age of twenty-one when he was elected churchwarden for Clase in the parish of Llangyfelach, but this early promise did not lead immediately to more elevated or distinguished public service. He was not elected to the Town Council of Swansea until November 1871. Thereafter, however, he served both as councillor and alderman for twenty-three years before finally retiring in 1894. He was elected Mayor in 1877 and in the same year he was appointed a County Magistrate.

William Thomas first drew attention to the need for open spaces in Swansea shortly after his election to the Council. In July 1874 a proposal for the enlargement of the Cwmdonkin grounds was debated. While supporting this scheme, William Thomas had reservations as to the propriety of making further provision for Swansea West, a less densely populated and far more favourably situated area than any other part of the borough. To him it seemed only reasonable that the Council should tackle this problem of providing open spaces and playgrounds in those parts of the town where the inhabitants, particularly the children, had no facilities other than the streets and the gutters in which to play. Encouraged by a favourable press, William Thomas decided to test further public opinion on this subject and accordingly offered substantial cash prizes for essays on "the desirability and advantages of providing play and recreational grounds for Swansea".

This competition brought forth a number of practical essays containing several invaluable suggestions as to the best sites for parks and recreation grounds. Prior to publication of the essays, William Thomas wrote to several local landowners apprising them of the suggestions made by the essayists. A consequence of this shrewd move was a gift by John Dillwyn Llewellyn of Penllergaer of 42 acres of land at Knapllwyd, Llangyfelach, together with a donation of £1,000 towards the cost of laying out the land as a public park. This public-spirited gift was readily accepted and the Town Council in return agreed that the land should be known as Parc Llewellyn. The occasion of its official opening and designation as a public park in October 1878 was a local holiday, highlighted by William Thomas entertaining a large number of friends to luncheon at the Swansea Music Hall and the distribution of 12,000 buns to the elementary school children of the district. The holiday was given a fitting climax with a grand fireworks display for the crowds which flocked to the park in the evening.

Having secured a park to serve the densely populated districts of Landore, Plasmarl, Brynhyfryd, Treboeth and Morriston, William Thomas now opened a campaign to provide similar facilities for other parts of the borough. Following his now established tactics, he brought the matter before Council in October 1875 and secured the appointment of a committee "to consider and report on the best site, or sites, for further recreation grounds". In October

1876 his new campaign achieved its first success. Council agreed to acquire by lease ten acres of land, now forming the Swansea Bay Recreation Ground, at a rental of £5 per acre per annum. In 1877 when the Corporation took steps to dispose of an unused part of Dyfatty Field to the Swansea School Board as a site for a school, William Thomas successfully moved the appointment of a committee to consider preserving the field as a children's playground. It was not until 1884, however, that Council agreed to the committee's recommendation that this land should be so preserved.

The campaign to preserve the St. Helen's Field—the present site of Victoria Park and the Guildhall—as a public park had its inception during the mayoralty of William Thomas. In July 1878 a Property Committee minute recommending the use of this land for building purposes came before council for ratification. In opposing this minute William Thomas publicly acknowledged his determination "to move heaven and earth to prevent this field being built upon". His vehement opposition was temporarily successful. Council agreed to defer consideration of the question for three months. This decision proved to be the forerunner of a series of successes and reverses for "The Welsh Pioneer of Open Spaces" in his fight to save the St. Helen's Field. The struggle was to continue for six years.

Both within and without the Council Chamber William Thomas met a determined opposition. While it was generally held that playgrounds were a necessity, the further provision of them in Swansea was considered to be unnecessary. No less a person than the Town Clerk claimed that with Parc Llewellyn, Townhill, Cwmdonkin, Brynmill, and the Sands "the lungs of Swansea were already to no inconsiderable extent provided for". There were others, no less influential, who based their arguments solely upon the question of finance and economy. The land should be sold and built upon. The rental obtained from leasing it was chicken feed, a mere five shillings per acre per annum.

Ranged against such opponents there was, fortunately for William Thomas, an equally vociferous body of opinion which favoured the retention of the St. Helen's Field not merely as a recreational site, but as a venue for galas, flower shows, agricultural shows and, in the last resort, volunteer manoeuvres. It was, in fact, an agricultural show which finally tipped the scales in favour of those who favoured retention of this land as an open space. In August

1878 the Glamorgan Agricultural Show was held on the field. Basking in the warm glow of a highly successful event, both the President of the Society, Henry Hussey Vivian, and the Lord-Lieutenant of the County, C. R. M. Talbot, publicly urged the Town Council to preserve the site and not to be swayed in their decision as to its future by "the sordid appeal of pounds, shillings and pence".

Despite this powerful and pointed advice, the preservation of the St. Helen's Field was still not a *fait accompli*. Several further attempts were made to let this land for building purposes, but each was resisted and finally defeated by the indefatigable William Thomas. Eventually, in June 1884, the Town Council made its decision and agreed to the retention of this site as an open space. There is, however, more than an element of drama in the fact that this resolution was only carried in Council by the casting vote of the Mayor.

On 20 June 1887, Victoria Park, as the site was now called, was officially opened by the Mayor, Frank Ash Yeo, as part of the local celebrations to commemorate Queen Victoria's jubilee. Before the end of the nineteenth century the original parks had been extended and others such as Brynmelin, Jersey, and St. James' Gardens, had been added to them.

Swansea owes an immense debt of gratitude to William Thomas, its redoubtable "Pioneer of Open Spaces". Sometimes, however, debts of gratitude to distinguished public servants are paid in a most peculiar fashion. In 1934, when the greater part of his beloved Victoria Park was utilised by the Corporation as the site for its new Guildhall, the statue which had been publicly erected in his honour was turned so that his back is forever towards the park for which he had fought so long and so valiantly.

The establishment of museums, art galleries, and public libraries provides further evidence of the widening scope of municipal administration in the late nineteenth century. Their foundation, in Swansea as elsewhere, is further testimony to the persistence and progressiveness of those pioneers and dedicated enthusiasts who campaigned for the provision of such public amenities in the teeth of considerable official and unofficial discouragement.

The *Museums Act* of 1845 enabled boroughs with a population of 10,000 or more to levy a halfpenny rate for the purpose of establishing what were euphemistically called "Museums of Art and Science". The statutory encouragement given to the establishment of public libraries was equally meagre at first. The *Public Libraries Act* of 1850 empowered the town council of a borough with a population exceeding 10,000 to levy a halfpenny rate for the purposes of building and maintaining a library. But no part of this rate income was to be used for the purchase of books. Five years later an amending act increased the rate to 1d. in the pound and authorised the purchase of books and newspapers out of the proceeds. In 1866 a further *Public Libraries Act* abolished altogether the limitations imposed on its adoption by population requirements and provided a majority of the ratepayers favoured the establishment of a public library the town council was free to avail itself of the provisions of the act for this purpose. Parliament had cleared the way to a vast extension of the public library system. It was now up to the local authorities to avail themselves of the opportunity and make provision for this new social service.

Swansea was not among the pioneers in this field. The responsibility for establishing and maintaining a museum, art gallery, and library was left initially to the Royal Institution of South Wales, a private organisation founded in 1835. The museum of the Royal Institution was specialist in character, comprising some three to four thousand specimens of a zoological, botanical and geological nature. To arouse public interest in these exhibits, it was decided in 1839 to open the Institution to the public free of charge on at least four occasions in the year. The Whitsun week-end proved particularly popular. In 1842 there were 9,000 visitors on Whit Monday and Tuesday. In 1845 the number had risen to 11,000 and in 1856 admissions totalled 12,200. This experiment in popular recreational philanthropy did not meet with universal acceptance. Members complained of the "unpleasant overcrowding" which had occurred on a number of occasions and their disgruntlement prompted the Council of the Institution in 1873 to discontinue the free admission of the public and instead impose an admission charge of 1d. on every day except Fridays,when the charge was 6d.

The library of the Royal Institution was equally specialist at first, consisting almost entirely of works of little interest to the general reader. The demand for books of a less specialist and more popular nature prompted innovations which considerably changed the character of the library. The first of these innovations was the formation in October 1848 of the Royal Institution Book Club. Reading matter purchased by this club was presented to the library of the Royal Institution after it had been in circulation for two years. The rules of the club, however, precluded the purchase of novels and general works of fiction. The ever-increasing popularity of this type of literature, however, could not be ignored and prompted further changes. In 1853 the Council of the Royal Institution agreed to the appropriation of part of its annual income to the purchase of general fiction, while in March 1857 a reading-room was established at the Institution. Its success was immediate. Membership rose; so much so, that it was recommended that the reading-room should be recognised as an essential part of the Royal Institution and should be maintained even at the expense of other parts of the society.

These changes in the character of the library of the Royal Institution of South Wales, important as they were, did not turn it into a public library. Indeed it was unlikely that it could ever become such. There were two basic reasons why this was impossible. Firstly, the Council of the Royal Institution while appreciating the value of a reading-room and a library of popular literature, remained stolidly middle-class in outlook. The possibility of their august society "degenerating into a superior Mechanics Institute, or being merely regarded as the Swansea Library and Reading-room" was anathema to the Council and the majority of the members. Secondly, the Royal Institution was supported as a private society limited in membership to those who could afford the annual subscription of one guinea. It is true that in 1865 a new class of subscribers was created to render the Institution more generally useful, particularly to those whose leisure time was restricted to the evenings, but these associate members, who paid an annual subscription of 10s., belonged almost exclusively to the better educated classes. Not one of them belonged to what the nineteenth-century sociologist termed "the working handicraft population".

The first conscious attempt to provide library facilities for the general public was made at a public meeting held in July 1868 to consider the adoption of the *Public Libraries Act*. Referring to the success of the Cardiff Public Library which had been established some three years earlier, the Mayor of Swansea, George Browne Brock, pleaded that by means of a penny rate a similar institution could be established in Swansea. Furthermore, he stressed the need for a public library in the town to supplement the work of the schools and to occupy profitably the leisure time of the working-man. If any further reason was required for the adoption of the libraries acts, he said, then it must be adopted in terms of political expediency. As the working-man was given more political power it was essential he argued, that he should be able to use it intelligently and be able to form correct opinions on the great issues of the day. These reasoned arguments, however, were insufficient to overcome the opposition of the Morriston ratepayers attending the meeting. They were vehemently opposed to the imposition of a penny rate which, in their opinion, would benefit the townspeople at the expense of inhabitants of other parts of the borough. Led by Alderman John Glasbrook, who had industrial interests in their locality, three canal barges of Morriston workmen had "sailed down" the Swansea canal and now outvoted the supporters of the public library project in the public meeting.

A fresh effort to establish a public library in Swansea was made in 1870. A bequest of 6,000 books, the library of the late Dr. Rowland Williams, supplied the nucleus for a town library: the establishment of the St. Helen's Workman's Institute and Reading-room in 1869, together with a growing consciousness of Swansea's gradual subordination to Cardiff as the metropolis of South Wales, supplied the impetus. A series of public meetings now held to reconsider the whole question of a town library gave full and ample opportunity for the airing of all possible and impossible arguments for and against this proposition. To those who opposed the establishment of a library on the grounds of expense, the champion of the project countered that the town which levied a library rate would easily recoup its expenditure in savings on the cost of other remedial social services such as its workhouse and prison. It was, perhaps, more difficult to make a suitably polite rejoinder to John Glasbrook who, in answer to the plea that working men needed education and culture, replied that "they knew too much already . . . the more education they received the more difficult they were to manage".

Adoption of the *Public Libraries Acts* was eventually approved at a lively public meeting held on 11 October 1870. It was a hairsbreadth victory for those who had fought so hard to achieve it. The motion in favour of adoption was put to the meeting twice. On the second occasion the number of hands raised against the proposal exceeded the number raised in its favour. Whereupon the Mayor claimed that nearly half of those voting against the motion had held up both hands. In his opinion the meeting was in favour of adopting the *Public Libraries Acts*. He therefore declared the motion carried. As *The Cambrian* commented: "Two attempts having failed the Mayor cut the Gordian knot . . . by the light of his own wishes, and declared the motion carried". Some members of the Town Council were equally suspicious and sceptical of this result and in December 1870 adjourned indefinitely the appointment of a Library Committee. Four years, in fact, were to pass before this committee was appointed under the chairmanship of Alderman (later Sir John) Jones Jenkin.

The primary task of the Library Committee was to establish a central library for the town, with branch libraries in the more populous suburbs. In August 1875 the Town Council placed two old houses in Goat Street at the disposal of the committee and on 1 May 1876 the lending department of this central library was officially opened to the public. Reading-rooms were established at St. Helen's, Landore, and St. Thomas, though the last mentioned was closed in 1877 as it had become "the resort of children who committed a considerable amount of damage to the furniture". The establishment of a branch library in Morriston was due entirely to the munificence and public-spiritedness of private individuals who raised sufficient money and books to form the nucleus of a good library. Moreover, they agreed to pay the librarian's salary. The Morriston branch library was opened on 16 January 1878.

The Town Council's parsimonious and grudging acceptance of responsibility for this new social service was further highlighted as lack of space at the Goat Street premises affected the efficacy of the central library and its associated art gallery. Both in the Lending Department and in the Reference Department, the size and position of the rooms used was such that it was impossible to arrange the books so that they were easily accessible to the public. While the generally dilapidated condition of the building made it "dangerous to allow any considerable number of persons to congregate on its upper floors" for the purpose of viewing its art exhibits.   In these circumstances it was gradually realised that if the townspeople were to derive full and proper benefit from the library and art gallery, then a new and far more commodious building was absolutely necessary.   Between 1878 and 1882 the Library Committee repeatedly brought this matter before the Town Council.   Finally its persistence in the teeth of considerable discouragement and opposition was rewarded.   In April 1882 the Council agreed to erect a new central library, art gallery and school of art on the present site in Alexandra Road.   The foundation stone of this new building was laid in November 1884 and on 6 June 1887 the completed premises were officially opened by the Right Honourable William Ewart Gladstone.

BIBLIOGRAPHICAL NOTE

An unpublished source from which material has been drawn is the author's M.A. thesis (University College, Swansea, 1955) on "The development of municipal government in Swansea in the nineteenth century".   Published sources include the following works:

Beanland, W. A.   *The Royal Institution of South Wales, 1835-1935.* Swansea, 1935.

Davies, R. R. and Roberts, J.   *Prize essays on the desirability and advantages of recreation grounds for Swansea.*   Swansea, 1875.

Francis, G. G.   *On the St. Helen's and other sites for a public park at Swansea.* Swansea, 1878.

Wright, A. C.   *The Welsh pioneer of open spaces.*   Swansea, 1878.

SWANSEA PORCELAIN:

SOME FACTS AND OPINIONS

by

ELIS JENKINS

WITH the publication in 1897 of William Turner's *Ceramics of Swansea and Nantgarw*, the scattered facts of a curious Glamorgan enterprise were brought together for the first time to give some coherence and homogeneity to what had hitherto been either hearsay or the loyal adherence of a few Welsh collectors of china. In June 1914, just before the outbreak of the first World War, a special Loan Exhibition was staged in the Glynn Vivian Art Gallery, Swansea, as part of the celebrations to mark the only visit to Swansea of the Museums Association, and, for the first time since the end of the short working life of the nearby China Works, some five hundred pieces of Swansea pottery and porcelain were assembled in one building. The impressive Catalogue included an introduction, "Ceramics in Wales", by Frederick Lichfield, then considered an authority on European porcelain, in which there is a profusion of erroneous statements, including such absurdities as this: "The greater part of the more highly and ambitiously decorated Swansea china was sent to London . . . the mark is generally *Nantgarw*, impressed", which recalls the old music-hall catch-phrase, "The next song will be a dance". But the same Catalogue contains a short history of the Swansea potteries and their wares by Herbert Eccles, a Neath industrialist and collector who, like William Turner (with his fund of local gossip), relieved a factual account of the various Swansea "bodies" (to obtain which even a precious Bevington-Gibbins plate had to be broken) with some enthusiasm for the beauty of the objects themselves.

This noteworthy Exhibition also contained sections showing other Welsh products such as the lacquered iron ("japanned") ware of Pontypool and Usk, and the work of Welsh crafstmen in oak, all pointing to a new awareness of the contribution which Wales had made over the years to the decorative arts. But nobody noticed, except for a casual aside by Eccles, that 1914 was the centennial anniversary of the beginning of porcelain manufacture in Swansea; and certainly few realised that two small associated Welsh manufactories had turned out a porcelain body which in its finished decorated state was to be regarded by informed opinion as comparable with the best porcelain made in Europe, in some respects having a slight edge even on the famous pâte tendre of Sèvres. Today it shares with the "Mabinogion", the poems of Dylan Thomas and the landscapes of Richard Wilson, the distinction of being recognised and acclaimed outside Wales.

Since the Swansea Loan Exhibition of 1914, the scientific and scholarly approach of Herbert Eccles has been followed by others. In 1942 E. Morton Nance, a Cornishman who at the end of the last century had been classics master at Swansea Grammar School, published a massive work on the pottery and porcelain of Swansea and Nantgarw, which at the time seemed the definitive history, though it modestly admitted that many questions remained unanswered. In 1948 and 1958, Mr. W. D. John of Newport, in whom a love for Welsh china was joined with a talent for lucid exposition, published from his own press two sumptuous volumes on the Nantgarw and Swansea potteries. Then, in 1949, the late Kildare S. Meager, after a lifetime of studious dedication to the subject, wrote a concise account in an introduction to the Catalogue of the Welsh China in the Glynn Vivian Art Gallery, following this up six years later with an illustrated chapter in the second volume of *Glamorgan Historian*.[1] One can only regret that such a scholarly collector, with his incomparable knowledge of the subject, should have written down so little of it for those who came after.

Apart from a six-page extract from the section dealing with earthenware, in the Catalogue of the Glynn Vivian Gallery,which was reprinted in the Catalogue of the Kildare S. Meager Bequest in 1968, there is very little accessible material dealing with Swansea porcelain and pottery.[2] The more extensive treatises by William Turner,

[1] See *Glamorgan Historian*, vol. II, pp. 104-114.
[2] Since this was written Mr.W. J. Grant-Davidson's paper has come to hand. It is mentioned in the bibliography.

Morton Nance and Mr. W. D. John are now available only to the specialist reader at enhanced saleroom prices or in the larger libraries; and so great is the interest in all that has to do with Glamorgan that volume II of the present series, with its informative chapter by Kildare Meager, published as recently as 1965, is already out of print, and must either be borrowed or purchased in a rare-book department.   Yet while the reading matter is becoming scarcer, the researches of scholars and collectors bring fresh evidence to support new theories; death duties, death without issue and the whims of previous owners bring hitherto unrecorded treasures into the salerooms, and a prosperous and expanding middle class, discriminating or merely acquisitive according to its background and disposition, imposes new trends and fashions on the prevailing taste. Among collectors of china one may find flamboyance, vulgarity and a lowly urge to out-plate the Joneses, but even at a slightly more sophisticated level porcelain has more variety and surface area to look at than postage stamps.

Swansea porcelain appeals to people in different ways and at many levels.   There is first the dramatic content of its short but complex history, which in an oversimplified and distorted re-telling of the sufferings and frustrations of William Billingsley has made a successful radio feature.   Then a lot of the china happens to be attractive to look at, not only for its finely-modelled unfussy shapes but also for its tasteful decoration.   The best of it is just as beautiful when viewed by transmitted light, for the translucency of both the glassy variety and of the finer grades of duck-egg can delight the sense.   If Greek sculptors and architects attained perfection in a limited way, their reach not exceeding their grasp at such close range, the makers of Swansea china aiming at a goal far beyond any hope of realisation achieved something substantially worthwhile, but only by breaking the first law of a commercialised society, losing money.   Lastly, there is always the challenge to complete the unfinished, to fill in the blank spaces in a ceramic puzzle by finding the answers to so many questions.   How much of the Nantgarw recipe was made at Swansea?   Did Billingsley paint the hundreds of roses that get by as his, or is that which we call a rose by any other man just as puce?   How much china did the Bevingtons make from Dillwyn's two recipes?   How many recipes did Walker try out besides the glassy, the duck-egg and the trident?   Who painted what? And were there a Colclough, a De Junic and a David Evans? Those who have access to what has been written on the subject since 1897 will have noticed the frequent use of words and phrases that are either preludes to guesswork or misty evasions of the admission that many problems remain unsolved. Words like "perhaps", "doubtless", and "probably" appear on every page, sometimes varied by their more leisurely equivalents "it would appear", "one can reasonably assume", and "it is more than likely". Still, every schoolboy knows, or would know if he were not so sharply specialised, that Swansea porcelain is a brief flowering that came midway between the early growth and the long decline of a hundred years of local ceramic history.

In 1764 a Cadoxton-juxta-Neath industrialist named William Coles leased from the Swansea Corporation a piece of land on which he built a small pottery for the manufacture of simple domestic ware. Twenty-two years later, Coles's son John was carrying on the now flourishing business in partnership with George Haynes, a very able manager and administrator who would today be called an executive. In the closing years of the eighteenth century, under the proprietorship of Haynes, the quality of the creamware and other earthenware was considered fully equal to that being manufactured by Josiah Wedgwood at Etruria in Staffordshire. Then in 1801, a prosperous Quaker, William Dillwyn, during his second and more protracted visit to the town, bought the lease of the Pottery, known since 1790 as the Cambrian, for his son Lewis Weston, then aged twenty-three. It was a shrewd deal that ensured the controlling interest for the Dillwyns while retaining the administrative skill and the local business connexions of Haynes as manager. From 1802 until 1810, the "Haynes, Dillwyn & Co." era, young Dillwyn was virtually in partnership with a man thirty-five years his senior. But if in these early years Dillwyn was a studious botanist devoting much of his time to publishing his scientific work, he was also learning to be an astute business man, and when the agreement with Haynes lapsed in 1810, Lewis Weston Dillwyn became the sole proprietor until December of the following year, when another Quaker, Timothy Bevington (who had succeeded Haynes as manager) and his son John, were taken into partnership. From the end of 1811 until near Michaelmas 1817, the firm traded as "Dillwyn & Co.". Although Haynes is known to have produced a little experimental porcelain just before the Dillwyns came on the scene,[3] the period beginning in 1814, when Dillwyn was associated with the Bevingtons, is that in which the fine porcelain we are concerned with was manufactured and decorated. For three anxious years, in which the fortunes of the businessman and the artist-potter, both in their way perfectionists, alternated between success and failure, with vexations and disappointments continually harassing them, Dillwyn and his practical associates persisted in the hopeless efforts to make a porcelain that was both beautiful and profitable, until in 1817 the attempt was abandoned. In the same year, family commitments prompted Dillwyn to lease the Pottery and the China Works to the Bevingtons and others who, not succeeding with either porcelain or earthenware, in 1824 allowed the two concerns to revert to Dillwyn. Thereafter the entire works was given over to the manufacture of earthenware. In 1831 Dillwyn was joined in its management by his third son, the seventeen-year-old Lewis Llewelyn, who had just left his school in Bath. Five years later, Dillwyn senior, whose social and political engagements were taking up much of his time, assigned the whole of the assets of the works to his son. In 1850, about two years after the attempt by the younger Dillwyn and his wife Elizabeth (the daughter of the eminent geologist, Henry De la Beche) to impose the pseudo-classical Etruscan wares on an unappreciative public (a rejection which has since made them extremely rare), the Cambrian Pottery was transferred to David Evans and J. E. Glasson, a partnership whose wares were marked "Evans & Glasson". In 1862 the works were taken over by Evans's son, D. J. Evans, who for eight years traded as "D. J. Evans & Co.". Having now reverted to making the kind of simple domestic ware, the manufacture of which had characterised its beginnings a hundred years earlier, as well as quantities of smokers' clay pipes, the pottery closed down for good in 1870.

Porcelain-making at Swansea is in broad perspective inseparable from the mysterious curtain-raiser which preceded it at Nantgarw. Of the four men who were at various times associated with one another in the two ventures, one had little to do with the Nantgarw works, another had an even slenderer connexion with Swansea, while the remaining pair divided their time equally between the two places. In 1808 William Billingsley (1758-1828), one of the outstanding china

[3] Mr. W. J. Grant-Davidson states that these early experiments were "around 1796".

decorators[4] and potters of his time, if not of all time, was employed by the Worcester china-making concern of Flight and Barr, not primarily as a decorator, but to improve the Worcester body. Billingsley had two daughters, Sarah (*b.* 1783), and Lavinia, twelve years younger, and in September 1812 Sarah had married Samuel Walker, a practical potter and kiln-builder of some repute. Two months later, on 17 November, Billingsley and his new son-in-law, whose joint experiments had produced a very beautiful white translucent china body, signed an agreement with their employers not to divulge the recipe to a third party, though there was nothing to prevent them from using it themselves to manufacture china. In consideration of their undertaking to withhold the secret from any other person the two men were paid £200 in cash, and also agreed to a clause stipulating a payment of a thousand pounds to the firm of Barr, Flight & Barr in the event of their disclosing the formula to anyone else.

Sometime in the summer or autumn of 1813, Billingsley (now calling himself by the more convenient works name of Beeley) and Walker were in Nantgarw. For over seventy years there has been a good deal of surmise as to why they chose this obscure Welsh village, exactly seven miles north of Cardiff castle; and there has even been a snide suggestion that they had decamped from Worcester. However, the evidence available supports the view that Nantgarw was selected for very practical reasons, such as its plentiful supply of coal for firing the kilns and the availability of a cheap waterway in the nearby canal for transporting the wares to Cardiff, Merthyr and Bristol. They can hardly have been absconders, for there was nothing in their agreement with their last employers to prevent them from setting up in business on their own account.

With a capital estimated by Young to be £250, much of it being the £200 hush-money from Flight & Barr, the little family party consisting of Billingsley and his eighteen-year-old daughter Lavinia, with Walker and his wife Sarah, settled into Nantgarw House, which they rented from Edward Edmunds. With their modest assets they

---

[4] In the jargon of ceramics, the artist who painted on the china was known as a *decorator*, though sometimes the ambiguous word *modeller* was used. It is assumed that the reader is familiar with the distinction between earthenware (pottery, ware) and porcelain (china). The former is quite opaque, while the latter is translucent to a greater or lesser degree, depending on the power of the illumination and the thickness and composition of the body.

had to house, feed and clothe themselves, purchase materials to build at least two kilns,[5] then wait for some china to be made and sold before they could expect any return from this shoe-string operation. After a few months, the impoverished potters had the good fortune to meet William Weston Young,[6] a Newton surveyor, who later had enough faith in the quality of the china being manufactured in a Glamorgan back-garden to support it with all the money he possessed, which amounted to some £600. When this subsidy was spent, Young could give no more financial help, as he was made bankrupt for the second time before the end of the year; but now a partner in the business and the only literate member of the trio, he addressed an appeal to the Secretary for the Lords of the Committee of Council for Trade and Plantations (the equivalent of our Board of Trade) with a covering letter to his friend Sir John Nicholl of Merthyr Mawr, who was to forward the request to London, asking for a grant to enable their mini-factory to compete with the famous state-aided Sèvres china works, and appealing to the Committee to increase the tariff on French porcelain which was, even then, less than two years before Waterloo, being imported into Britain. The Memorial (as it is usually called) signed by Walker, "Beeley" and Young was submitted to London forthwith, together with Young's explanatory letter in which the sum of £500 is mentioned as an acceptable figure for a subsidy, and Nicholl's covering note; but the petitioners quickly received a polite refusal saying there was no government fund from which the Committee could obtain money for such a purpose. Sir John Nicholl, who acted as go-between in this exchange, shortly afterwards sent a specimen plate or plates (for it is unlikely that any other kind of china was available then) to London. A notable dilettante member of the Committee, Sir Joseph Banks, explorer, botanist, Fellow of the Royal Society and a discerning collector of china, must have seen the Memorial and the sample, for within days he had written to his friend Dillwyn, himself an F.R.S. at twenty-six, suggesting that the latter visit Nantgarw to report on the little factory and the quality of its products.

Dillwyn, who was already interested enough in the making of porcelain to have had two Coalport men, Biggs and Burn,

[5] At least two kilns were essential, but during his visitation Dillwyn mentions "a kiln" and "a small kiln", probably the one that was being fired that day.
[6] A fuller account of Young's involvement with Billingsley and Walker will be found in *Glamorgan Historian*, volume V, pp. 81-88.

experimenting independently of one another at the Cambrian factory, and whose initiative in doubling its earthenware capacity from four to nine kilns and overriding the trade recession of the previous four years had prompted him to consider such an extension of the pottery's manufactures, immediately got in touch with Young at Newton, following this up with the Nantgarw visitation. Throughout the month of September 1814 Young, as shown in his fact-book for that period, was continually coming and going from Newton to Nantgarw, from Margam to Swansea, from Swansea to Newton and Nantgarw; on one occasion accompanied by his partners Billingsley and Walker, on another by Walker and Thomas Pardoe,[7] and throughout acting as go-between for Dillwyn and the potters. The speed of the events is incredible when one realises that the period from 5 September, the date of the Memorial, to the 29th, when Dillwyn records an agreement with Young and Walker for the transfer of the Nantgarw venture to Swansea, including a government department's reply to the Petition, was only three and a half weeks.

Dillwyn was elated at the prospect of manufacturing fine porcelain at Swansea, and in a letter of 29 September to his father-in-law at Penllergaer, he is bubbling over with enthusiasm. "I never have done a better day's work in my life. I am to be put into immediate possession of every circumstance relative to the making of porcelain, and the entire management, both as to the scale and the manner in which the manufactory is to be carried on is without restriction, to be placed at my discretion, on my giving a Bond not to communicate their secrets to others, and agreeing to pay them half the profits arising from the sale, as my Agents". The same letter reveals a bit of modern salesmanship on the part of the Nantgarw men, who had hinted to Dillwyn that there was a take-over offer from a certain "L.D." (assumed by Nance to be Lord Dumfries, shortly afterwards to become the second Marquess of Bute, a man who always manifested an interest in Glamorgan enterprises, as his later relationship with Young was to show). In this letter Dillwyn also proposes to spend a few days in Nantgarw "to make myself

[7] Young and Pardoe had known one another when Young worked for Dillwyn at Swansea between 1803 and 1806. Subsequently Pardoe had set up as an enameller and glass stainer at Bristol, and was to come to Nantgarw in 1820 to decorate the china that Billingsley and Walker had left there when they departed for Coalport.

master of the process", and adds, "I expect the agreement to be signed on Monday" (i.e. 3 October).

At Nantgarw, Dillwyn was delighted with the fine appearance and translucency of the china, and despite some reservations about the firing losses, wasted no time in arranging for the move to Swansea. Thirty-five years later, soured by his recollections and embittered against Walker and "Beeley", he was to recall those early days in a letter to Joseph Marryat, who was gathering material for his *Collections towards a History of Pottery and Porcelain* (1850). "From the great number of broken and imperfect articles which I found, it was quite plain that they could not be produced with any certainty, but I was made to believe that the defects arose entirely from the inconveniences of their little factory, and was induced to build a small china works adjoining the pottery, that the granulated[8] body might have a fair trial". About the same time Dillwyn had given similar information to Sir Henry De la Beche:[9] "Upon witnessing the firing of a kiln at Nantgarw I found much reason for considering that the body used was too nearly allied to glass to bear the necessary heat, and observed that nine-tenths of the articles were either shivered, or more or less injured in shape by the firing. The parties, however, succeeded in making me believe that the defects in their porcelain arose entirely from imperfections in their small trial kiln, and I agreed with them for a removal to the Cambrian pottery, at which two new kilns, under their direction, were prepared".

According to Young's fact-book, the actual move to Swansea was on 8 October 1814. After the building of the kilns, which must have taken some months, a few trial firings of the Nantgarw body were attempted, but despite better facilities and the improved conditions, with the same disastrous failure-rate. In a letter printed in *The Cambrian* newspaper on 18 October 1822, Young refers sadly to these events of 1815 (for the kilns can scarcely have been working to capacity before the New Year). "An agreement was entered into with the proprietors of the pottery, and the work was removed there. Here seemed everything that could be wished for; but unfortunately a new body and glaze were proposed and entered upon before sufficient experiments were made; this occasioned great loss, both

[8] "Granulated" was the "lump-of-sugar" fracture of a soft paste (pâte tendre) body as seen in the texture of the edge of a broken fragment.
[9] Published in the 1855 catalogue of the ceramics section of the Museum of Practical Geology in Jermyn Street, London.

of time and money: the parties disagreed; and Mr. Beeley returned to Nantgarw".

There has been some difference of opinion in recent years about the extent to which the Nantgarw formula was used in these early trials before Dillwyn insisted on introducing modifications that would cut the losses. Dillwyn states that the first pieces were impressed with the Nantgarw mark (he calls it "Nantgarrow") and later authorities have noted that a number of these plates were lobed and embossed with scrolls in the Sèvres-type early-Nantgarw fashion, the later Swansea ones being usually round or notched. The work of building the two kilns can scarcely have been completed when Walker received a surprise letter from Flight, Barr & Barr.[10] Dated 12 November 1814, it reproached the two men for their sudden and inconsiderate departure from Worcester after the kind treatment they had received; expressed astonishment on hearing ("we are now told . . .") that Walker and Billingsley had formed "some sort of connection with a Person of the name of Young" and were about to make the secret "composition" for Dillwyn and Bevington; and, lastly, informing Walker of their "firm resolution of instantly giving our attorney instructions to commence an Action against you for the amount of the Penalty of one Thousand Pounds named in the Bond given to us the 17 day of November 1812". In his letter to Marryat, written on 5 June 1812, Dillwyn recalls that "while engaged in some experiments for strengthening this body, so the articles might retain their shape in the kilns . . . I was astonished by receiving a notice from Flight & Barr, of Worcester, that the persons who called themselves Walker and Beeley had clandestinely left their service, and warning me not to employ them. Flight & Barr, in the most gentlemanlike way, at the same time convinced me that this granulated body could never be made any use of". At this stage the businessman in Dillwyn must have been convinced that the Nantgarw recipe could not be made to pay, and that if a new one could be devised, he would also be safe from any legal trouble with Flight & Barr. Because of the decision to make an attempt to modify and improve the Nantgarw body, Billingsley went away in a huff to Nantgarw, and when second thoughts brought him back to

[10] Until 1807 this Worcester firm was known as "Flight and Barr"; from 1807 till the death of Martin Barr, senior, in 1813 as "Barr, Flight and Barr"; and after 1813 as "Flight, Barr and Barr".

Swansea, it was as designer, decorator and instructor in the painting-room. Walker, too, now in charge of the china-making, had to find a way of strengthening the Nantgarw body in order to eliminate the heavy losses without at the same time reducing the quality, especially the translucency. In his letter to *The Cambrian* in October 1822 on the subject of the impending sale of china at Nantgarw, Young, as we have seen, refers to these experiments with their loss of time and money, and adds that "the parties disagreed; and Mr. Beeley returned to Nantgarw". There is some confusion as to which "return" this was, for according to Young's fact-book, Billingsley left Swansea for the second, perhaps the last, time on 23 December 1816, and is not heard of again until the middle of the following September. As so little is known of the movements of the two men during these months, there has been a good deal of surmise. Mr. W. D. John's guess is that Billingsley was still in Swansea applying his expertise to making soft-paste china, while Morton Nance infers that he was in Nantgarw. He could equally well have been reunited with his wife in Derby, or even making one of his devious tours round the English potteries seeking employment or some other employer to exploit his remarkable recipes. At Swansea, Walker's dilemma was to decide whether to improve the Nantgarw body by altering the proportion of each ingredient in turn or to make a different body by introducing an entirely new constituent like soaprock.[11] On the very day of the 1814 agreement between Dillwyn and the two potters, the former had entered into a seven-year contract with Lord Falmouth to "search and dig for soaprock in Cornwall" (actually from Gewgraze, near the Lizard Point) at a cost of £75 per annum for fifteen tons. It has been assumed from this that Dillwyn intended using soaprock from the outset to strengthen the porcelain body during the firing, especially when the proportion of bone ash had been reduced; but this contract could also have been made for the purpose of including it in the earthen-ware body, a practice that was not uncommon in Staffordshire. It is generally agreed that Walker was experienced enough to know that the body could have been made more manageable, that is, more plastic and less frangible, by using more china-stone and less of the Lynn sand, or even by increasing the proportion of china-clay; but

---

[11] The hydrous bisilicate of magnesia, often called steatite, soapstone or even french chalk, was found in natural deposits mixed with china clay.

always at the expense of the translucency which was so desirable a quality of fine porcelain. The London dealers and agents, to whose decorating-rooms so much of a porcelain factory's output was sent, were uncompromising in their insistence on what William Barnes would have called "the see-throughableness of the stuff". This quandary in which Dillwyn, Billingsley and Walker found themselves has been described in some detail because in any account of Swansea porcelain, it is the heart of the matter, the essential reason why its manufacture lasted only a little more than two and a half years. Perhaps the nub of the whole affair is that Billingsley wanted it beautiful, while Dillwyn wanted it profitable as well. The factory's agent did not announce the availability of the new product until the summer of 1816, so for nearly two years Walker was persevering in his attempts to find a body that was not only stable but also acceptable to the London enamellers; and he may well have kept on trying even until he joined Billingsley at Nantgarw on 25 September 1817.

About the middle of 1816 Walker, by substituting Cornishstone and lime for the Lynn sand of the earlier body, produced a porcelain with a near-white translucency which is still much admired. In the autumn of the same year came the confection which because of its slight greenish tinge when seen by transmitted light has come to be known as the duck-egg, or duck's egg, its tint being caused by an impurity in the blue ball clay.[12] Thomas Baxter, who arrived in Swansea in July 1816 to work as a freelance, or perhaps part-timer, as a rule used the better of the two variants, though the slightly off-white glaze, which Dillwyn in his note-book designated "Glaze No. 2" was the same for both. Dillwyn euphorically hailed it as "a beautiful body", and his approbation has since been confirmed by most judges, from the London decorators of the time to modern collectors. It has been estimated that from a quarter to a third of the porcelain produced at Swansea was of this kind. But as the kiln losses were still too high, in the spring of 1817 Walker, by adding soaprock, devised yet another body which despite its glassy appearance both in transmitted light and in the fracture was nevertheless china and not glass. Notwithstanding Robert Drane's apt

---

[12] Some observers have seen a bluish tint in the body, but the writer is familiar only with different hues and intensities of green, except when the thickness of some pieces adds a brownish tinge.

description of it as "sodden snow" the epithet "glassy" has stuck. In transmitted, not reflected, light it is a little whiter than the almost ivory-white Nantgarw body, and it has less of the surface pitting known as pigskin than has the later soaprock body.

Just as there are at least two distinguishable varieties of duck-egg, so there are two soaprock bodies: the glassy containing one part in fourteen of the steatite, and another (later to be known as the trident because of the impressed trident, or sometimes two, criss-crossing in what heraldry calls "in saltire") containing twice the quantity. As its soaprock content was too low, the glassy porcelain had been very difficult for the factory potters to handle and shape, and impossible to throw; and since this shortcoming made it costly to manufacture, very little of it was in fact made. Yet what has come down to us is sometimes mistaken for hard-paste porcelain, except when marked with the word "Swansea" (as it often was) in red, gold or even green script. Yet your collector has no doubts even when a piece of local china is not marked, for like the subject of one of Lamb's "Imperfect Sympathies", his wisdom is born in panoply, and he has only to candle a piece to give you his categorical judgment that it is Nantgarw, glassy, duck-egg or trident. Not that the choosing is always difficult, for the later trident, resembling its ancient Roman counterpart in being the instrument of the coup-de-grâce, brought an end to the brief life of Swansea porcelain. When held against even a bright light, this ill-favoured thing has an unexciting auburn tint which by contrast with the duck-egg is depressing. Someone has written of it as "clouded, and nearly always yellow or olive-brown to a dense smokey-brown", a description that seems more appropriate to tropical sun-glasses than to porcelain. From its gloomy translucency to its hard, thin, pigskin or orange-peel glaze, which Dillwyn thought was "well suited to the body", it is dismal stuff, which the London enamellers turned down out of hand. No doubt pleased with its easier working and cheapness to produce, Dillwyn thought it a marked improvement, yet though disappointed with its rejection by London, it is significant that he used it for quality show-pieces like cabinet cups, cabaret sets or vases because its plasticity made it more manageable for delicate or difficult shapes. Its decoration presented difficulties, too, for the glaze and the enamel colours did not always get on well together, so that the painting can sometimes be felt by the fingers as

Lewis Weston Dillwyn

*By permission of the Royal
Institution of South Wales,
Swansea*

The Cambrian Pottery in 1791, from an engraving by Thomas Rothwell

By permission of the Royal Institution of South Wales, Swansea

Swansea porcelain transfers and set patterns

Rear:	Plate with underglaze blue floral transfer from the Lady Seaton service
Left Centre:	Plate with filled-in transfer, "mandarin" pattern, No. 164
Right Centre:	Plate, set pattern No. 232
Left:	Cup and saucer, set pattern No. 231
Right:	Cup and saucer, set pattern No. 219, with reserves decorated by Henry Morris

Swansea porcelain comport or centre stand.   Mark: *Swansea* and *No. 223*, in red script

Mr. and Mrs. W. E. Jenkins Collection, Neath

a slightly raised pattern. Turned down by London, the factory stock-pile, which was considerable, had to be decorated on the spot. In the meantime other events were moving fast. As Dillwyn's father-in-law, John Llewelyn, sometime of Ynysygerwn in the Vale of Neath, then of Penllergaer, had been a sick man for many months before his death in July 1817, family affairs had taken precedence over the business of the pottery and china works, which were then being managed by Timothy Bevington and his son John. Walker's failure to produce a perfect china, as well as his own daily commuting between The Willows in Swansea and Penllergaer seven miles away, had discouraged Dillwyn from continuing with the experiments. The situation was further complicated by the departure of Walker to rejoin his father-in-law Billingsley at Nantgarw which, according to Young's fact-book, he did on 17 September. It had been a sad year for all, with death and disappointment all round. On New Year's day, Sarah Walker had died in Swansea and was buried in St. Mary's Church. On 8 September, at the age of twenty-two, Billingsley's younger daughter Lavinia died suddenly in Nantgarw and was buried at nearby Eglwysilan. Billingsley was desolate, and his letter to his estranged wife, Sarah, still living in Derby, is a most moving document. By the end of the month he was reunited with Walker and Young at Nantgarw, for Young as a friend of both Dillwyn and the potters had discreetly acted only as a third party in the negotiations for the move to Swansea in 1814, and could at last renew his associations with Billingsley and take an active part in reviving the Nantgarw pottery without compromising his loyalty to Dillwyn, who in any case had now discontinued the manufacture of porcelain. Walker, a widower since the death of Sarah in January, may have realised that Billingsley, who was a skilled potter as well as decorator, was able to continue the making, and even the improvement, of the old body; so on 28 September he wrote from Swansea to Etruria asking Josiah Wedgwood for a job, and giving, perhaps in advance, a Nantgarw address. From this time on, Billingsley and Walker[13] disappear from the Swansea porcelain scene, and only William Weston Young pays the occasional visit to decorate or fire a few trial pieces.

[13] On 14 February 1827, nearly ten years after his departure, Samuel Walker called at the Cambrian Pottery to discuss with Dillwyn the possibility of another attempt at manufacturing porcelain. But the China Works had now closed and Dillwyn was not disposed to reopen it. Walker in due course emigrated to the United States and is said to have prospered.

Back at Swansea, Dillwyn was not only finding that family affairs and the Llewelyn Trust were taking up much of his time, but was also getting heavily involved in public affairs. The Cambrian works was being managed by Timothy Bevington, a Stratford-upon-Avon Quaker who had been employed by Dillwyn for fifteen years, first as chief clerk and, since the departure of George Haynes in 1810, as works manager, with his son John acting as salesman and clerk. In 1811 Dillwyn had taken the two Bevingtons as partners in the firm, which then traded as "L. W. Dillwyn & Company", with Dillwyn holding seven-tenths of the shares, the total value of which was given as £13,500. As the profits were shared proportionately, and the Bevingtons were not paid salaries, they cannot have been sorry to see the last of Samuel Walker and his porcelain experiments, which had not only lost money for the China Works but had been carried on to the neglect of the earthenware section. Early in 1817 Dillwyn had offered to sell his interest in the pottery, and by the month of May the Bevingtons had found enough backing to accept, but fearing that Walker might take over the China Works, insisted that the deal must include both concerns.

On 23 September 1817 the Bevingtons, with their three new partners, George Haynes, senior, and his son (also George), and John Roby, a Tamworth man who had money invested in coal mines, concluded the take-over by paying Dillwyn £9,100 for his share in the concern. They took a lease on the earthenware works for 21 years with a year's notice at an annual rental of £1,000. The new company also took a separate lease of the China Works for £200 per annum, with two years' notice either way. Dillwyn was to keep the Garden Scenery dessert service decorated specially for him by Thomas Baxter (see *Plates VI* and *VII*) as well as the sum of £340 owed to him by Billingsley and Walker for the cost of setting up the porcelain kilns in 1814. On their side, the Bevingtons were given two of the porcelain formulas (the duck-egg and the trident), as well as their glazes, and also the large stock of porcelain in the white, which Dillwyn valued at £2,500, an astonishing amount when it is realised that this was one-fifth of the total valuation of the whole business.

As none of the five partners in this new concern of "T. & J. Bevington & Co." was qualified to make practical use of the two porcelain recipes, and the take-over coincided with a post-war recession in trade, the new company had decided to concentrate on earthenware manufacture, and on 7 August 1820 gave Dillwyn the contractual two years' notice to terminate the lease of the China Works. The following year Dillwyn was at cross purposes with four of the partners, who accused him of having grossly overcharged them for the stock of porcelain taken over, mostly trident; of having over-estimated the total amount of the debts due to him that could be collected as assets; and of having insisted on exorbitant rents for the Pottery and China Works. A Bill in Chancery was filed against Dillwyn who, convinced that Haynes, who had left the Cambrian works in March 1810, was the main instigator, was firmly determined not to accept any sort of liability or even a compromise; and when, in September 1821, the case was dismissed with the award of costs to Dillwyn, the two Haynes,[14] father and son, and Roby, gave up their interest in the Pottery, leaving Timothy and John Bevington to carry on alone. But not for long, for in 1822 they gave the stipulated two years' notice to Dillwyn,who in 1824 once more took possession of the works which his father had purchased for him in 1802 and where he had been closely and continually associated with Timothy Bevington for the whole of that time. In order to concentrate on the making of earthenware, Dillwyn successfully merged the two sections of the works into a more efficient unit than the Bevingtons had achieved, with Isaac Wood, Billingsley's former modeller, as manager.

The stock of china taken over by the Bevingtons in 1817 must have been enormous, representing the accumulation of several years of slack trade followed by the piling up of unsaleable trident. Haynes's claim in 1821 that £2,500 was an overvaluation by Dillwyn of china that was worth only £1,000 is manifest nonsense, for not only did he have an established reputation in the town as a shrewd and efficient businessman, but he had been in charge of the Pottery for years, and at the take-over had accepted Dillwyn's valuation without demur.

There is no evidence that the Bevingtons manufactured any

---

[14] Haynes also had banking and brewing interests in Swansea. Resentful at leaving the Cambrian Pottery in March 1810, he and his son-in-law started up a soap works on land adjoining the pottery, and till Dillwyn took legal action to abate the nuisance, the latter's 150 employees were near vomiting with the noisome stench. Haynes was also associated with the rival Glamorgan Pottery (1812-39) which adjoined the Cambrian.

quantity of porcelain; at most, only a few successful firings. Apart from a dozen or fewer small biscuit rams fashioned by Isaac Wood, for several years the modeller at the Cambrian, which have the mark BEVINGTON & CO. SWANSEA impressed, together with his initials I.W., there is only one other piece bearing the impressed mark BEVINGTON & CO., which, since it must have been added when the body was in a plastic state before firing, may be considered as evidence of its provenance. This is the base or stand of a very large tureen in the Bevington-Gibbins dinner or dessert service, cheerfully decorated in the Castled Gatehouse or Tower pattern, which is one of three Swansea services decorated in underglaze-blue transfer.[15]

Dillwyn, as we know, had passed on to Timothy Bevington the recipes for a duck-egg and a trident porcelain, but as Walker for some unascertained reason had not been re-employed by the new firm, there was now no skilled practical potter at the works who could use the recipes. Dillwyn, who at the take-over had expressed willingness to give advice if and when called upon, and who records in his diary that he was helping with experiments at the Pottery late in 1817, could not have been very helpful once he had passed on the recipes to Timothy with an injunction to keep them secret even from his partners. Of the two older partners, Timothy Bevington was nearing sixty and George Haynes, senior, well over seventy; both were managers and administrators rather than technicians, and were even less qualified than Dillwyn to turn the formulas to practical use. Since the porcelain made in 1815 was largely experimental, and only in 1816 was enough produced to enable Dillwyn's agents to advertise it to the public, as two of them did that year; and since by mid-1817 there could not have been large quantities of fine quality duck-egg china that had not already been sent to London for decorating, the undisposed stock at the works must have been for the most part either rejected trident or discarded seconds. It is not surprising, therefore, that the Bevingtons, who had themselves suffered directly from the losses sustained during Dillwyn's recent enthusiasm for china-manufacturing, should have decided from the outset to concentrate

---

[15] The two others are the Lady Seaton service with floral spray decoration, and the oriental-inspired willow-tree and peony service which, because of the curious shapes of the stylised rocks in the right foreground, is commonly known as the "elephant" pattern. This transfer was earlier used on the earthenware.

their efforts on making earthenware, and as regards porcelain, to be content with decorating in Swansea (as Dillwyn had suggested) the thousands of pieces that had accumulated in the store-rooms. That this is in fact what they did is borne out by Henry Morris's important statement.[16] "The following information", wrote his interviewer, "I take down *viva voce* from Mr. Henry Morris, of Swansea, who was duly apprenticed to Mr. L. Weston Dillwyn as a pottery painter in the year 1813".[17] Recalling those early days, Morris continues: "It unfortunately happened that owing to some peculiarity in 'the body' whole kilns of this precious material were destroyed or rendered useless, and many a load was carted away to a hollow in the field at Hafod above the pipe works, whence on some future day choice fragments will doubtless be disinterred". Referring more specifically to the Bevington period (1817-1824), Morris is reported as saying "On the departure from Swansea of Walker & Bailey, the management devolved upon Mr. Timothy Bevington, the then manager of the earthenware department of the Cambrian Pottery. The 'China' continued to be manufactured from the recipes of Walker and Bailey up to about 1823, when the make was finally abandoned on the expiring of the lease to Bevington, the pottery returning into Mr. Dillwyn's hands. The existing stock of china in the white was removed to the pipe works about half a mile further up the river Tawe and there it was ornamented, enamelled, and sold. An enamelling kiln was next constructed at the Brewery premises in the Strand,[18] so as to be near Mr. John Bevington's offices, and there the last remnants of 'Swansea China' were painted and sold, the very last portions being painted by my present informant".

Morris, who lived until 1880, was a most prolific painter of Swansea porcelain, though there were many others with him in these later years, including David Evans, William Pollard and George Beddow. As a group working on into the Bevington period, rather than as individuals, their handiwork may sometimes be identified by the use of the word SWANSEA in red transfer, usually

[16] This statement made to Col. George Grant Francis on 14 August 1850, and published by his son in *The Cambrian* newspaper on 3 January 1896, the year before William Turner's book appeared, is one of the few first-hand accounts of the Pottery, and with its many hitherto unrecorded facts is a most valuable document.

[17] Henry Morris was then a child of fourteen.

[18] This was the Cambrian Brewery.

on cleanly-finished pieces, for it was not often that they had to fall back on discarded wasters as poor Young was so often compelled by circumstances to do at Nantgarw. Some idea of the sheer quantity of stock taken over from Dillwyn may be inferred from the fact that at least half a dozen china painters were employed continuously for eight years in the mammoth task of preparing it for general sale, as well as for the public auction of 30 January 1826 when, as will be seen from the following announcement that appeared in *The Cambrian* newspaper on 21 January, there was still some china remaining undecorated.[19]

Elegant Swansea & Nantgarw China

To be sold by auction by Mr. Dan¹ Harris on Monday, January 30th 1826 and following days, at the Public Rooms, Burrows, Swansea, the undisposed stock of the late Cambrian China Manufactory consisting of various specimens of richly-painted ornamental pieces in Vases; Cabinet & Chocolate Cups; elegant French ink-stands (painted by Evans); Candle-sticks; Pen & Wafer Trays; several Dinner, Dessert and Breakfast services; a very handsome complete Breakfast service, Paris fluted, broad gold bands; with a great variety of shapes both useful and ornamental in white china.
The Public are particularly invited to attend the above sale, as such an opportunity is not likely to occur again.
N.B. Either of the Swansea Bank Notes will be taken for the above ware.

So the unsold china that began life in the kilns of the Pottery was carted, after a long stay in the stock-rooms, to William Bevington's Pipe Works half a mile upstream, then back again to Haynes & Morgan's Brewery near its birthplace, and finally half a mile down-river to be sold by public auction. Many of "the great variety of shapes in white china" were purchased by Henry Morris, from whose flowery production-line the numerous services and single pieces were to be dispersed in the neighbourhood for many years. "The very handsome complete Breakfast service, Paris fluted, broad gold bands", one of the most elegant tea-sets sold by the Bevingtons, is the Sayers service, named (like the Lysaght, Lady Seaton, Burdett-

---

[19] If one may venture a guess that pieces of trident and other porcelain in the white would not have cost more than sixpence each, then Dillwyn's valuation of the stock at £2,500 in 1817, though considered excessive by the Bevingtons in 1821, would have represented some 100,000 pieces.

Coutts and Vachell services) after a one-time owner.[20]   The
inkstands in the French style are specifically attributed to "Evans",
a shadowy figure who is mentioned by Turner as a person who
had been named by Henry Morris in a conversation with friends.

Of the many specialised porcelain painters whose names have
been linked with the large quantities of china in the white that became
available for decorating between 1815 and 1825 the best known are
William Billingsley, Thomas Baxter, David Evans, William Pollard,
Henry Morris and George Beddow.   The importance of Morris's
statement is again confirmed by his references to his fellow artists:
"The truly beautiful paintings which adorn this manufacture were
executed by or under the direction and superintendence of a Mr.
Bailey; by the artist Baxter, who had been a student at the Royal
Academy; by De Junic from the Royal Manufactory at Paris, and
other artists, several of them natives of Swansea, amongst whom
was my present informant.   The modelling was entirely performed
by Isaac Wood, of Burslem, in Staffordshire, but who came from
Nantgarrow with Walker & Bailey.   The biscuit flower modelling
was executed by a man of the name of Goodsby, of Derby, and it
was then considered excellent.   Mr. Bailey not only painted our
china, but designed many beautiful forms for the modellers".

Despite Morris's important information there are still many
hiatuses in the sequence of events and in the lives of the men closely
connected with them, many enigmatic silences and the vexation of
lost records.   There is no letter, diary, newspaper cutting, not even
hearsay, that gives a clue to Billingsley's movements in the crucial
period between December 1816 and his reunion with Walker and
Young at Nantgarw nine months later, nor is there any indication
of how his work was apportioned between decorating, instructing
and experimenting with recipes in the two years he spent at Swansea.
The chronicler need not be discouraged, however, for men like
Morton Nance have demonstrated how by years of painstaking
enquiry much new and relevant material can be brought to light.
Nor, apart from satisfying a natural curiosity, is the biographical
fill-up always essential, for once it has left its maker's hands, a work
of art, whether it be the Jubal cup or "Hamlet", exists *in vacuo*,
independent of Baxter or Shakespeare, self-sufficient in its greatness

---

[20] According to Mr. W. D. John, a hundred pieces of this service were purchased
from "an old Swansea family" in 1932 by Mr. Edwin Sayers of Newport.

and its wonder. But we are human and we are curious, and most of us want to know whether the plate we possess is a Swan or a goose, in the jargon of the dealer, whether it is "right" or "wrong"? It is an exhilarating experience to see the knowledgeable appraiser at work, for expertise in others (unlike the tattered contents of the rag-bag one's own mind seems to be) is exciting and convincing, even though no two of the Seven Sages agree. The connoisseur evaluates a piece of china by examining its potting and body, its glaze, decoration and (when it has one) its mark; the shape being perhaps the feature that is first noticed as being most characteristically Swansea.

It has been customary to distinguish four kinds of Swansea porcelain body: the conjectural Nantgarw paste of the first trials, the duck-egg, the glassy and the trident; but nowadays collectors who have examined large numbers of representative pieces are agreed that there are certainly as many as the eleven that are entered in Dillwyn's notebook, and more if we include the gradations and nuances in each group. The Nantgarw body is not invariably ivory-white, and some duck-egg is tinged with blue; for Walker and Billingsley were continually experimenting to improve their paste. In the summer of 1816 Walker, as we have seen, hit upon a body that was as translucent as the early Nantgarw, but whiter, though it resembled the later duck-egg except for its lime content and a smaller proportion of china stone. Mr. W. D. John, who was himself a research chemist, has pointed out that this recipe differed from the early attempts, which merely altered the proportions of the Nantgarw ingredients, in that it contained a completely new, non-fritted constituent. The best known example of this beautiful but un-economic porcelain is the cabaret set decorated by Thomas Baxter with sepia cupids in various attitudes.

There were many differences in the hues and in the intensity of pigmentation of the duck-egg porcelain evolved late in 1816, the most attractive being the one that Dillwyn hailed as "a beautiful body which in all respects answers".[21] Alas, the following months were to show that there was one crucial respect in which it did not answer: it was not profitable to make. Still it was a glorious failure, which Thomas Baxter, who was fastidious, used for most of his best work.

---

[21] Nance, who made sardonic capital of the mistakes of others, has misquoted Dillwyn's comment on p. 275 of his own book, but transposes it correctly on p. 461.

When held against a light this porcelain is only slightly tinged with green, and thinner parts like the sides of cups and the rims of plates appear as luminous as those in the best Nantgarw. Slight changes in the recipe, the presence of impurities, variations in the firing temperature, and rule-of-thumb methods, often resulted in a more pronounced green, though it was still agreeable. The problem in identification is that Spode and several other factories later turned out porcelain with a greenish tinge though for different chemical reasons. Walker's compromise was beautiful enough to satisfy the London decorating establishments, but the kiln losses were still high, and since the factory's earthenware was its breadwinner, less of it was sent to London than one would expect; yet it was attractive enough to invite imitation, and Dillwyn took gentle counter-measures by announcing in *The Cambrian* in May 1817 that henceforth the word SWANSEA would be stamped on his china. No sooner had his warning been published than he was offering to the world the Swansea factory's great flop, the china made from the soaprock recipe, the so-called trident body, which has already been described.

The china bodies preceding the trident had the good fortune to be decorated by two of the most celebrated china painters of their time, perhaps of all time. William Billingsley (1758-1828) and Thomas Baxter (1782-1821) had been trained in England, and both had already distinguished themselves in their art at other factories before coming to Wales. Billingsley, on whose activities as a potter in Worcester and Nantgarw we have already dwelt, had been apprenticed at Derby where he remained for thirty-four years, and had also worked in Pinxton, Mansfield and Torksey. This restless key-figure was fifty-two years old when he came to Swansea,[22] and after more than three years in Nantgarw (from late 1816 till early 1820), he was still to work for John Rose at Coalport. Opinion is divided about the extent and nature of Billingsley's activities at Swansea, but because his style of painting is known from signed examples of his work at other factories, there is agreement about many of the landscapes, flowers, shells and figures that are assigned

[22] Billingsley, accompanied by his daughters, had walked to South Wales in 1808, looking for work, without success. The sad little party stayed with Thomas Pardoe, who was then the chief decorator of earthenware at the Cambrian Pottery, and who was to come to Young's help at Nantgarw in 1821 when Billingsley and Walker suddenly left for Coalport.

to him. Although he is everywhere acknowledged as the supreme
master potter and painter, it is for his depiction of flowers, especially
the rose, that he is best remembered. Breaking away from the
artificial French fashion of the time, he painted flowers with great
naturalness and restraint, never using his colours garishly or crudely,
but always with disciplined good taste. He is credited with introducing a new technique of obtaining his highlights by wiping off the
pigment with a dry brush, a method which was adopted by some
of his pupils at Swansea. His admirers praise his individual
treatment of the rose, with his fondness for a pink that seems to be
tinged with puce or purple, and the subdued palette of his low-key
landscapes, which are sometimes even sombre, though, as Kildare
Meager has said, there is a harmonious blending which is always
pleasing. Like the lexicographer who admitted that he could not
define an elephant but knew one when he saw it, many of us when
stirred by music or painting attempt to define kinds of awareness
that are beyond the reach of words. Few people will have difficulty
in recognising Billingsley's finest work at Swansea, and there is a
measure of unanimity about its attribution to him. Where
controversy and doubt arise is with his less ambitious routine
productions, the run-of-the-mill work in the painting room when
the master joined in with the rest in keeping the production-belt
moving, or just gave a hand to his apprentices with some deft
gilding or retouching. As painting on china is considered one of
the lowlier manifestations of decorative art, its lesser achievements
do not often attain an "after-the-school-of" designation.

Although we cannot be certain of the reason for Billingsley's
departure from Swansea at the end of 1816, we do know that it was
some five months after the arrival of a sophisticated young artist who
brought with him the new Royal Academy School notions of art and
certainly a different style of painting. Thomas Baxter was a third
generation china painter who had received his early training in his
father's decorating shop in Gough Square, London, near the house
where Dr. Johnson had lived thirty years earlier. He had attended
Fuseli's lectures, published books on classical costume and architecture, painted at Flight & Barr's works in Worcester and started
an art school in the same town. At Swansea he was virtually a
part-timer, and is mentioned in the Directory as "artist" or "drawing
master". We can imagine the impact of his arrival on Billingsley,

then nearing sixty and described in the records as just a "china painter". Baxter's supreme accomplishment during his three-year stay in Swansea was the garden scenery dessert service of over forty pieces which was made specially for Dillwyn, possibly as a factory sample, and, having been named in the Chancery Bill against Dillwyn, shares with the "Paris fluted; broad gold bands" (the Sayers service) the distinction of being mentioned in a contemporary document. Baxter's birds, shells, flowers and figures are executed in a delicate stipple with a miniaturist's perfection, and are much prized by collectors and museums not only because they are so readily attributable but because they are even scarcer than anything indisputably by Billingsley, if we exclude the profusion of rose-decked masterpieces that pass for his work. Since Billingsley taught so many able youngsters, and the rendering of flowers on Swansea china is consequently very good, that which we call a rose by any other man is often just as sweet.

Henry Morris (1799-1880) was an apprentice of barely sixteen when Billingsley took over the superintendence of the painting-room, and was not only employed at the Pottery until the end of the Bevington period, but claimed to have painted the very last of the Bevington left-overs in the Strand Brewery just before the 1826 auction sale. He is credited with an enormous amount of Billingsley-style decorating, and any competent arrangement of garden flowers which cannot with confidence be assigned to others is sometimes ascribed to him. One of his more impressive performances was on the Lysaght service, most of which was purchased by Mr. Sidney Heath in Devon not long after the last war. After the Swansea period, Morris worked in London and Staffordshire before returning to his native town, where he set up a muffle in his back garden and for another thirty-five years decorated Staffordshire china for sale locally. Some of this is signed and dated, but since the workmanship is undistinguished, Morton Nance and Kildare S. Meager were troubled by the thought that the earlier and better Swansea decoration attributed to him could not be by the same hand; yet the two styles are not incompatible if we bear in mind that Morris, once freed from the rigid discipline of the pottery painting-room, may have been less painstaking when churning out quantities of mediocre stuff for the local market.

William Pollard (1803-1854) was too young to have come under the direct influence of Billingsley and Baxter, and was not even working at the Pottery until the Bevington era. After that, he free-lanced in Swansea, Carmarthen and elsewhere, decorating china from Staffordshire. His work on Swansea porcelain, usually on the duck-egg body, shows skill in both landscape and flower painting, but he is best known for his representation of wild flowers, as is the shadowy, half-mythical David Evans, who received his only contemporary mention in the 1826 auction-sale announcement, "Elegant French ink-stands (painted by Evans)". In Turner's book, *The Ceramics of Swansea and Nantgarw* (1897), he not only achieves a local habitation and a christian name, but also acquires an uncle, one Evan Evans, who painted on earthenware. Turner refers to his reputation as a painter of wild flowers, and retells the hearsay picked up from interviewing very old men who had worked at the Pottery and remembered the artists. Although the Pottery persisted until 1870, the China Works had closed down nearly fifty years earlier, and at the time of Turner's enquiries anybody with alert faculties and a retentive memory who claimed to remember Evans would have been eighty or ninety years old. There clearly was a china-painter named Evans working with the Bevingtons, and as some of the finest wild flowers were on the earlier and better duck-egg body, there must have been an older artist than the teenage Pollard working with Billingsley and Baxter, with whose skill his own bears comparison. While this gifted man may well be David Evans, there is some evidence for the existence of another highly talented artist of the calibre of Billingsley. In his *Ceramic Art of Great Britain*, Llewellyn Jewitt includes a certain "Jenny, a gold tracer", in his list of artists who were at Swansea during the porcelain period; Morris, in his statement, mentions a "De Junic from the Royal Manufactory at Paris" (i.e. Sèvres); and Turner records a tradition that a French artist was employed at the China Works. So the discredited De Junic or even the missing Colclough may still come forward to claim the fine workmanship that has not yet been satisfactorily assigned.

For many years a good deal of ingenuity and skill, sometimes amounting to virtuosity, has been applied to this ceramic game of whodunnit. The conformation of Billingsley's "most secret and inviolate rose" ("in puce", rather) has been contrasted with that of Pollard and Morris; Pollard's speedwell has been minutely analysed, almost dissected, even to the publication of close-ups of its diverging stamens, to distinguish it from that of Evans; there have been six beard-splitting attributions of the tulip in an attempt to isolate the mythical De Junic. Of the Swansea flora the nasturtium alone remains undivided, for only Morris painted it. If chaos consists o disordered opinion as well as unformed matter, then this is it: no two experts agree about anything. Still, there is promise of a breakthrough to a more detached way of deciding who decorated what, of an altogether more accurate yardstick. Sir Leslie Joseph, for instance, has had photographs taken of several hundred pieces of the china bearing the word "Swansea" in script, sometimes with other written matter as well, and when the work of sorting and analysing is done, this graphological approach should yield some interesting, even startling, results.[23]

There is one class of decoration which in its serene anonymity is above the disputations and uncertainties that beset those considered so far. The Conventional (or Set) Patterns, as they are called, are quite different from the naturalistic or representational paintings of flowers, landscapes, birds and figures which have always been so much in demand. They consist for the most part of abstract geometrical forms, sometimes with stylised flowers, trees or birds in colourful juxtaposition, and very often with some discreet gilding. Some of the motifs are based on the Japanese Imari and Kakiemon designs, while others, like the well-known cornflower or Bourbon sprig patterns, are simple adaptations of emblems, badges and such-like. Billingsley used a numbered pattern-book when he was at Derby, may have introduced a similar system to Swansea, and even designed some of them himself. About sixty different conventional patterns have been noted, of which some forty have borne numbers on one or more key pieces. Morton Nance had already listed and described most of those indentified up to the time of the publication of his book in 1942; and, in 1958, Mr. W. D. John placed them in numerical order, thereby facilitating future reference.[24] Since then,

---

[23] Sir Leslie has already given cogent reasons to support his view that the Nantgarw plates with chocolate edge were decorated by William Weston Young. My only reason for coming to the same conclusion about some of them was that Pardoe would not have written "Young Newton" on the back of one in the National Museum of Wales.

[24] The pattern numbers named by Mr. W. D. John are: 30, 31, 164, 180, 193, 194, 216, 219, 223, 227, 231, 232, 233, 236, 237, 251, 255, 257, 262, 264, 405, 409, 419, 436, 449, 470, 478, 544, 556.

more than a dozen others have turned up, and no doubt there are many yet to come, for there are quite a lot missing in the numerical series between 30 and 556.[25] Some of the patterns were copied from Worcester, Derby, Spode and other factories, and although it must have been a two-way traffic, it is not always possible to say which got in first.[26] Morton Nance and Kildare S. Meager, notable as scholars and discriminating collectors, thoroughly familiar too with both the individual freehand painting and the stylised arrangements, had in their last years come over to the view that this latter form of decoration was perfectly suited to the medium of porcelain. At different times each expressed his mature belief that despite the immediate appeal of the recognisable and the representational in landscapes, flowers and birds, it was the abstract and stylised compositions on Swansea china, with their finely-blended colours, that constituted the factory's finest expression. There are a growing number of sensitive and discerning people, who, tired of the banal and the pretty-pretty on porcelain (roses and birds being perhaps the typical clichés, the truly "conventional" in its decoration), turn with relief to the numbered patterns.

Conventional in a less impressive way are the two kinds of transfers, the plain and the filled-in. The best known of the latter is the "mandarin" pattern, in which a delicate transfer has been filled in with bright greens, reds, blues and browns, except where it has been left uncoloured to reveal such features as the lineaments of faces or the ripples on water. Although the plate in Sir Leslie Joseph's collection seems to be the only piece of "mandarin" bearing a number (164), the frequency with which the quaint colourful oriental façade turns up makes it unquestionably a set pattern. Other filled-in transfers are the flowers copied from Curtis's Botanical Magazine, much as Pardoe's were shortly after the arrival of Dillwyn in 1802. The bird, shell and landscape transfers believed to be from drawings by Baxter and James Brindley, and a group of landscapes, were not filled in.

[25] Even when he was engaged on these notes the writer came into possession of No. 247, hitherto (as far as he is aware) unrecorded. Other numbered pieces not included in Mr. John's list are in the collections of Mr. Harold Davies, Mr. R. J. Maddock and Mr. Sydney Heath. In the Glynn Vivian Art Gallery "Croeso 1969" Exhibition of 300 pieces of Swansea porcelain from Sir Leslie Joseph's Collection the following additional numbered patterns were shown: 23 (or 235), 164, 259, 404, 410, 418, 469, 471 and 493.

[26] In the writer's collection, Swansea pattern number 194 is as near as can be to Spode number 967.

Lastly, there are single pieces and even whole sets that were decorated in London. There were several enamelling establishments in or near the City which are known to have received supplies of china from Swansea, particularly Mortlock's of Oxford Street and Pellatt and Green's[27] who had their premises in St. Paul's Church-yard and who placed their name underneath an occasional piece. Although some of this London-decorated porcelain was skilfully and tastefully painted, a lot of it followed the mode set by Sèvres of using bright, sometimes even garish, colours with a tendency to overdo the gilding. This fashion of excessive ornamentation followed the taste of the time, for the wealthy manufacturers and landowners emerging from the Industrial Revolution were eager to flaunt their wealth and importance by embellishing their homes with the showy and colourful china that was being marketed by the London enamellers. Intended for display, it attracted attention to itself in showcases and cabinets; but moving farther and farther away from the simple functionalism of domestic ware, even from the restrained elegance of the porcelain decorated at Swansea, it assumed a lifeless artificiality, especially in more sophisticated forms like cabaret sets and cabinet cups. It has been described as degenerate, debased and decadent, which at its most extravagant it certainly was; but it is in great demand today, perhaps in an age as unsettled and unstable as its own, and those who pay large sums of money for the more ornate specimens will feel very much at home in their company. The best known and the largest example of this London-Welsh porcelain is the Burdett-Coutts service, of which at least 250 pieces have survived. It has been called "resplendent", "gorgeous" and "majestic", is of fine-quality duck-egg, and is, in fact, London at its sumptuous best.[28] *Plate XI* in our colour section, illustrating a rectangular "twig" dessert dish with a colourful seascape and lively foreground figures, looks like the work of James Plant, one of the best of the London artists. Some years ago, Mr. W. D. John and Mr. B. A. Williams showed that Nantgarw china decorated in London could be identified by a narrow band of iridescence surrounding the enamel colours, but they had not noted it in connexion with Swansea's London-decorated porcelain.

[27] The writer has an engraving by Thomas Hornor of St. Paul's Cathedral and St. Paul's Churchyard, which shows Pellat and Green's premises occupying a corner site. The engraving was made in the Bevington period.
[28] Some 249 pieces of this service were sold in Christie's in 1922 for £1,627 10s. 10d.

Recently, Mr. Harold Davies showed the writer a number of such pieces in one of which, a comport or centre stand, the iridescence was over a quarter of an inch wide.

The foregoing, which at the outset was intended to be an introduction to the colour plate supplement, has grown inordinately into an ouline history of the Swansea factory's short-lived experiment in making porcelain. The colour plates are by no means representative of the china that a new collector will come across, for they illustrate individual pieces that in shape and decoration are much more elaborate than the cups, saucers and plates commonly (perhaps less commonly now) found in shops and sales. Even in its day this china was for the well-to-do, and the dresserfuls of it that are often said to have been seen in cottages and farms are either later earthenware or "Swansea cottage", that useful euphemism for common Staffordshire sold in South Wales markets. Should a reader succumb to the humblest bit of Swansea porcelain, he will have no regrets, for he will either enjoy its company over the years, or, in time of famine, sell it at a profit. Until Turner's book appeared in 1897 Swansea porcelain and pottery had remained in the same families for several generations. It was not until this century that it was discovered by collectors, some of them driven by the urge to gather things together, others attracted by its beauty or by its history. In recent years a rapid depreciation of currency has persuaded yet another group of people to buy china, pictures and silver as an investment,[29] and it is surprising how even this ignoble introduction to the visual arts can sometimes kindle an interest in such objects if only by quickening a dormant instinct like curiosity or love. Few material objects can tease us out of thought as does a piece of Swansea china.

[29] It may be worth recording that a Swansea "mandarin" plate which could be bought in 1939 for a day's wage would cost a month's salary in 1969.

Plate I Swansea cabinet cup and saucer with landscape decoration by William Billingsley.

Mr. and Mrs. M. R. Morgan Collection, Penllergaer, Glamorgan

Plate II

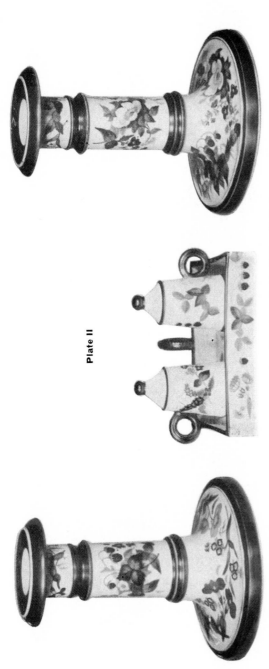

Above: Pair of Swansea candlesticks decorated by David Evans and snuffers decorated by William Pollard.
Sir Leslie and Lady Joseph Collection, Newton, Glamorgan

Above: Pair of Swansea miniature watering cans and a round inkstand decorated by Henry Morris. *(left) Lady Evans-Bevan Collection, Margam, Glamorgan (centre and right) Sir Leslie and Lady Joseph Collection, Newton, Glamorgan*

Plate III

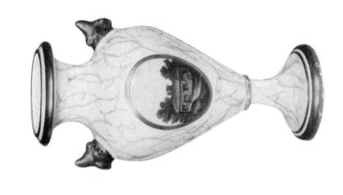

Pair of Swansea vases with floral decoration.

Derek S. Hutchings Collection, Newport, Monmouthshire

Centre: Swansea vase with landscapes.

Miss Betty Tucker Collection, Bishopston, Swansea

Plate IV   Swansea tureen, cover and stand from the Lysaght service, decorated by Henry Morris.

Mr. Sidney Heath Collection, Burry Green, Swansea, Glamorgan

Plate V Swansea round stem dish, decorated by William Pollard.

Mr. Sidney Heath Collection, Burry Green, Swansea, Glamorgan

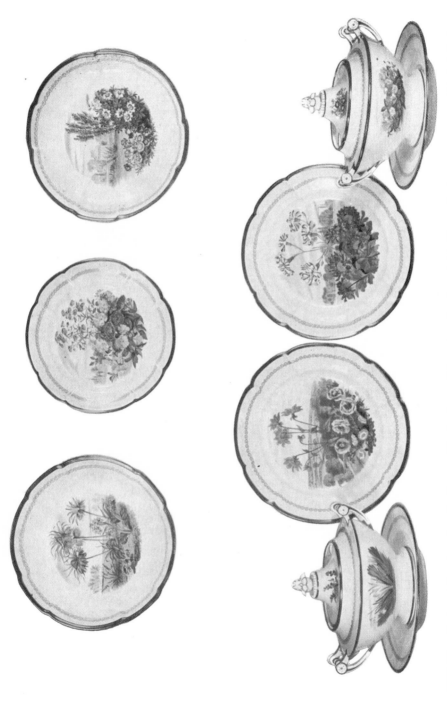

Plate VI   Representative pieces from the Swansea "Garden Scenery" dessert service, decorated by Thomas Baxter.

Private Collection

Private Collection

Plate VII   Part of the Swansea "Garden Scenery" dessert service, decorated by Thomas Baxter.

Plate VIII   Swansea cabinet cups and saucer, decorated by William Billingsley with garden flowers, rose wreath and shells.

Sir Leslie and Lady Joseph Collection, Newton, Glamorgan

Plate IX   Large Swansea comport or centre dish, decorated with garden flowers and butterflies.

Formerly in the Harry Sherman Collection

Plate X Part of Swansea cabaret tea service, decorated by Thomas Baxter.

Mr. Sidney Heath Collection, Burry Green, Swansea, Glamorgan

Formerly in the Harry Sherman Collection

Plate XI   Swansea rectangular dessert dish with seascape and figures, London decorated.

Plate XII   Swansea breakfast cups and saucers with birds, decorated by Thomas Baxter.

Mr. Sidney Heath Collection, Burry Green, Swansea, Glamorgan

Plate XIII

Left: Swansea cabinet cup and saucer, decorated by Henry Morris.

Miss Caroline Snowden Collection, Newport, Monmouthshire

Right: Swansea cabinet cup and saucer, decorated by William Pollard.

Sir Leslie and Lady Joseph Collection, Newton, Glamorgan

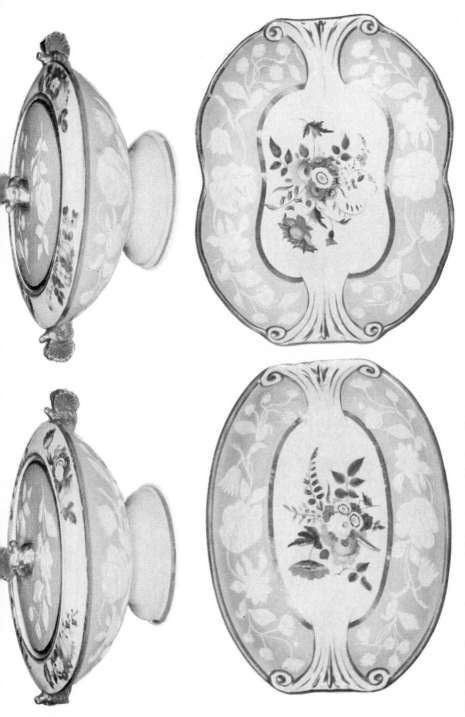

Plate XIV Swansea tureens and dishes, decorated by Henry Morris.

Formerly in the Harry Sherman Collection

Plate XV Swansea pot-pourri vase and cover, with landscape decoration by William Billingsley.

Mr. and Mrs. M. R. Morgan Collection, Penllergaer, Glamorgan

THE COLOUR PLATES

PLATE I—One of the most beautiful of the Swansea cups and saucers, comparable with Baxter's "Jubal" cup. *Mark:* "Swansea" in red script, and "Veiw near Eaton Hall", which is four miles south of Chester. I am indebted to Mr. Morgan for drawing my attention to the similar mis-spelling of "View" by Billingsley on the Paris "De la Courtille" plate (illustrated Nance, p. 240, pl. 100 B, C) and to Mr. W. D. John's teapot signed "Billinsgley Mansfield". The saucer is inscribed "Ouse Bridge Yorkshire", a favourite scene with the nineteenth century artists. *Body :* duck-egg.

PLATE II—Of the candlesticks, only the one on the left is marked, with "Swansea" in red transfer. *Body:* too opaque for certain diagnosis, but as there is no pigskin effect on the glaze, it is more likely to be duck-egg than trident. *Snuffers:* —*Mark:* "Swansea" in red transfer. *Body:* duck-egg. The handle is similar to that used on some cabinet cups. *Watering-cans:* These are virtually the ordinary coffee cans with accessories. *Inkstand:* Is really as much penholder as inkstand, for the base has three quillholders. *Mark:* "Swansea" in gold script in a hand resembling Billingsley's. The painting is not his, but the gilding may be.

PLATE III—Much of the china of the late Mr. Harry Sherman has been dispersed in recent years, and it has not been practicable to trace all the present owners of the pieces illustrated. It was quite by chance that Miss Tucker told me she had purchased the middle one of these.

PLATE IV—This service must be Morris's most finished work. Kildare Meager thought that, like the Lady Seaton service, it was incomplete in the white, and was made up to its full size by using spares from Staffordshire. He believed the heavy, notched plates were not Swansea; but quite recently I have seen a notched duck-edge Lady Seaton plate which is from the same mould as my own, yet mine has a dirty-brown translucency.

PLATE V—This is a bird's-eye view of a very attractive dish. Mr. M. R. Morgan, Sir Leslie Joseph and Lady Evans-Bevan have similar ones.

PLATES VI AND VII—Some people have expressed disappointment
     after seeing this part-service, but from the two pieces which
     I have personal knowledge of, and these colour plates,
     it seems to me very handsome work.

PLATE VIII—These four cabinet cups and the odd saucer are
     superb examples of Billingsley's best work. *Mark:* All
     have "Swansea" in script, but the colours (reading clock-
     wise from top left) are: black or dark grey, red, light
     brown, gold. The saucer also has "Swansea" in gold script.
     Bodies: All four cups are glassy, the saucer duck-egg.

PLATE IX—A typical Swansea centre-piece for a dessert service.

PLATE X—With its quaint figures and blue scale-border this is a
     colourful cabaret set, and it is a pity the page-size did not
     allow room for the inclusion of the tray with its centre
     group of a peasant with his wife and daughter on their way
     to the fields. *Mark:* "Swansea" in red transfer. *Body:*
     duck-egg.

PLATE XI—Mr. W. D. John and I have been unable to trace the
     present owner of this attractive dish. The painting is
     of very fine quality, and is almost certainly by James
     Plant.

PLATE XII—Typical Baxter rendering of birds. On the left, a
     woodcock (saucer) and scarlet ibis (cup); on the right, a
     bittern (saucer) and a parrot finch (cup). *Marks:* Each
     piece has the name of the bird and the word "Swansea" in
     sepia script. Sir Leslie Joseph, who has made a special
     study, and a very rewarding one, of the handwriting of
     Swansea decorators, informs me that Baxter was the only
     one who separated the letters in the script mark
     "Swansea".

PLATE XIII—I have not seen Miss Snowden's cabinet pair; but
     Sir Leslie's is a most beautiful example of Pollard's very
     best work. *Marks:* None. *Body:* duck-egg.

PLATE XIV—I have failed to discover the present owners of these
     four attractive pieces. The dishes illustrate two very rare
     shapes. The uncoloured part is an embossed raised
     border. *Marks:* "Swansea" in red transfer.

PLATE XV—This is without doubt a pot-pourri vase, for it is very unlikely that anyone would burn a pastille lozenge in such an immaculate vessel. Mr. Morgan tells me that it was potted by Goodsby, and that the moulding is of two continuous bands of acanthus leaves and three circles of applied bead ornament. The landscape is cycloramic, i.e. it runs continuously right round the vase, ignoring the two handles.

BIBLIOGRAPHY

Turner, William. *The Ceramics of Swansea and Nantgarw*. London, 1897.

Nance, E. Morton. *The Pottery and Porcelain of Swansea and Nantgarw*. London, 1942.

John, W. D. *Nantgarw Porcelain*. Newport, 1948.

—— *Swansea Porcelain*. Newport, 1958.

—— *William Billingsley*. Newport, 1968.

Meager, Kildare S. *The Swansea and Nantgarw Potteries, together with a Catalogue of the Collection of Welsh Pottery and Porcelain in the Glynn Vivian Art Gallery, Swansea*. Swansea, 1949.

—— "Swansea and Nantgarw Porcelain". *Glamorgan Historian*, vol. II, pp. 104-114. Barry, 1965.

Eccles, Herbert and Rackham, Bernard. *Analysed Specimens of English Porcelain, Victoria and Albert Museum, Department of Ceramics*. London, 1922.

Grant-Davidson, W. J. "Early Swansea Pottery, 1764-1810". *Transactions of the English Ceramic Circle*, 1968.

Young, William Weston. Original manuscript Fact Books deposited in Glamorgan County Record Office, Cardiff.

Jenkins, Elis. "William Weston Young", *Glamorgan Historian*, vol. V, pp. 61-100. Barry, 1968.

ACKNOWLEDGEMENTS

I wish particularly to thank Mr. W. D. John of Newport whose generous loan of the colour blocks has added distinction to the whole volume; and Mr. Harold Davies of Neath whose expert knowledge of the porcelain bodies and the styles of the various decorators has saved me from many a pitfall. I also wish to thank the following not only for their help but for allowing me to view their collections: Lady Evans-Bevan, Sir Leslie Joseph, Mr. Sidney Heath, Mr. R. J. Maddock, Mr. Maldwyn Morgan, Mr. John Owen and, of course, Mr. W. D. John and Mr. Harold Davies. Others who have at all times been generous with information and advice are Mr. Rollo Charles (National Museum of Wales, Cardiff), Mr. John Bunt (Glynn Vivian Art Gallery, Swansea), and Mr. W. J. Grant-Davidson (Royal Institution of South Wales, Swansea).

THE SENGHENYDD COLLIERY DISASTER

by

NORMAN WILLIAMS

TUESDAY 14 October 1913 started like any other day in Senghenydd, a village at the head of the Aber Valley, twelve miles north-west of Cardiff. Like many of the Welsh valleys its claim to fame was in its coal. Houses clung to the mountain-sides like limpets, their inhabitants were human moles enslaved to the two collieries sunk between the hills. The lower one, the Windsor, was a "wet" colliery taking most of the water from the twin-shafted one higher up the valley called the Universal. But this colliery, too, was capricious, for it was one of the most gassy pits in the whole of the South Wales coalfield. However, miners couldn't be choosers, so to this valley they came seeking employment. Young men from North Wales lodged with the homely landladies of Senghenydd, and almost became members of the family. They were completely absorbed into the local community, most members of which, of course, were employed by the collieries either below ground or in the many other duties that go to run a pit. Workmen's trains from Cardiff also spilled out their daily quota of tea-carrying shift workers for the three eight-hour shifts that constituted a whole day.

The money for the time was fair, about £1 16s. 0d. a week, with a half day Saturday and the whole of Sunday off except for those who were engaged on maintenance work in preparation for the incoming Monday shift. The tradesmen flourished and little shops sprung up almost all the way down to Caerphilly. Local girls courted the more guttural North Walians, perhaps making the local boys a little jealous. But the dangers of coal-mining, with lives daily at stake and death all too near at hand, bonded them all together as "butties". There had been a sharp reminder of this fact some time after the Universal colliery had first sunk its shafts in 1891, for on 21 May 1901 the whole mine had been devastated by an explosion and eighty-one men died.

148

On that occasion only one man was saved. The subsequent inquest was not conclusive. It seemed probable that the explosion was the result of a "blasting shot" and suggestions were put forward to "water the roof and sides of the mine as a precaution". This was to try and reduce the amount of coal dust suspended in the air.

Twelve years later, on that Tuesday morning at 8.10 a.m., just after the day shift had descended, the people in the Senghenydd Valley heard a noise, as a survivor told the writer, "like the crack of doom". A gigantic explosion had occurred somewhere underground and blown the top shaft, called the Lancaster or "downcast", to pieces. So severe was the explosion on the surface that the blast blew the head clean off the shoulders of a banksman who had returned to duty after already working a night shift. A young boy of fourteen who had gone to fetch him looked on terrified and helpless. Underground 439 miners died, and in the village of Senghenydd every other house had lost an average of two members.

To obtain a clearer picture of the disaster it is necessary to know something of the layout of the mine and the conditions under which the miners worked. The Universal colliery was owned by the Lewis Merthyr Consolidated Collieries Ltd., and managed by miners' agent Mr. Edward Shaw. He had the services of two under-managers, one for the east and one for the west side. On the west side the under-manager had three over-men, one for the Ladysmith and Kimberley districts, one for the Mafeking, and one for the Pretoria. Under these were fourteen firemen, each having a separate district. Altogether the number of staff employed underground amounted to 950 men, there being 440 working on the west side. Coal had been worked in the Universal colliery since 1896. Two shafts, the Lancaster or "downcast" and the York or "upcast", were both 650 yards deep, and coal could be wound up either shaft, though it was the Lancaster that was most used. Underground there were three seams of coal, the 4 feet, the Universal, and the 9 feet. The workings were divided into two main divisions, the east and west sides. The west side was further divided into six districts: 1. West York, 2. Pretoria, 3. Mafeking, 4. Kimberley, 5. Ladysmith, 6. Bottanic. All these districts branched away from the main intake known as the main west level. It was in the west side that the explosion occurred.

Coal was mined by the long wall method, the stalls being

11 yards centre to centre.   Although it was recognised that it was better and safer to take out face timber after use, the peculiar characteristics of the Universal colliery made this impossible, thus adding to the fire risk.   It was a rare occurrence in this mine to use much explosive, as its use would be confined to "hard ground" only and there was not a great deal of this.   When used, however, the explosive would be Roburite.   The last time "shots" had been fired in this mine was on Sunday 12 October.

The main haulage of coal from the Mafeking, West York, Bottanic, and Pretoria districts was via the return airway.   This airway may well have contained more than $\frac{1}{2}$ per cent of inflammable gas and this usage contravened the *Coal Mines Act* of 1911, section 42 (4).   However, since the mine was opened before 1911, it was exempt from this clause.   Another clause in this Act, section 62 (2), states that all trams carrying coal must be sealed against dust escaping through side ends and floor.   As far as the Universal colliery was concerned they had already ordered a few hundred of this type, so presumably other types not conforming to this requirement were in service at the time of the explosion. Electric signalling was employed at most collieries and the Universal was no exception.   The method of signalling was somewhat crude. Two bare wires supported on insulators 12 to 18 inches apart were shorted together by a file or some similar object, the whole system being powered by a number of dry cells of the "Dianna" type.   The bells used were of the trembler pattern, the coils and contact breaker being protected by an iron cover not necessarily gas-tight.

The colliery was ventilated by a 24 feet steam driven surface fan which exhausted the air via the York upcast shaft.   This fan supplied 200,000 cubic feet of air per minute.   At the time of the explosion arrangements for reversing the air current to conform with section 31 (3) of the *Coal Mines Act*, 1911, had not been quite completed. The date upon which this clause should have been operative was 1 January 1913, but in April of that year the owners had applied for an extension of time in order to make the necessary structural alterations. This extension was granted and a deadline date fixed for 16 September.   However, the work was not completed until 30 September.   The Act called for an arrangement whereby an immediate reversal of air current could be affected.   The arrangements at the Universal colliery needed two hours.   A further requirement of the 1911 Act was "that the quantity of air in the main and every other split and at any other such points as may be determined should be measured at least once per month and entered in a book for the purpose". These "points" were:

1. At the main intake airways as near to the "downcast" shaft as possible.
2. At every "split" at the point where the split commences.
3. At each ventilating district at a point 100 yards back from the first working place.

The latest measurements taken before the explosion were made on 25 and 26 September, but were not entered in the form prescribed by the Secretary of State and were not countersigned by the manager and under-manager. It would therefore be difficult if not impossible to say what was the volume of air current that traversed the working face. The Universal colliery was a notoriously gassy mine—indeed, it was stated by some to be the most gassy in the whole of the Welsh coalfield. It had been proved that the amount of inflammable gas generated was 1,200 cubic feet per minute. It was also stated in the official report that the air in the Mafeking heading would contain the whole of the fire damp generated in the Kimberley and Mafeking districts as well as part of that generated in the Pretoria district. Thus the Mafeking and Kimberley districts should have had their own separate intake and return of air quite independent of any other. This was not the case.

The official report of the disaster, from which this information is drawn, also mentions that the safety lamps in use were not fitted with the regulation glasses, although the management were not aware of this. Lamps were lit and locked, and issued to the men at the surface, and were again inspected underground at what were called "locking stations". There were cabins, one in the east and one in the west side, where each incoming shift was met by a fireman. Should a miner's lamp go out, and in those days of oil lamps this was very frequent, he had to go to the lamp cabin to have it relit. Apparently this was also an unofficial arrangement. The west side lamp station was 440 yards from the shaft and this was one of the suspected sites of the explosion.

Another aspect of this colliery was the dusty nature of the conditions underground, aggravated by the way trams were piled with coal, and in the Kimberley, Ladysmith and Pretoria districts hauled against the air currents. So much coal dust was produced that during each afternoon and night shift eight men were engaged in shovelling up the dust from the floor. To try and minimise this nuisance the trams were sprinkled with water from an upright pipe about 6 feet high connected to the water pipes across the tram roadway. But sometimes, as in the Ladysmith district, it was necessary for the trams to travel some 700 yards before the sprinkle was reached.

In order to safeguard the mine and to test for gas it was normal for the day fireman to precede the other colliers by some two hours. Shift times were as follows:

	Descended	Ascended
The day fireman	3.30 a.m.	1.00 p.m.
Colliers and others	5.10-6.00 a.m.	2.00 p.m.
Coal drawing between	6.00 and 2.00 p.m.	
Repairing shifts	2.00 p.m.	10.00 p.m.
Repairing shifts	9.00 p.m.	5.00 a.m.

The amount of time necessary for the firemen to go from their lamp stations to the working face of their district, adequately examine it, and come back again to meet incoming colliers was approximately two hours. This was an extremely responsible duty. In many collieries there is a meeting station in each district giving the firemen more time to examine their area. At the Universal colliery at the time of the explosion there was only one for the whole of the west side.

As coal is mined, cavities caused by slips or falls in the coal or rock are formed. In the Universal colliery these were timbered up and constituted areas where gas could accumulate. The usual method used to locate gas in these pockets, certainly in Senghenydd, was to secure a miner's lamp to a 5 feet pole, raise it to the cavity and observe the lengthening of the flame. Much play was made in the official inquiry about this method, for it was contended that accuracy was in question as the angle of vision had now been altered.

These were the conditions that set the scene on that Tuesday morning, 14 October 1913, when 700 men descended the Lancaster shaft to start a day's work. On the surface a fan man kept watch, oiling the big ventilating fan and reading the water gauge every fifteen minutes. The fan house shift was a long one, sometimes as

The Great Welsh disaster at Senghenydd. Removing some of the Victims.

By permission of Cardiff Public Libraries

"Universal Pit, Senghenydd.
The Canary that was carried down the Mine
to test the air.

The "Universal" Pit, Senghenydd, After the explosion of Oct. 16th 1913.

By permission of Cardiff Public Libraries

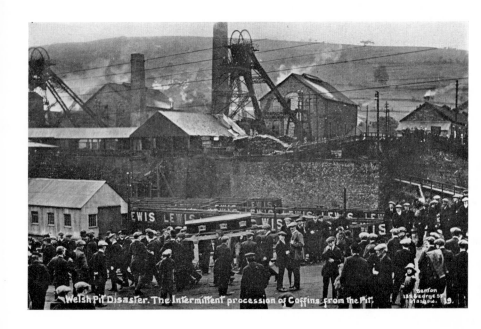

Welsh Pit Disaster. The Intermittent procession of Coffins from the Pit.

The scene outside the mortuary at Senghenydd at the Universal Pit.

Senton
138 George St.
Glasgow.   6.

By permission of Cardiff Public Libraries

Welsh Pit Disaster. One of the many sad scenes at Senghenydd.

Senton
138 George St.
Glasgow   22.

Welsh Pit Disaster. Mr. Keir Hardie. M.P. & Mr. Winston in car speaking to Mr. Brace. M.P. at the scene of the disaster.

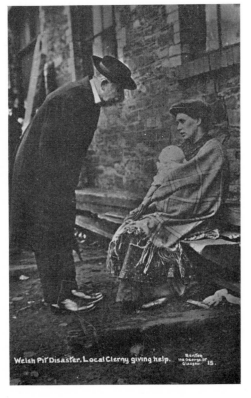

Welsh Pit Disaster. Local Clergy giving help.

By permission of Cardiff Public Libraries

much as twelve hours a day. The speed of the fan was constant, nothing was unusual, routine was being followed. At 8.10 a.m. Senghenydd heard the explosion, the fan man heard it, but deep underground those that survived the initial blast and the falls of coal heard nothing but a "swoosh" of air. In the east side the miners heard nothing at all, but they knew something was wrong as their lamps had suddenly dimmed. Manager Shaw was in the lamp room on the surface at the moment of the disaster, his under-managers were underground investigating a report from the night shift. He went straight to the Lancaster shaft and saw it had been wrecked, and here too he saw the headless body of his banksman. He hurried back to the York upcast shaft and with a party of men descended the mine. When the cage was halfway down they saw in a tram in an ascending cage the body of a man, his legs hanging on the crossbar. He had been blown into the tub in the cage at the pit bottom. Both cages were stopped and the body of the miner was pulled in. Shaw and his companions then continued their descent. When the cage reached the bottom it was impossible to get near the west side because of the fire and smoke. The east side also was burning but it was impossible to control the flames and proceed to the Lancaster shaft which was about 50 yards away. Dead men were lying all around, it was like looking into a furnace, all the timber arches were ablaze. It was obvious that nothing could be done until the fires were controlled and breathing apparatus was available. Unfortunately the Universal did not possess any, the nearest being at Porth Rescue Station eight miles away. Porth did not receive the message until 10.00 a.m., and rescue workers were at Senghenydd by 11.00 a.m. By this time the water pipes had been reconnected but there was an insufficient water supply to fight such an enormous blaze. There was a suggestion to switch the water main over to the compressed air pipes in order to give a greater volume of water underground, but this was impractical as the hundreds of entombed miners needed the air.

Underground the situation was appalling. The west side was a raging inferno with over 400 men trapped. On the east side things were somewhat easier. Mr. T. O. Davies, 78 years of age at the time of writing, was amongst those who came out. He sat patiently waiting at the top of number one incline for the word to go. Survivors were allowed out twenty-eight at a time. The air was so thick with smoke that they tied their scarves around their faces soaked in the cold tea that was to have refreshed them at breakfast. Mr. Davies reached the surface at about 1.00 p.m. At 3.00 a.m. the next day he joined the rescue teams going down to try and reach the hundreds still trapped in the west side. It took about the whole of one shift to get anywhere near this side of the mine. The colliery was operating four rescue shifts a day. By Wednesday morning the daily papers had heard of the tragedy and a typical paper, the Swansea *South Wales Daily Post*, reported:

ENTOMBED IN BLAZING PIT
Tremendous Welsh Colliery Disaster.
Feared loss of 150 miners.

AT NOON THE POSITION IS OFFICIALLY STATED TO BE 327 MEN BROUGHT UP ALIVE. SIX DEAD BODIES RECOVERED. DEATH ROLL ESTIMATED 150. DUE TO THE SERIOUS CONSTERNATION THAT IS PREVAILING IN THE DISTRICT A DETACHMENT OF 120 POLICE FROM SWANSEA AND DISTRICT HAVE BEEN HURRIED TO THE SCENE TO KEEP ORDER. THE MOUNTAINSIDES AROUND THE COLLIERY ARE BLACK WITH THOUSANDS OF PEOPLE FROM NEIGHBOURING DISTRICTS.

By Thursday 16 October the same paper was saying:

THERE NOW SEEMS NO HOPE OF PREVENTING IT RANKING AS THE BIGGEST MINING DISASTER THAT HAS OCCURRED IN SOUTH WALES. THE OPTIMISTIC RUMOURS THAT GAINED CURRENCY ON WEDNESDAY OF VOICES AND KNOCKING UNDERGROUND IS UNFOUNDED. THERE IS NOW NO JUSTI-FICATION OF ENCOURAGING THE HOPE THAT ANY OF THE ENTOMBED MEN WILL EVER BE FOUND ALIVE. THE TERRIBLE FACTS ARE BEST TOLD IN FIGURES.

NUMBER IN PIT 924
NUMBER RESCUED ALIVE 507
DEAD BODIES RECOVERED 44
DEAD SINCE RESCUED 4
NUMBER STILL MISSING 373.

Shortly after 1.00 p.m. on Thursday a telegram of deep sympathy was received from the Queen Mother, while an official communication stated that "By command of the King and the wishes of the Prince and Princess Arthur of Connaught, the wedding presents of their Royal Highnesses will be on view to the public at St. James'

Palace daily. One shilling admission per person will be charged, the proceeds to form a fund to be devoted to the relief of the sufferers". The Prince and Princess Arthur had been married the previous day. His Majesty the King, who from the first had expressed a heartfelt sympathy with the victims, gave £500 to a fund organised by the Lord Mayor of Cardiff.

Back at Senghenydd the fire was still being fought by water, and it was not until Friday 17 October that sand was requested to fill sandbags and seal off certain parts of the west main, the water pipes still pumping thousands of gallons into the inferno. With all hope completely gone recovery work went on week in and week out. The bereaved of Senghenydd resigned themselves to the dreadful fact that they would never see their husbands, brothers or sons alive again. Indeed in many cases they were even denied the solace of identifying their loved ones except by the possessions found on the bodies. As the bodies were recovered they would be conveyed to the makeshift mortuaries in the carpenter's shop and the smithy. They would then be covered with a sheet and the personal belongings of the man placed on his chest. All would be allocated a number and the district in which they were found. This number would correspond to a name listed on a board. As the bodies were identified the boots would be removed. Later that day those so identified would be placed in a coffin, a supply of which had been built crossways to a great height alongside the shaft.

As the weeks went by more and more bodies were recovered, some in groups of twenty-eight or more. Indeed the view has been expressed to the writer by a rescuer that it was possible that some miners may have lived on for as long as a week after the explosion. He also expressed the view, shared as well by one of the rescued, that somewhere down in a dingle on the west side to this day lie the bodies of some twenty-six miners.

How did this disaster, the worst mining disaster in Great Britain, occur? How could circumstances arise whereby 439 men could die in a blazing pit 1,950 feet below the surface? To find out, an Official Inquiry was opened at the Law Courts in Cardiff on 2 January 1914. It lasted until 1.15 p.m. on 21 February. Altogether 21,837 questions were put to witnesses. In answer to the first part of the question, "How did the disaster occur?", no conclusive decision was reached. Two schools of thought existed. There were those who believed that the point of origin was in the Mafeking incline and was caused by a fall of coal liberating a pocket of gas which in its turn was ignited by electrical sparks caused by shorting the bell wires.   The resulting methane gas explosion would disturb the coal dust causing this to explode and ignite.   The whole thing would behave as a chain reaction, sweeping up and down the west side.   To support this theory evidence was offered to show that the bell wires were carried past the place where in October 1910 a large outburst of gas had occurred, and also that these bell wires ran into the west Mafeking district past a place known as Beck's Old Heading where some little time prior to the explosion the existence of gas had been reported in such quantities as to prevent men working there. In defence the management stated that experiments had proved that no sparks could have been produced by the electrical pressure exerted by the batteries.   In any case the mine was exempt in respect of that part of the *Coal Mines Act*, 1911, as this method of signalling was in use before 1911, and it could continue to allow such an arrangement until 1 June 1920, unless the inspector of a district raised an objection.

    The other school of thought believed that the explosion was caused by the naked flame kept in the lamp room 440 yards from the pit bottom.   Again it was suggested that a big fall occurred in this area just before the explosion, releasing clouds of gas.   To add weight to this argument it was revealed that the roadway at this point had been widened by 4 feet the night before and this would have tended to weaken the roof.   Objections to this theory were that the lamp room had only been whitewashed two months prior to the explosion, and yet on being examined after the disaster the walls were so discoloured as to suggest that they had been swept by an explosive mixture of coal dust and smoke, whereas if the lamp cabin had been the originating point of the explosion one would not have expected discolouration.   With regard to this argument, as the writer of this article required some clarification, the point was raised with the Safety In Mines Research Division at Sheffield. Their reply stated:

> Nearly all coal dust explosions in mines have been initiated by an ignition of firedamp which provided the large amount of energy required to raise and ignite a cloud of coal dust, which in turn raised and ignited further dust and so propagated the

explosion through the workings.   If the flame travelled only outwards from the point of ignition, as is usual, then only firedamp would have burnt in the lamp cabin and no appreciable deposit of coked dust would have been deposited on the walls.   In addition, the intensity of the blast could have been relatively small so that little dirt would have been raised and the damage observed around the lamp station would not be expected.   However, blast may sometimes travel back through the area of ignition (see *Transactions of the Institute of Mining Engineers*, vol. 112, pt.3, Dec. 1952, pages 157-167).   Therefore the indications of violence and, more particularly, signs of the passage of a coal dust explosion at the lamp station point to the source of ignition being elsewhere; but they do not prove it.

Both of these theories require a fall of coal of some magnitude just prior to the explosion.   Such a fall would be expected to cause a variation of the speed of the air circulating fan on the surface, but the fan man was emphatic in his evidence that he had noticed no such variation in the speed.   Whether or not the bell wires produced a spark at Senghenydd is an academic point, but the following letter circulated to all mine owners a year before is certainly revealing. It refers to the explosion at Bedwas Colliery on 27 March 1912.

123 Cathedral Road,
Cardiff.

Gentlemen,   28 August 1912.

I am directed by the Secretary of State to inform you that an explosion of firedamp occurred recently in the South Wales Inspectors Division, by which twelve men were burnt, three of them so severely that they subsequently died.

The explosion was proved beyond all reasonable doubt to have been caused by the sparking of an electrical signalling bell which ignited an accumulation of gas resulting from a dearrangement of the ventilation due to the breakage of air pipes.

It was afterwards proved experimentally that sparks from the bell in question worked by a battery of $11\frac{1}{2}$ volts would ignite an explosive mixture of lighting gas and air, and the mixture was also ignited by sparks from signalling wires produced by a current of only 4 volts pressure.

I am instructed therefore to call your attention to the necessity of strict observance of the Electrical Special Rule 15 (1) with reference to signalling apparatus.

Yours faithfully,

W. N. Atkinson.

The second part of the question "how could circumstances arise whereby 439 miners could be entombed?" was also debated at length in the inquiry.   The arguments revolved around two aspects of mining:

1. The advantage of reversing the air currents.
2. The greater need for water in a dusty mine.

Before briefly discussing these points it should be borne in mind that Mr. Shaw, the mine manager, had lost most of his officials and technicians in the disaster.   Firstly it was argued, the fire spread so rapidly because the air currents were not reversed.   It was claimed that men may have died because fumes were carried to them.   Any reversal of the air currents would have brought all the fumes up the Lancaster shaft, so allowing more exploration behind the fire.   It was further argued that it may have saved the men in the West York district who were found within a short distance of the York pit bottom before being overcome.   The reversed air current would also have blown clean air down to the West York, Pretoria, and to the "return" from the Bottanic district.   Men, it was said, were overcome by smoke fumes and not afterdamp.   However, there was a counter argument against the efficacy of reversing the air.   It was possible that it may have saved the men in the West York area but it would have killed those saved in the Bottanic district.   This district was not entered until 10.00 p.m. on Tuesday and it was not until 11.30 p.m. that the first of the eighteen saved men was rescued. They were all unconscious.   The management stated that repeated attempts to reach these men had been made at 9.00 a.m. and 1.00 p.m. but the rescuers were driven back even with breathing apparatus.

When the inquiry discussed the other question of watering a very dusty mine it was offered in evidence that this had been tried but had to be discontinued for two reasons.   One was the enormous amount of water required, the other a much more important reason, the fear of structurally weakening the roof and sides.

So there the matter rested.   No conclusive answer was found as to where or how the explosion occurred.   There is a postscript, however.   Recently the writer was talking to one of the eighteen men rescued alive from the Mafeking district.   At the time of the explosion an air way was being driven to improve the ventilation in one of the Mafeking headings.   Digging with the other miners was a well known character called "Good Boy Dick". A culvert carrying cold air was in use for the miners on the working face. So near to each other were the miners either side of the wall of coal that they frequently signalled to each other by knocking "tap . . . tap . . . tap . . .tap . . .tap . . ". It was their intention to make a small hole in this dividing wall to allow the cold air from the culvert on one side to mix gradually with the much hotter air on the other. However, the brittle coal wall collapsed and the hot and cold air rushed together, causing thermal currents. Possibly there was a pocket of methane gas released which would be brought to floor level by the turbulence. Then came the explosion. "Good Boy Dick's" body was never found. Was this the solution to the mystery? It is impossible to tell.

What of the relatives who remained? Life had to go on, babies had to be fed. There were two sources of income. An official one that gave dependents about £300, and a public subscription which only recently was exhausted, giving them a further ten shillings a week.

Great as the disaster had been it was not the end of the Universal colliery. It continued to give employment until it finally closed in March 1928. Today a timber works covers the area, but the site of the two shafts is still visible, the Lancaster downcast and the York upcast. It is the York upcast that has the final word. A notice on the corrugated iron paling surrounding the shaft reads "Danger— Explosive and Poisonous Gas".

NOTE

Afterdamp: A non-inflammable heavy gas, carbon dioxide, left after an explosion in a coal mine.

Methane: A natural gas, highly explosive when mixed with air, then called firedamp. Coal gas contains a large proportion of methane.

LLANHARRY: A BORDER VALE MINING VILLAGE

by

DAVID J. FRANCIS, B.A.

LLANHARRY is a parish of some 1,629 acres comprising the original village of Llanharry, now greatly extended by a rather featureless housing estate, two outlying hamlets at the Gwaun and Tylagarw and a number of isolated farmsteads of great antiquity. Situated on the edge of the Vale of Glamorgan, the parish for the most part lies on a low, undulating plateau of about 250 to 300 feet. The visible monuments of history are few; indeed the chief landmark in the parish is the familiar pit head and winding gear of an iron ore mine. They belong in fact to the only surviving iron ore mine in Wales.

The rocks and soils of the parish have from man's first appearance been conditioning factors in the history of Llanharry. Geologically, Llanharry is unlike most of the Border Vale in that it is an island of carboniferous limestone projecting out of the mantle of glacial drift, which although present in parts of the parish, is more extensive in the surrounding parishes. Along the narrow belt of carboniferous limestone, which extends from Llanharry eastwards to Taffs Well, rich deposits of haematite occur. These deposits have in turn attracted the Romans, Elizabethan smelters and the twentieth century nationalised iron and steel industry. Millstone grit and lower coal measures conformably succeed the limestone in the northern part of the parish. As the coal measures outcrop near the surface, coal as well as iron mining has often challenged the agricultural predominance of the economy. Overlying the carboniferous rocks in places are younger rocks of triassic age, which give the soils to the WNW of the village their distinctive red colouring.

Many English local historians have noted how sensitive to the quality of land were the earliest settlers. On the whole, primitive man favoured light, freely-drained soils. Such soils have developed at Llanharry, not only on the trias and carboniferous rocks which project through the glacial drift, but also on the glacial drift itself. These contrast sharply with the impeded clay loams and clays which cover much of the eastern Border Vale parishes of Pendoylan and Welsh St. Donat's. It is probably no accident therefore that Llanharry is the site of one of the few important archaeological discoveries of the Border Vale, that of a Beaker burial dated about 1800 B.C.

Enough of the skeleton is preserved to tell us that the person buried in the barrow opposite the house called Naboth's Vineyard was a pronounced beaker man of about 5 ft 9 ins in height, broad headed and probably under 35 years of age. He was lying on his right side, with his head towards the north, and his knees up to the chin. With him was found a pot, 8 ins tall, of Abercromby's type C. It was boldly designed and delicately made, similar to other examples found in Somerset. How these first inhabitants of the parish were able to wrest a living from that strange, unfamiliar world is difficult to tell. It is likely that they were pastoralists and semi-nomadic in economy. Their flocks of sheep and herds of cattle must have roamed in the temporary clearings that were made in the moderate forests of oak and beech which then flourished on the light soils. Neither can we really hope to know how the Beaker folk ever reached these parts; it is possible that they followed the river Thaw up from its mouth, but it is equally likely that they were following the open country over the hills above the river valleys from West Wales or Nash Point.

A bronze axe, found recently on the northern edge of Coed-y-Tranches, affords further evidence of prehistoric visitors to the locality. The axe bears traces of simple tooled decoration of the kind characteristic of Irish axe-heads of this type, and it is quite possibly an import from Ireland somewhere about 1500 or 1600 B.C. This early type of axe-head was cast in an open mould and hammered further into shape after casting; it was intended to be mounted in a slot in a wooden handle rather like the stone axe-heads which it displaced. The people who used it probably lived partly by agriculture but mainly by stock-raising in small villages comprised of very lightly constructed huts.

Taking into account the above discoveries, together with a bronze rapier found at City,Llansannor,and an iron age millstone at Breigan, one begins to doubt the applicability of theories of geographical determinism to the "Border Vale" in general and the Llanharry area in particular; far too much has been made of the role of the Border Vale as a barrier in the early days. It is much too narrow to have been a real barrier to communication as Lady Fox and H. J. Randall claimed. It is not realistic to suggest that primitive man could not get through from the Vale to upland Glamorgan, and vice versa, when he wanted to, or settle in the more favourable parts of the Border Vale.

It was the rich deposits of iron ore, often exposed at or near the surface, which next attracted early man to Llanharry. It is now widely believed that the deposits were worked by the natives for their local use before the Romans came. Iron ore, thought to be from Llanharry, has been found in an Ancient British settlement near Cowbridge.

Although no recognizable Roman workings are to be found here, evidence of a secondary nature does suggest that the Romans were interested in extracting the iron ore. A writer in 1859 actually claimed to have found some old workings at Llechau, which appeared to have been of Roman origin. It is far more likely, however, that they belong to the Tudor period of iron mining when Llanharry was a manor belonging to the Lords of Coity. Some pieces of coarse pottery, said to have been Roman, were found at the bottom of an ancient stall working at Ty-isaf. More recently, in 1967, a shard from the rim of a Roman cooking pot of the third century A.D. was unearthed at Redlands, a few hundred yards from the site of the present mine.

We must try to picture local people rather than Roman soldiers or civil servants extracting the iron ore from shallow pits wherever it outcropped conveniently, and taking it away to smelt either in ancient British homesteads or villas of the Roman type, such as those at Ely and Llantwit Major.

Long before the Normans came, small hamlets like Llanharry must have grown up around a Celtic church, but when and by whom the first church was established remains a mystery. All we can say with certainty is that Llanharry and the neighbouring churches of Llanilid, Llansannor, Ystradowen and Welsh St. Donat's are sited on the more favourable parts of the Border Vale, where the freely drained

soils have developed. Only Pendoylan is located in the more un-
favourable eastern part of the Border Vale, where the soils, being
impeded, would have discouraged early settlement. The church in
Llanharry is in fact dedicated to Illtud, founder in the late fifth
century of the great monastery at Llantwit Major.

But Iolo Morganwg, puzzled by the name Llanharry, tried to
connect it with "Garrai Sant O Gor Bangor". In a list of saints
which was drawn up by Iolo, we read "Garrai ap Cewydd ap Caw
Cawlwyd; ei eglwys Llanarrai, Morganwg", (Garrai, the son of
Cewydd, the son of Caw Cawlwyd; his church Llanarrai,
Glamorgan). But no credence can be given to this flight of fancy.

The author of a recent M.A. thesis on place names in the lordship of Tal-y-fan was also unable to explain the meaning of Llanharry. The earliest version of the name which he found was Llanhari,
in a document of the third quarter of the twelfth century. This he
suggests is the correct Welsh form. This is the version found in the
works of Dafydd Benwyn, Meurig Dafydd, and Gronw William,
all poets of the sixteenth century. It is rather interesting that he
suggests the correct pronunciation is like the present day vulgar
pronunciation. Hence also the suggested spelling with only one
r, for doubling the r would require a short a in standard Welsh
phonetics. The primary and secondary schools of the village have
incidentally adopted the form Llanhari.

When the Normans conquered Glamorgan, Llanharry became
part of the member lordship of Tal-y-fan. It was part of the demesne
land of that lordship, and about 1246, as a result of Richard
Syward's dispute with the Lord of Glamorgan, it escheated with the
lordship. In the west of the forfeited possessions of Syward,
Richard de Clare installed his sheriff, Stephen Bauzan, giving him
Breigan and Llansannor. Bauzan, a soldier of renown, is reputed
to have built Breigan castle, the remains of which stand in a wood
called Coed Breigan in the parish of Llansannor. I do not know
whether Bauzan ever had a castle in this locality, but the site marked
Breigan castle (or Gelli-garn) on maps does not seem to have any
military feature, and the large ring motte at Llanilid and the smaller
one at St. Mary Hill are the only medieval fortified sites in the district.

Bauzan may well have held Llanharry also, for Clark says that
Bauzan's companion, William Scurlage, held that manor from him.

It is certain that Scurlage was enfeoffed of a quarter knight's fee at Llanharry in 1262.

Scurlage is said to have built a "strong house" which became known as Scurlage castle, and afterwards Trecastle. What we are less certain of is whether Scurlage held the whole of Llanharry at that time or only that part which is equivalent to the Trecastle estate. The only extant survey of the manor of Llanharry, dated 1631, clearly shows that Trecastle lay outside the manor as a separate estate then belonging to the Gibbon family. If Scurlage and his heirs held the whole of Llanharry, then we must postulate that there were two heiresses early in the fourteenth century, one taking Trecastle, and the other what is the manor of Llanharry, as described in 1631.

The earliest member of the Gibbon family to have lived at Trecastle was Gibbon ap Llewelyn, who was there about 1428 or thirteen years after Agincourt. The family, who claim to be direct descendants of Einion ap Collwyn, lived right down to the eighteenth century in their residence at Trecastle, whence they moved to Newton House, near Cowbridge. The Hearth Tax returns of 1662 show clearly that Trecastle was easily the largest mansion in the parish for as many as eight hearths were to be taxed there; the next largest house had only four hearths.

The Gibbon crest and coat of arms in their original form can be seen in the village church, and the most striking form in which they appear is in iron on the wall, "emblematically representing the ancient industry of the district". The crest is a boar's head and the name of the inn near Tylagarw, *The Boar's Head*, is obviously derived from it. Part of the Trecastle estate is still owned by descendants of the Gibbon family, the present owner being Mr. John Samuel Gibbon of Bristol. It is a matter of regret, however, that nothing is left of the original Scurlage castle.

Trecastle apart, most of Llanharry appears to have become a part of the Coity estate by 1350, if not earlier. By an inquisition post mortem of that year it seems that Gilbert de Turberville held Llanharry manor. The manor passed from the Turberville family to their descendants the Berkerolles and Gamages.

Finally, in 1584, through the marriage of Barbara Gamage to Robert Sidney, brother of the famous Elizabethan poet, it became part of the Sidney possessions in Glamorgan. In the document whereby Robert Sidney received the livery of his wife's estates, we find the "manor of Llanharrys, held of the lord of Tallavan as of the manor of Tallavan, the annual value £4".

Tracing the boundaries of an ancient manor is a difficult task when many of the field names have become lost. However, it appears from the 1631 survey that the manor of Llanharry was separated from Trecastle by a little stream called the Nant Felin-fach, from Ruthin by the common lands of the Gwaun, and from Tal-y-fan by a rather indeterminate boundary running south-eastwards from Pantiscoed, and passing near Llwynbarcud, Pant-gwyn, Tydiffrwyth and Gelligneuen farms. In the east, the boundary with Tal-y-garn coincides in part with an extension of the Morfa Ystradowen peat bog.

The manor itself, though it retained certain Welsh features such as gavelkind, seemed to have been organised on the lines of an English manor. The current opinion is that the native Welsh developed social and economic institutions which were rather like English manors, where favourable geographical conditions permitted. Who can say that the Norman rulers made that much difference at places like Llanharry? Perhaps they only brought the existing arrangements into line with their own concept of how to organise a farming community. The distribution of demesne land and copyhold land is not easily recognisable at Llanharry, but there certainly seems to have been a sizeable parcel of demesne land at Llechau. Known as the mansion house in Stuart times, and situated on the red fertile soils of the trias, it may well have been the home farm of the manor.

There were other parcels of demesne lands intermingled with the strips of the copyholders in the open fields. Surrounding the church, and especially at Ty-isaf and Pantgwyn were the open fields, in which the tenants were allocated so many strips each according to their position on the manor roll. By 1631 the copyholders at Llanharry seemed to have bargained themselves into a strong position in relation to the lord. Unlike the copyholders of Ewenny who all died out in the eighteenth century, those at Llanharry survived. At the end of the last century, their descendants were still meeting at the *Gronow Arms* to attend the Court Leet and undertake the duties of reeve, constable and hayward.

The remainder of the cultivated part of the manor was in the hands of freeholders, leaseholders and tenants at will. The freehold lands had over the centuries been carved out by private enterprise from the wastes of the forest.   Here, on the outer limits of the manor, stood the old farmsteads of Gelligneuen, Tydiffrwyth, Coed-y-Wiw, Pen-y-Waun, Torgelli and Rhydycastell.

Finally, there was the wasteland, which had never been worth the farmer's while to plough.   In the following extract from the 1631 survey there seems to be a survival of tribal limitations as to the number of beasts which could be pastured on the waste:

> There is a common within the said manor lying on the north part thereof called by the name Llanharry Common containing by estimation 50 acres, which do properly belong to the Lord of the manor for the having, taking and receiving of all such royaltys as come out of the same, and that the herbage and pasture thereof do belong unto the tenants and resiants of the said manor for the time being, and that every tenant and resiant of the said manor may turn his beasts to grass upon the said common, according to the value of the lands which every of the said tenants and resiants do occupy and enjoy for the time being. And they also present Morgan Llewellyn and Thomas David, two of the resiants of the said manor for surcharging of the said commons by turning more beasts than they ought to turn after their several occupying of lands within the said Manor.

Associated with the old farming economy of the open fields was the nucleated village, with a compact grouping of the church, farmsteads and cottages. Whether there was ever a village of Llanharry in this sense is difficult to judge.   Over most of the parish, the isolated farmhouse is the general pattern of settlement, but there may well have been a "nucleated village" around the church. H. J. Randall certainly seems to think that Llanharry more than any of the neighbouring villages of the Border Vale resembled the compact village of the vale proper.   According to an estate plan of 1775, two farmsteads, the *Bear Inn* and a group of cottages, some of which were in ruins, surrounded the church.   On part of the village green was the parish house, situated on the exact spot where Prospect House now stands.   The parish house had been built upon a plot of land given by Sir Thomas Gamage of Coity in the late Middle Ages for the use of the inhabitants of the parish.   The parish house may well have been used as the village hall at one time.   In the seventeenth century the manor court sat there, and in the nineteenth century it probably housed the church school.

By Tudor times, the significance of the rich iron and coal deposits occuring at Llanharry came to be realised, and industry on a small scale began to challenge the predominance of agriculture. The Sidney family were important iron masters, and they found in the Llanharry district plentiful supplies of timber and good pockets of iron ore. It is quite possible that the old workings at Llechau attributed to the Romans really belonged to this period. From the plan of one of these old workings it appears that the depth of the shaft was about 30 feet, which was approximately the depth given for Tudor mines. The other dimensions were likewise appropriate to a mine of those days.

Coal mining was also being carried on at Llanharry, as is witnessed by a lease dated 10 May 1602 from Sir Robert Sidney and Lady Barbara his wife to Edward Davie of their coalpit at Llanharry and "all vaines of coles" within or under their waste or common of Llanharry at a yearly rent of 10s. By 1631, further pits were being opened on the common for a yearly rent of £7. Even if these early ventures had only a marginal effect on the economy of the parish, something of the future had been foreshadowed.

Of the three hundred clergymen who were ejected from their livings in Wales during the Civil War and Commonwealth periods none suffered more acutely than Edmond Gamage, the Rector of Llanharry. John Walker's well known book gives interesting information about him:

> He was Turn'd out some time before the year *1649*; and not only *Dispossest* of his *House, Glebe &c* but the very Tythe-Corn, that he had brought in some Weeks before, was Seiz'd upon; and not a grain of it, or any *Fifths* allowed him towards the *Subsistence* of his *Large Family:* So that he was forc'd to *Quit* the Place, and Retire to a *small Pittance* of his own, until the *Restoration.* Upon which he Returned to his *Living;* but Enjoyed it a very little while. One *Howel Thomas*, and one *Thomas Joseph*, both *Anabaptists*, Occasionally held forth in his *Church* during the *Usurpation.*

Dr. Thomas Richards, a leading authority on Welsh Puritanism, refers to Howell Thomas and Thomas Joseph as two of the immediate followers of John Myles of Ilston. This is not surprising since Myles had founded an early Baptist church in the neighbouring parish of Llanharan about 1650.

The Visitation Return of 1763 gives an insight into the state of religion in the parish in the eighteenth century. The curate at that time was David Griffiths. He lived in the parsonage at Llanilid. Being in charge of the combined parishes of Llanilid and Llanharan he received £20 a year, but he was also curate of Llanharry, for which he got another £12 a year. He took services once every Sunday in each of his three churches, and he claimed to preach a sermon at every service, which was rather exceptional at that time. Holy Communion was administered four times a year, the usual frequency in the eighteenth century, but there were only about thirteen communicants in Llanharry.

From as early as 1730, when a house on Gwaun Llanharry was licensed for preaching, the meeting houses of the Congregationalists were slowly becoming the spiritual homes of the people of the locality. By 1780 Bethlehem Chapel was built at Llanharan, and by 1802 Maendy Independent Church was established. It was the early decades of the nineteenth century which saw the breakthrough of Nonconformity at Llanharry. The impetus came from Maendy when the members of Maendy Chapel began to hold a Sunday school in Llanharry about 1820, first in the house of one Richard Richard and later at Rhiwperra. At this time the Llanharry district was noted for its ungodly games, and the young men of the adjoining villages used to meet there on Sundays to play ball. One Sunday, soon after the school had started at Rhiwperra, it appears that the Minister of Maendy, the Rev. Shadrach Davies, approached the boys playing in an adjoining field, picked up the ball when it came near him, and cheerfully led the astonished lads to Rhiwperra school. Certain it is that the Sunday School flourished; for in 1847 there were 70 pupils on the books, 33 of whom were over 15 years of age. In 1824 Nonconformity had made such an impact that it was necessary to build a chapel at Llanharry and Peniel Chapel came into being. By 1848 the curate Arthur Griffiths was forced to admit that the majority of his parishioners were Independents.

As regards education in Llanharry, there does not seem to have been a school there before the nineteenth century, apart from the Griffith Jones' circulating schools. In 1818 the rector, R. P. Sidney, reported to a Government inquiry that there was no school and added an interesting comment: "The rector believes the poorer classes are without sufficient means of educating their children and he fears they would not be thankful to possess them".

Notabilities of Llanharry present at the discovery of the Beaker burial

By permission of the National Museum of Wales

The Llanharry iron ore mine—the only surviving one in Wales

Photograph by Haydn Morris

Llechau, the home farm of Llanharry Manor

Photographs by Haydn Morris

An ancient farmstead, Gelligneuen, with Mynydd Garth Maelwg in the background

The "Mountain School", Llanharry, a National School built about 1870

Photographs by Haydn Morris

The *Bear Inn*, Llanharry. The club room of this inn was the location of the village school about 1870

The crest of the Gibbon family—a boar's head—in a
window of Llanharry Parish church
By kind permission of the Rector and Church Wardens

In 1845 a church school was started.   This was the dame school
mentioned in the Reports of the Commissioners of Inquiry into the
State of Education in Wales, 1847. The following extract from the
report brings the education of those days alive for us:

> The dame could speak English correctly, and she seemed to
> have her pupils well under her command. They were very orderly
> and well-behaved. I heard a class of 18 reading the 11th
> chapter of the gospel of St. Mark: 15 read with ease; neither of
> them could translate a verse that I gave them into Welsh,
> though I selected the simplest of those which they had read.
> The dame told me that when she came there (21 months ago)
> few of the children could speak English. Several of those with
> whom I talked could speak English very well, and they answered
> a few simple questions which I gave them out of the chapter
> pretty correctly.   The Rector guarantees the dame £10 a year.

The Commissioner, being of the opinion that the Welsh people
would never progress economically or morally so long as they spoke
Welsh, must have been pleased at what he saw happening to the
Welsh language at this particular school.

In another part of the report, the Rector, the Rev. John Powell,
answered a questionnaire about the parish in which he proposed a
scheme for uniting the parishes of Llanharry, Llansannor and
Ystradowen, so that the children of each could come to one central
school. By the Tal-y-fan enclosure award of 1863 an allotment of
one acre was made for a school for the three parishes; but this acre
was never used for the purpose, since four years earlier the parishes
had been granted a plot by Alexander Young Spearman of Llansannor,
and a national school, known locally as the Mountain School, was
built in 1872.   The Mountain School is still in existence and celebrated its centenary in 1959 (i.e. one hundred years after the site of
the school was granted).

The school at Llanharry village meanwhile had been held in the
Bear Inn for some time.   By 1870 it was being run privately by a
master reputedly 85 years of age.   Prior to 1870, and long after in
some places, schoolmasters were a motley crew, being made up of
wooden-legged soldiers and sailors, gravediggers, sextons etc.   Both
at Llanharry and Tonyrefail about this time, a journalist tells us,
there were pedagogues named Hopkins.   The one at Llanharry was
a farmer's son and this is the journalist's account of him:

He hardly had the ability of his Tonyrefail contemporary, and certainly not his irritability, except on rare occasions, when Twmi'r Teilwr's[1] shop had run out of snuff, which the old master kept loosely in his capacious waistcoat pocket. On such occasions, the pupils, many of whom—I mean the male pupils—had whiskers, and not a few of whom are alive to-day, said he was a very devil, and a terror to be near. The school was kept in the club-room of the Bear Inn, and was often visited by the dear old Rector of those days—Rev. W. Williams—who was deeply attached to the younger children, whom he seldom or never failed to regale liberally with apples from the Rectory orchard, or sweets from the village shop, if apples were out of season. By arrangement, or otherwise, the gentle Rector's welcomed arrival generally meant an opportunity for the old pedagogue to pop into the adjoining inn for a wee drop of the elixir of life, yclept chwys-y-ci. Hopkins was a firm disciplinarian, but the Rector had but a very vague notion, if, indeed, any such, of discipline, and would not have hurt a fly. When the cat is away the mice will play, and while the master was at his glass, the little school soon became a Bedlam, and dogs, cats, and birds gave it a wide berth, so terrific was the noise. The Rector walloped one of the tables which served as desks, with his walking-stick, and shouted for silence at the top of his voice, but the more he walloped and shouted, the more the uproar grew, till the pedagogue's tool box hat appeared passing the window towards the door, when silence reigned supreme instantly. In reply to the master's inquiry about the children's behaviour in his absence, the Rector's invariable reply was, "Very fair, on the whole, Mr. Hopkins".

Today the educational needs of the village of Llanharry are provided for by an ever expanding junior school and a County Secondary school of ten years standing.

There had been great changes meanwhile in the ownership of land in the parish. The seventeenth and eighteenth centuries saw the increasing control of absentee landlords over the lives of the inhabitants. By 1843, out of the 1554 acres of titheable land, 1324 acres were in the hands of six powerful landlords, all of whom lived away. They were Robert Savours of Cowbridge, the Rev. William Gronow of Neath, Joseph Bailey (Llansannor estate), Lord Dynevor, R. H. Jenkins of Llanharan House and C. R. M. Talbot of Margam. There were only two owner occupiers, who could manage just 12

---

[1] Thomas Thomas, a tailor from Caerphilly, who had rebuilt the church house and kept a general stores in Llanharry. The present day village shop known as Prospect House is in the hands of his direct descendants.

acres between them.   A fairly high proportion of the farm land was in arable in the middle years of the nineteenth century; over 40% of the land had been at some time or another in arable in the seven years preceding 1843.   This is a high proportion for a Border Vale parish.

The enumerators' books for the censuses of 1841-61 show clearly that Llanharry was by mid century still a fairly self sufficient community with a wide range of rural crafts, two shops, four public houses, a mill and a dame school run by the local church.   The village community was becoming less closely knit, however.   The growth of industry within the parish itself was bringing in newcomers: iron miners from Cornwall, chemical manufacturers to run a distillery at Rhydycastell from Gloucestershire and London, and colliers from West Wales.   Conversely, more people were leaving the parish to find work in the adjacent industrial belt.   By 1861, only 40% of the population of the parish had actually been born in the parish.

It appears from the 1875 ordnance survey map that Llanharry underwent its own private industrial revolution in the 1850's and 1860's.   On Llanharry common at this time there was a colliery, a brick works, a coke oven and a distillery.   The colliery is of a much earlier origin, however.   It dates as far back as 1775 and possibly much earlier.   In 1816 the following advertisement appeared in *The Cambrian:*

> To be let and entered upon 1st May next a colliery in full work ...and very advantageously situated close to the high road leading from Llanharran to Cowbridge, on Llanharry Meadow . . . and directly on the line of a tram road to be made from that part of the country to Cowbridge.   The coal is of excellent quality both for fire and lime coal, and is worked at very trifling expense. There is a good engine of 10 h.p.   This colliery has commanded a very extensive trade from the vale of this county for some years, and is now enabled to sell as much as can be rose.

By 1817, the Trecastle Coal Works were also in full operation, and prospects for mining appeared so bright by 1825 that ambitious plans were being made to construct a tramway from Trecastle to Cowbridge.   In 1826 it was even proposed to extend the line to Aberthaw.   Nothing came of the venture however until the Cowbridge—Llantrisant Railway was built in 1865.   Not many years later, coal mining was abandoned in the parish, mainly because of legal disputes over royalties.

If the first half of the century belongs to coal mining, the second half saw a sudden growth in the production of iron ore.   As early as 1858, iron was being discovered in large quantities in the parish, and a London firm had sunk a trial pit on the Tregroes estate.   By 22 December 1862 the Llanharry Haematite Iron Mine was a flourishing concern, but the most important of the late nineteenth century workings was the Trecastle Iron Works.   The mine was opened about 1878, and about 120,000 tons of high quality ore was extracted from one large pocket.   The mine was forced to close in 1891, mainly through the competition of cheaper imported ores from Spain.

No further iron was raised in the parish until the present mine was sunk in 1901.   It produces high class iron averaging about 55% pure iron, with only traces of phosphorous and sulphur.   Some 3,000 tons of ore a week are railed from Llanharry to Guest Keen Iron and Steel Works at East Moors, Cardiff, where it is used to produce high quality pig iron for castings. About 350 men work at the mine, including about twenty-five Italians, the remnants of an original batch of sixty-five who were recruited from Italy after the Second World War.   The great hazard at the mine is water, and consequently a favourite recurring joke of the engineering maintenance department at Llanharry Mine is that the Glamorgan Haematite Iron Ore Company is there to produce water with iron as a by-product.

The large scale housing development of the post war years has completely altered the face of Llanharry.   More change is imminent: the proposed open cast mining on the Gwaun will, temporarily at any rate, increase the scars of industry in the parish, and the advent of the new motorway will ensure that Llanharry will not escape the noise and bustle of the modern age.   With the distinct possibility that the new town of Llantrisant will eventually extend into the parish, it is to be hoped that Llanharry will not completely lose its identity, and that the pleasant farming land to the south west of the village will be retained as an adjacent miniature green belt.

BIBLIOGRAPHICAL NOTE

The most important document the author has consulted is the 1631 Survey of the manor of Llanharry, or rather an eighteenth century copy of it in the Blandy Jenkins collection at the Glamorgan County Record Office.   He would also like to acknowledge the aid he has derived from Mr. B. D. Harries's unpublished M.A. thesis on "Enwau lleoedd hen Arglwyddiaeth Tal-y-fan" (University College, Cardiff, 1956).

Copies of the enumerators' schedules for the 1841, 51 and 61 censuses have been kindly supplied by the Public Record Office, while the Visitation returns have been obtained through the co-operation of the National Library of Wales. The author wishes to thank Mr. T. J. Hopkins, Archivist at the Central Library, Cardiff, Dr. H. N. Savory, Keeper of the Department of Archaeology at the National Museum of Wales, Mr. Brian Ll. James, Assistant Librarian of the University College Library, Cardiff, and the staffs of County Library, Bridgend, and the National Society, London. Finally, he is indebted to the Glamorgan Haematite Iron Ore Co. for supplying him with information on present day iron mining. He has also consulted the following books, reports, articles and maps:

Clark, G. T. *Cartae et alia munimenta quae ad dominium de Glamorgancia pertinent.* 2nd ed., 6 vols. Tal-y-garn, 1910.

—— *Limbus patrum Morganiae et Glamorganiae.* London, 1886.

Evans, C. J. O. *Glamorgan, its history and topography.* 2nd ed. Cardiff, 1943.

Nicholl, L. D. *The Normans in Glamorgan, Gower and Kidwelly.* Cardiff, 1936.

North, F. J. *Mining for metals in Wales.* Cardiff, National Musuem of Wales, 1962.

Randall, H. J. *The Vale of Glamorgan.* Newport, 1961.

Rees, T. and Thomas, J. *Hanes eglwysi annibynol Cymru,* vol. II. Liverpool, 1872.

Richards, T. *The Puritan movement in Wales, 1639-53.* London, 1920.

—— *Religious developments in Wales, 1654-62.* London, 1923.

Walker, J. *An attempt towards recovering an account of the numbers and sufferings of the clergy of the Church of England . . . in the late times of the Grand Rebellion.* London, 1714.

Williams, T. (ed.). *Iolo manuscripts.* Llandovery, 1848.

Historical Manuscripts Commission. *Report on the manuscripts of Lord de l'Isle and Dudley,* vol. I. London, H.M.S.O., 1925.

Reports of the Commissioners of Inquiry into the State of Education in Wales, vol. I. London, H.M.S.O., 1847.

Evans, John. "Silurian's notes and paragraphs". *Glamorgan Gazette* (weekly newspaper), 17 September 1926.

Nash-Williams, V. E. "A beaker-burial from Llanharry, Glamorgan". *Archaeologia Cambrensis,* vol. LXXXV (1930), pages 402-5.

Watson, J. J. W. "The haematitic deposits of Glamorganshire". *Geologist,* vol. II (1859), pages 241-56.

Crampton, C. B. and Webley, D. "The correlation of prehistoric settlements and soils in the Vale of Glamorgan" (with a map). *Bulletin of the Board of Celtic Studies,* vol. XVIII, pages 387-396.

Rees, W. (Map of) *South Wales and the border in the fourteenth century.* Southampton, Ordnance Survey, 1933.

MEDICAL MEN OF GLAMORGAN :

(6) P. RHYS GRIFFITHS (1857-1920)

by

PETER H. THOMAS, M.D., B.CH., F.R.C.G.P.

OF all the townships in the South Wales coalfield none can boast a topographical situation as fine as that of Aberdare where Philip Rhys Griffiths was born. An account of the development of the town and neighbourhood has already appeared in this series,[1] but for our present purpose we must enlarge a little on the town centre in its mid-nineteenth century setting. According to W. W. Price, the outstanding historian of the area, the present Town Hall was at that time the Market Hall, opposite which and separated from it by a narrow street was the *Wellington Inn*. To the left of these landmarks stood the ancient parish church of St. John the Baptist with its well-filled but unenclosed churchyard—a stark reminder of the ravages resulting from the nationwide cholera epidemic of 1848-9. To the right an observer could see Evan Griffiths' large shop or warehouse (now called Tŷ Mawr). It was built, probably as a residence, towards the end of the eighteenth century by Richard Richards, son of Theophilus Richards of Blaengwawr. The latter's tomb can still be seen in St. John's churchyard and according to the inscription upon it he was an "eminent drover" who reached his ninetieth year. Buried on Christmas Day 1794 he is a noteworthy figure inasmuch as in the capacity of a drover he was one of the first local businessmen of whom we have any record. In the middle of the nineteenth century his farm at Blaengwawr became the home of the well-known Davis family who sank pits in the Aberdare and Rhondda Fach Valleys, and in the meantime it has also given its name to a part of the Aberdare urban area.

Up until 1846, the year in which the Taff Vale Railway was opened, the main link between Aberdare and the outside world was the Canal which took its name from the township. Built to serve

[1] R. Ivor Parry, "Aberdare and the Industrial Revolution", *Glamorgan Historian*, vol. IV, pp. 194-203.

the local ironworks and opened in 1812, it joined the Glamorganshire Canal at Abercynon. The Evan Griffiths to whom we have already referred was a grocer, draper, and ironmonger who owned a number of boats on the waterways and acted as freight carrier to and from Cardiff. As we shall see in due course, one of his sons was Evan, P. Rhys Griffiths' father. It is of some interest that two more of his sons, William and Daniel, were also hardware merchants at Aberdare, the latter having business premises at 6 High Street.[2] Of the remaining sons, Lewis, who became a prominent elder at Bethania Calvinistic Methodist Church, was a grocer living at Clifton Cottage, while Griffith[3] was brought up with his uncle "Twmi" at Ffynnon Dwym, Llanwynno, and moved with the latter to Gelliwen Farm (near Miskin Manor) where he brought up a family and spent the rest of his long life. Daniel is also said to have had no superior as a musical adjudicator.[4] We would like to know much more about each one of the brothers than we actually do.

When Evan Griffiths died on 25 September 1852 tribute was paid to him as one of the oldest and deservedly one of the most popular inhabitants of the area.[5] At one time he had kept the only shop in the village of Aberdare, and as the village grew into a town, the shop grew too. He was of so benevolent and charitable a disposition that he never took legal proceedings against his debtors. When the Vale of Neath Railway opened to Aberdare, Evan Griffiths was selected by his fellow-parishioners to present the address to Lord Villiers.[6] In *Y Cylchgrawn*,[7] a Calvinistic Methodist monthly magazine, he was described as an elder well-known through all the counties of Wales because he gave hospitality to the itinerant ministers and preachers of the day. This obituary notice together with three *englynion* in memory of him was contributed by David Williams (Alaw Goch)[8] and twelve months later a lengthy dirge by another

[2] *Slater's Directory of North and South Wales*, 1880.
[3] See his obituary notice in *Cardiff Times*, 11 May 1912.
[4] This and other facts about the Griffiths brothers are drawn from William Thomas (Glanffrwd), *Plwyf Llanwyno* (Pontypridd, 1888), page 121.
[5] *Cardiff and Merthyr Guardian*, 9 October 1852.
[6] Ibid., 27 September 1851.
[7] Vol. II (1852), p. 352.
[8] A most interesting personality because he was an industrialist, poet, and religious leader combined. He was the father of Judge Gwilym Williams of Miskin Manor, grandfather of Lieutenant-Colonel Sir Rhys Williams, Bart., K.C., D.S.O., and great-grandfather of Sir Brandon Rhys-Williams, Bt., the present M.P. for Kensington South. When Griffith Griffiths moved to Gelliwen *circa* 1865, he became one of the future Judge Williams' tenants.

local poet appeared in the same magazine. It is evident that Evan Griffiths had wholeheartedly embraced the Calvinistic faith and that his death was a very great loss to the Church at Carmel, Gadlys. Prior to the building of Carmel in 1829 he might well have been a member at Pentwyn-bach, Heol-y-felin, where the Calvinistic Methodists had established their first cause in the area.

Since Evan Griffiths and his descendants were so closely connected with nonconformity in Aberdare and elsewhere, it is perhaps fitting at this point to mention briefly some of the main stages in the rise and progress of dissent in the Aberdare area. By extending liberty of private worship to Dissenters, the *Toleration Act* (1689) did much to protect and promote nonconformity throughout the country. Across the mountain from Aberdare a congregation of Presbyterians straightaway took out a lease on a remote mountain farmhouse near Blaencanaid called Cwm-y-glo. In the early years of the cause's existence a certain amount of internal friction and dissension was experienced because of the conflicting doctrinal views of the Arminians and Calvinists. Roger Williams, an Arminian, was pastor from 1689 until his death in 1730 but about 1720-1 a Calvinist co-pastor was appointed in the person of the Reverend James Davies, Llanwrtyd. Heated disputations between the two factions continued to take place for a long period and in 1747 a number of Arminians left Cwm-y-glo and commenced what later became the Unitarian cause at Cefn-coed-y-cymer. When the lease on Cwm-y-glo ran out in 1749, some members of the remaining congregation took out a lease on a piece of land near the centre of Merthyr and built Ynysgau chapel. Of greater and more direct importance to us, however, is the fact that by 1751 the Arminians who lived on the Aberdare side of the mountain had erected their own meeting-house—the first "Hen Dŷ Cwrdd"—at the edge of Hirwaun Common. Like its counterpart at Cefn-coed-y-cymer it later became a Unitarian cause.

The earliest recorded pastor of Hen Dŷ Cwrdd was Owen Rees, whose son Josiah[9] became minister of Gellionen near Pontardawe. Owen Rees was followed by a succession of capable and eminent

[9] He was the father of Owen Rees, a member of Longmans, the London publishing firm; the Reverend Dr. Thomas Rees, author of *The Beauties of South Wales* (1815); and Josiah Rees, Malta.

pastors[10] who to this day have led their flocks along the path of Unitarianism, steering them well clear of Trinitarian doctrines like "hereditary depravity (*pechod gwreiddiol*)". One such shepherd was the colourful Reverend John Jones (1802-63) who on 2 July 1833, in the first year of his ministry there, opened a very progressive school, the Trecynon Seminary, in a room above the meeting-house stable, a room which was replaced in 1850 by a purpose-built School House. An expert in Greek, Latin, and Welsh, he taught successfully at the Seminary for a period of thirty years before his death. His successor as minister of Hen Dŷ Cwrdd and as principal of the Seminary was his eldest son, Rees Jenkin, who came to have a very close connection with the Griffiths family.

Despite the early ascendancy of the Presbyterians or Unitarians they had ceased by 1811 to have any dominance as far as numbers were concerned. By then Calvinistic Methodists, Independents, and Baptists, all of whom inclined to Calvinistic persuasions, had established meeting-houses in the neighbourhood. Together with the Wesleyan Methodists the three denominations just mentioned continued to increase in membership and to open new chapels throughout the nineteenth century. The same can hardly be said of the Unitarians. As we shall soon see the original Hen Dŷ Cwrdd gave way to a bigger and better building in 1862. A few branches were also established but the one at Highland Place is the only branch that has continued to function. For many years it has been an English chapel whilst Hen Dŷ Cwrdd has remained Welsh.

Mention of the rebuilding of Hen Dŷ Cwrdd leads us back to Evan Griffiths, junior. Born in 1824, he supposedly could have joined his father's business but decided instead to become a surveyor and architect. We know very little about young Evan's early education but it is possible of course that although he was a Methodist he might have had a thorough grounding in many subjects at John Jones' Seminary. He might also have obtained more advanced technical instruction at the local Mechanics Institute which was founded in 1838 with John Jones as its first secretary. About the same time he probably became apprenticed to a local architect and surveyor. The apprenticeship system still offered adequate training in the building professions, for there was little in contemporary

---

[10] They include the two well-known literary figures, Edward Evans (1716-98) and Thomas Evans (Tomos Glyn Cothi; 1764-1833).

building technique which demanded an academic discipline. As the century advanced, constructional methods developed in scope and complexity with the result that higher standards than those offered by the average surveyors' and architects' offices were needed. Evan Griffiths must have been an extremely competent young trainee because his first assignment as a professional architect came his way as early as 1848 when he was a mere twenty four years of age. In that year he was invited to plan the Park School[11] ("Ysgol y Comin"), the first British School in the Aberdare Valley.

Before describing the contribution made by the Griffiths family towards the setting up and development of the first British School, we should at this stage like to summarise some of the main facts concerning the history of elementary education in Aberdare and district during the last century. Several National Schools, promoted after 1811 by the Church of England and state-aided after 1833, had been established in the valley twenty years before the Park School was opened. On the other hand the nonconformists, ever suspicious of any Governmental interference in religious and educational matters, were naturally slow and reluctant to accept Treasury support in launching a school-building programme. By 1843, for the reasons just mentioned, there were only a handful of British Schools in South Wales. In that year Mr. (later Sir) Hugh Owen,[12] a London-Welsh civil servant, issued an appeal to his countrymen through the current English and Welsh press, urging them to sink their differences and take full of advantage of the assistance rendered by the British Schools Society in order to supplement what they themselves could raise by voluntary contributions. His pleas had little immediate effect in South Wales.

In 1847, however, the Welsh nation was shocked, angered, and finally galvanised into action by the notorious *Reports of the Commissioners of Inquiry into the State of Education in Wales.* Their publication gave rise to the well-known expression "Brâd y Llyfrau Gleision" or the "Treachery of the Blue Books". In tone and content they were regarded by leading Welshmen of all creeds

---

[11] A major part of the original building still stands and is still in use as a school. A centenary brochure compiled by W. W. Price was published by the centenary Committee under the title *1848-1948, Park Schools Centenary (Canmlwyddiant Ysgol y Comin). Its History.* An illustration of the original building can be seen in *Glamorgan Historian*, vol. IV, facing p. 200.
[12] He has been aptly called "The Apostle of Welsh Education".

and parties as an unjust and biased indictment of the general moral behaviour, educational standards, and social conditions of the Welsh working classes. Meetings of protest were held throughout Wales because the people felt that the Commissioners had mis-understood and libelled the whole nation. On 23 February 1848 one such memorable meeting was held at Siloa Chapel, Aberdare, under the chairmanship of the versatile David Williams (Alaw Goch) who was well supported by all the leaders of nonconformity in the valley. The Reverend John Griffith, the young local vicar, was especially invited to attend in order to explain publicly some of the scathing and highly critical statements he had made in answer to the Commissioners' questions. Although the Vicar was, in the opinion of the writer, an exceedingly brave man to appear at Siloa in defence of his evidence, he was certainly no match for that born fighter, the Reverend Thomas Price, who was pastor of Calfaria Baptist Chapel. By weighty argument and the clever use of statistics Price demonstrated indisputably that the local contribution of the non-conformists towards the educational and spiritual needs of the people far exceeded the corresponding efforts of the Established Church. Be that as it may, the meeting was of great mutual benefit to all denominations, for from that day onwards they strove success-fully to put their respective "houses" in order. Paradoxically, the Blue Books turned out to be a blessing in disguise, since out of the fierce indignation that they had occasioned at the time there emerged a vigorous desire on the part of the inhabitants of the Aberdare Valley to do something constructive towards improving educational standards in the area. By the end of the century their efforts had ushered in a kind of Golden Age and given to Aberdare a justifiable claim to be regarded as the Athens of Wales.

The immediate effect of the Siloa encounter was to stimulate the nonconformists to act promptly in electing a formidable *ad hoc* executive committee. Alaw Goch was appointed chairman and remained in office until his sudden death in 1863. The influential John Jones, druggist, of the "Ceffyl Gwyn", No. 1 Commercial Place (now called Victoria Square), was elected treasurer, and he later succeeded Alaw Goch as chairman. The secretary of the committee was the very same Dr. Thomas Price of Penpound who had castigated Vicar Griffiths so severely at the Siloa assembly. It is worthy of mention that among their able colleagues was Evan

Griffiths, senior. With such dynamic leaders and businessmen in charge progress was ensured and things began to move very quickly indeed. The committee soon secured a quarter of an acre of land from the Marquess of Bute for a British School on part of the old "Comin"—the ancient Common of Hirwaun Wrgan. Evan Griffiths, junior, was instructed to draw up plans and the cost was worked out at approximately £530 with extras. Supported by contributions from all levels of local society the work of building proceeded without a hitch so that both the school and the master's house were ready for occupation within a matter of seven months. The first head was Thomas Taylor who served until 1851. On 3 February 1857 the deed of conveyance for the school site was received from the Honorable Sylvia Frederica Christina, Marchioness of Bute. Among the School Committee members at that time were John Jones the druggist, and the architect's brother, Lewis Griffiths.

Within a hundred yards or so of the British School—originally called Ysgol y Comin, afterwards the Park Schools and now Comin Junior School—there stands another building which has already figured in our article, namely the second Hen Dŷ Cwrdd. As we have seen, it was erected in 1862 to replace its dilapidated and crumbling predecessor. By this time Evan Griffiths, junior, despite his Calvinistic roots, had become actively connected with Hen Dŷ Cwrdd.[13] The task of designing the new building naturally fell upon his shoulders. It could have been ten or eleven years previously, perhaps just prior to his marriage, that he planned and built his own home "The Poplars", 41 High Street, on a small parcel of land immediately adjoining his father's emporium. It was in this house which stands to this day, albeit vacant and in a state of gross disrepair, that he and his wife brought up a large family of seven children—five girls and two boys. Philip Rhys, born in 1857, was the elder of the boys and the only one who grew to manhood. He possibly obtained his primary education at the British School and we know that later on in his boyhood he received instruction from Rees Jenkin Jones at the Trecynon Seminary.[14]

Destined for the medical profession, the young man may well

---

[13] He probably inclined towards Unitarianism through marriage to a member of Hen Dŷ Cwrdd. In Cardiff MS. 4.208, p. 75, however, there is a letter which suggests that his mother may have had a similar inclination.

[14] See article on "Hen Dŷ Cwrdd" in the Cardiff *Evening Express*, 9 September 1902.

have gone directly to London from the Seminary. He received his training as a doctor at University College Hospital, where Dr. (later Sir) John Williams would almost certainly have been one of his tutors in midwifery and gynaecology. The Gwynfe-born doctor was at that period on the staff of the hospital as an assistant obstetric physician. In 1880, at the age of twenty-three, P. Rhys gained his M.R.C.S. diploma and in the following year the M.B., B.S. degree of London University. Having obtained some experience as a clinical assistant at the Royal London Ophthalmic Hospital, the Central London Throat and Ear Hospital and the Hospital for Women, Soho Square, he returned to South Wales and settled down in practice at Cardiff for the rest of his life. Commencing in 1882, he served for two years as a house-surgeon at the Glamorganshire and Monmouthshire Dispensary in succession to C. J. Watkins. On relinquishing the post (D. R. Paterson was his successor), P. Rhys had to wait until 1886 before he was reappointed to join his seniors, F. W. Evans and Herbert Redwood Vachell, who had become honorary medical officers for outdoor patients at an earlier date. This newly-won status meant that as a medical man he now had a good foothold on the ladder of success. His future, like all futures, depended on his ability to work hard and wait patiently for vacancies on the hospital staff as they arose. Since he had undergone a surgeon's training, hard work and patience must have been very much a part of his make-up.

On 5 October 1882 P. Rhys attended an ordinary meeting of the Cardiff Medical Society held at the "Old Infirmary" in which he was invited to exhibit before his senior brethren a fine specimen of aortic aneurysm.[15] They must have been impressed by the young surgeon's demonstration, for he was immediately co-opted as a member of the pathological committee formed at the self-same meeting. On 14 March 1883 the society called upon him to display for the members' benefit several microscopical preparations of bacteria. Eight days later, with the subject obviously fresh in his mind, he read before the Cardiff Naturalists' Society an informative paper on "Disease Germs". It dealt with the origin, morphology, reproduction, and classification of bacteria in general and again was supported by a practical demonstration. As has been stated in our previous article on D. R. Paterson, the modern study of bacteriology,

[15] A pathological expansion of the main artery leaving the heart.

stimulated by the original researches of Pasteur, Koch, and Lister, was relatively new. In a popular lecture P. Rhys Griffiths, by the very choice of topic, seized a good opportunity of arousing interest among people drawn from all walks of life in these epoch-making scientific advances. He was probably the first man in Wales to demonstrate publicly actual specimens of such a pathogenic organism as the tubercle bacillus—a microbe discovered only in the previous year by the German, Robert Koch. Mr. Griffiths also showed a slide of the organism responsible for woolsorter's disease or anthrax. Although it is a rare malady in this country and one which attacks horned cattle, sheep and horses, it is occasionally transmitted to man. In addition he referred to spirillum obermeieri, a germ which causes relapsing fever. In his attempt to provide the gathering with a specimen of spirillum he enlisted the aid of Mr. Storrie, curator of the Municipal Museum, but their joint efforts were in vain. These incursions into the virgin field of bacteriology serve as early examples of Mr. Griffiths' contribution to and interest in the Cardiff Medical and Naturalists' Societies. It is noteworthy that when the biological and microscopical section of the Cardiff Naturalists' Society was founded in 1888 Dr. C. T. Vachell was elected president and Mr. P. Rhys Griffiths a committee member.

The new Infirmary built near the Longcross in Newport Road was ready for the admission of patients by 1884. At a meeting of the Cardiff Medical Society held in the new building on 7 October 1885, P. Rhys Griffiths was unanimously elected a member. It is of some interest that he was invited on that occasion to read some notes concerning surgical matters which were discussed that year at the annual B.M.A. meeting in Cardiff. On 11 March 1886 he addressed the society on "Some problems in the regional diagnosis of the nervous system". In May of the same year, at the house of the president, Dr. W. T. Edwards, he further showed his interest in bacteriology by demonstrating jointly with D. R. Paterson an interesting series of micro-organisms. The addition of Paterson's name, on the motion of the president, gave the pathological committee another member who could provide the impetus of youth. In January of the following year Griffiths was elected to the general committee of the society and, with some intermissions, he continued to serve until 1909. At the same meeting he presented a series of actual cases suffering from such neurological disorders as hemiplegia with epileptic attacks, spastic paraplegia, and paralysis of the musculo-spiral nerve.

To the medical historian the usual meeting of the society held on 10 March 1887 is of more than ordinary interest. In addition to showing a variety of splints made in Cardiff, Mr. Griffiths read a paper on "The birth and early years of medicine in Wales". He had obviously devoted a lot of attention to the subject and we are, indeed, exceedingly fortunate in that soon afterwards he published an account of his studies in the *Red Dragon*,[16] a quarterly periodical which was styled "The National Magazine of Wales". The results of further investigations which he made appeared by instalments in the Cardiff *Weekly Mail*. The instalments were subsequently reprinted in nine parts under the title "Welsh medicine in the 13th and 15th centuries" in *Cymru Fu*,[17] a journal designed by its editor George H. Brierley to include a variety of articles, notes, and queries relating to the past history of Wales and the border counties. Although P. Rhys Griffiths did not sit any professional examinations after obtaining his M.B., B.S. in 1881 he never ceased to be a student; and as he was the only man of his day to write extensively on early Welsh medicine, it behoves us to examine his contributions in some detail.

The first part of the *Red Dragon* article deals with the history of Welsh medicine from the earliest times down to the thirteenth century. The Druids, or more specifically the Ovates, figure prominently in the narrative, but there is little if any modification of the views put forward by John Williams (ab Ithel) in the introduction to his edition of *Meddygon Myddfai*.[18] Mr. Griffiths sums up the Roman period by stating that "through the Romans no doubt Hippocratic teachings became known in Wales". In dealing with the Dark Ages he closely follows ab Ithel once again; but when he comes to deal with Rhiwallon and his sons in the latter part of the article, he breaks entirely new ground.

To Rhiwallon and his three sons, Cadwgan, Griffith, and Einion, legendary figures though all four may be, the honour belongs of having first collected and documented the medical knowledge of their native country. Accordingly, Mr. Griffiths emphasises the

---

[16] Vol. 10 (1887), pp. 339-354.
[17] Vol. I (1887-9).
[18] *The Physicians of Myddvai; Meddygon Myddfai* (Llandovery, 1861).

fact that the appearance of Rhiwallon in the early part of the thirteenth century marks an important epoch in Welsh medical history. Rhiwallon can be regarded as one of the earliest medical writers in Great Britain. Tradition states that he was the household physician of Rhys Gryg, the son of Rhys ab Gruffydd, Prince of South Wales. Under the patronage of Rhys Gryg, Rhiwallon and his sons—all residents at Myddfai, Carmarthenshire—were able to dedicate their whole lives to the study and the care of the sick. Descendants continued to be domiciled at Myddfai and to practise there the art of their renowned ancestor until the middle of the eighteenth century, the last lineal descendant being a John Jones who lived in the early part of the eighteenth century and whose weathered gravestone can be seen to this day inside the porch of the local parish church. One of the last scions of the old doctors was Rice Williams, M.D., of Aberystwyth, who died on 16 May 1842, aged 85. Dan McKenzie remarks that heredity was one of the usual qualifications for admission to what we not improperly term the regular medico-priestly caste of savage communities. It is interesting in this connection to come upon the same circumstance among the folk doctors of Britain. In old Ireland the calling often ran in families, and the same is true of the Scottish Highlands. But the most remarkable instance, perhaps, is the medical scene at Myddfai, where the profession was carried on from father to son for half a millenium.

According to Iolo Morganwg another medical man called Hywel, a descendant in the direct male line from Einion and a general practitioner at Cilgwryd in Gower, compiled about three centuries later a corpus of recipes and cures from the writings of Rhiwallon and his lineal successors. If we can give credence to all that Iolo said about Hywel's manuscript, we can deduce that there was a copy of it in the possession of John Jones, the last of the Myddfai physicians. In the year 1743 a transcript of it was made by a North Carmarthenshire man, William Bona, and in 1801 Iolo Morganwg, so he himself tells us, made a copy of Bona's transcript. It was this "careful copy" of Iolo's that was printed by ab Ithel to form the second part of his text. The first part, for which one of Bona's actual transcripts[19] was used, represents the work of Rhiwallon and his sons, while both parts are followed by translations which are the work of John Pughe, F.R.C.S. of Penhelyg, Aberdovey. By today

[19] Cardiff MS. 58.

it is generally recognised by Welsh scholars that ab Ithel's text leaves much to be desired,[20] but as it has not been entirely superseded by an improved edition it is still as valuable to us as it was to P. Rhys Griffiths in the eighties of the last century.

Whatever the views of present day and future scholars may be regarding the historicity of Hywel the Gower physician, they can hardly affect our evaluation of P. Rhys Griffiths' work. He was the first man to attempt an interpretation of the wealth of medical material which John Pughe's[21] translation contained and he remains to this day the only man who has done so. We are therefore fully justified in allotting some considerable space to the fruits of his detailed studies in a field which was of such great interest to him.

One of the opinions which he expressed was that Eastern philosophy and culture were not unfamiliar to the early Welsh physicians. As evidence he quotes:

> The Latins, the men of Persia, and the Greeks (say), what we choose we love, what we seek we think of. Therefore let all men know that God has given the men of Greece a special gift, to discern every art, and the nature of all things, to a greater extent than other nations, with a view to the preservation of human health.

Towards the end of the second part of ab Ithel's text we are presented with a section entitled "The Essentials of a Physician" (Anhepgorion Meddyg), one of which reads:

> He (the doctor) should also have his warranted Books of Art authorized by a master, so that he may be cunning in the judgment and science of the wise and skilful Physicians who have preceded him, and who have written with authority in the Cymraeg, the Latin, and the Arabic.

According to Mr. Griffiths this particular essential is "worthy of note in that we find Welsh put alongside the Latin and the Arabic as one of the languages in which medical authorities had written". He does not comment, however, on the absence of Greek.

It is a well known fact that the humoral theory of disease[22] dominated the Hippocratic School. There is little doubt that

---

[20] See P. Diverres, *Le plus ancien texte des Meddygon Myddveu* (Paris, 1913) and G. J. Williams, "Meddygon Myddfai", *Llên Cymru*, vol. I, pp. 169-173.

[21] As Griffiths was writing in English he probably studied Pughe's translation rather than the Welsh text.

[22] Throughout the work of Hywel we meet with allusions to the four humours.

Rhiwallon followed the Arch-Mediciner of Cos in believing that the human body, apart from possessing the four fundamental qualities, hot, cold, dry and moist, was composed of four fluids or "humours" —blood, phlegm, yellow and black bile.   The health of the body was maintained so long as there was a right proportion and due combination of these several constituents.   Pughe's translation of Rhiwallon's precise view runs:

> The philosophers and wise men foreknew that man was formed of four elements, each being antagonistic to the others, and each consequently requiring continual aliment, which if it do not obtain, it will succumb.

Hippocrates and his followers also gave a prominent position to "Dietetics" and divided the principal causes of disease into two main categories, one being the influence of food and exercise. Throughout the Hippocratic Corpus we meet with detailed instructions on the hygiene of disease.   Rhiwallon and his triumvirate were apparently equally alive to the influence of food in the aetiology of morbid conditions of diet and exercise.   Mr. Griffiths cites several examples in which the text of Rhiwallon follows very closely the teachings of the Greek Master.   The resemblance between the statements is sufficiently striking to justify almost the assumption that Rhiwallon was at times actually quoting Hippocrates.

The article in the *Red Dragon* contains a detailed table of the maladies familiar to thirteenth century Welsh doctors.   Mr. Griffiths notes that Rhiwallon did not attach enough importance to the merits of the temperature and the appearance of the tongue in the diagnosis, prognosis, and treatment of sick people.   A careful systematic examination of a patient by Hippocrates and his followers always included observation of the pulse but, curiously enough, there is mention of neither this important physical sign nor the cardiac system in Rhiwallon's work.   It is noted that diseases of the heart and circulatory system also receive but scant attention in Hywel's account.   The foxglove (digitalis), the sheet anchor in modern treatment of heart irregularities and failure since its introduction by Withering in 1785, is mentioned in two places by Rhiwallon but only in connection with tumours. McKenzie states that the beautiful foxglove seems to have been unknown to the Greeks and the Romans.   It was Fuchs in 1542 who first called it "digitalis", remarking that until then there was no name for the plant in the "classical" world. As a medicament it receives its first mention from Rhiwallon—under the name, we ourselves note, of "ffiol y ffrud". Mr. Griffiths saw that Rhiwallon relied almost entirely upon the efficacy of herbs either in the form of infusions and decoctions to be taken internally or in the form of local applications —poultices, ointments and liniments. Although his materia medica included about one hundred and seventy five plants, flowers and roots, the inorganic world was represented by five substances only. There were apparently very few diseases which did not respond to the therapeutic effect of some simple or mixture of simples. When plant remedies failed, the old Welsh physician resorted to operative treatment with the knife and cautery, trepannation of the skull, lithotomy for bladder-stone, and drainage for lung abcess. The surgical skill of Rhiwallon was, perhaps, in Mr. Griffiths' view even more impressive than his medical expertise. The fact that such operations as these were being performed in the thirteenth century leaves us full of wonder. Rhiwallon's occasional use of charm-cures was, however, sufficient evidence to show that the sage of Myddfai had not quite discarded the superstitious shackles of his time.

Before passing on to the work of Hywel, the Gower physician, Mr. Griffiths evaluated Rhiwallon's position in medical history. It will be well to quote the passage in its entirety:

It has been customary in the past to single out for distinction the founder of any important movement, the originator of any industry, the pioneer of any new science, and to apply to him the distinctive appellation of Father. Justly does this title belong to Rhiwallon—the Father of Welsh Medicine—a man, if we may judge from the written record, remarkable no less for the strict integrity of his character than for the wealth of his understanding. The work which he has left to us will always remain as a monument to his remarkable skill and learning. It gives us in a clear and succinct manner a most complete account of the methods of treatment in vogue in the thirteenth century. Much of it is, no doubt, based upon pure empiricism. The theories which form, in many cases, the substratum for the treatment of disease may be speculative and specious in a high degree, but when we bear in mind how in the present day there are methods of treatment and theories of drug action which are not one whit less so than in the time of Rhiwallon, can we marvel at our old ancestors? On the other hand, there are many comments on subjects of great interest which are worthy of modern science—marked by great keenness of observation and remarkable shrewdness in deduction.

Although the second part of *Meddygon Myddfai* is ascribed to Hywel the text contains no mention of the date at which he flourished. It contains, however, a reference to the Sweating Sickness or English Sweat, a disease which ravaged the country in a series of five epidemics during the first half of the Tudor period. The last visitation, which began at Shrewsbury in April 1551, was observed and documented from actual experience by John Caius (1510-73), a practising doctor in the town at the time of the outbreak. The epidemic was an extraordinary phenomenon, inexplicable in its origin, and remarkable in that it disappeared never to return again. The fact that the Sweating Sickness is mentioned in the text of ab Ithel's book is of great importance because it enabled Mr. Griffiths to assign a date to Hywel's writings. Whether the disease spread to the Principality or not we cannot be sure. Our worthy feels there is strong presumptive evidence to show that the disease was not unfamiliar to the Carmarthenshire physicians and that their native country shared in the same dreadful disaster which some authorities contend only affected England. From this testimony we may conclude that Hywel's work was compiled after the appearance of the English Sweat.

Noting with concern that the medical profession was engaging the attention of charlatans, empirics and illiterate monks, often with the connivance of their bishops, Thomas Linacre (1460-1524), the royal physician, succeeded in establishing an authoritative body to control the practise of medicine throughout the country. This body was empowered not only to decide who should practice within the City of London but also to examine and license practitioners throughout the kingdom and inflict fines and even imprisonment upon those who broke the laws. Hywel states that the physician "should be . . . declared competent to practice by authority of the wise and learned masters of the art". From this quotation Mr. Griffiths deduces that the Gower doctor was a product of the new sixteenth century regime, one who had no doubt given a satisfactory account of himself before his august examiners.

Although surgery gets no mention in Hywel's work we must,

according to Mr. Griffiths, guard against the inference that the art was dormant in sixteenth century Wales. On the contrary, Hywel deliberately set out to write a book of remedies, and not a comprehensive treatise on medicine and surgery. It is, however, in the realm of materia medica and therapeutics that we encounter the most striking evidence of change and progress. As has been mentioned previously, Rhiwallon's materia medica comprised about one hundred and seventy five galenicals. The Cilgwryd doctor, on the other hand, could boast of using eight times that number, most of which he grew for convenience in his own garden. Hywel also employed far more inorganic substances than Rhiwallon, his pharmacopoeia including copper ore, verdigris, sulphate of copper, alum, mercury, red precipitate of mercury, sulphur, antimony, and white lead. The relationship between chemistry and medicine is of very long standing. In the opinion of A. G. Debus,[23] most of the early chemically prepared medicines were based on simple distillation techniques originally developed by the medieval alchemists. Indeed, it is through this pre-Paracelsian alliance of chemistry and medicine that chemical remedies were first introduced into Britain. Many British physicians of the Renaissance period had been trained at those continental universities which were prominent for their advocacy of chemical medicines. The interest in the new cures may be seen in all branches of the medical profession in the fifteen seventies and eighties and, not least, in Hywel's writings. One can almost hear him say that "if I finde . . . any thing that may be to the good of the Patients . . . be it either in Galen or Paracelsus; yea, Turke, Iewe, or any other Infidelle: I will not refuse it, but be thankfull to God for the same". Unfortunately, as Mr. Griffiths notes, Hywel fails to state in his prescriptions the relative quantities of the various ingredients given and does not lay down any definite instructions as to the doses of the different preparations used. This, in the writer's view, is a serious omission.

In Rhiwallon's treatise there is no evidence to show that the Welsh mediciners of his period laboured under the yoke of astrology. Mr. Griffiths sees that this is not the case with Hywel, for in a few sections the latter demonstrates very clearly that he is influenced to some extent by the doctrine that the stars of the firmament had some

[23] See his article "Paracelsian doctrine in English medicine" in F. N. L. Poynter's *Chemistry in the service of medicine* (London, 1963).

special control in directing the actions and destinies of mankind. Astrological bias is exemplified in a section entitled "A Snake's Skin":

> The following are the twelve characteristics of a snake's skin, which Alphibam testifies of, and states to be true and effectual to those that use it.   I have translated them out of the Arabic to Latin, and from Latin to Cymraeg also.
>
> When the moon is in her first increase, under the sign called Aries, or the Ram, which falls about the middle of the month of March, on the third day of the Calends of April, when the first seed under this sign are formed, then burn the skin of a snake, which has been cast in the time of harvest.   Take the ashes, and keep them carefully, for they are the most precious application which any human tongue can order.   Let the first instance at hand suffice: whosoever has a fresh wound, let him cover it with a little of this ash, and it will heal it in three days.

Largely due to the introduction of the telescope by Galileo (1564-1642) medical interest in astrology virtually disappeared by the end of the eighteenth century.

Despite his rampant empiricism, Hywel does make a genuine attempt to systematise the knowledge of the properties and uses of the medicinal plants at his disposal.   In summing up, our worthy notes that although Hywel distinctly advanced the theory of medicine, he did not make, even with a vastly increased armamentarium, any striking therapeutic progress.   The Gower doctor delighted in superstitions and charm-cures to an extent which quite eclipsed the practice as set out in Rhiwallon's treatise.   Some of the charms were the fruit of the vivid imagination of the early Welsh; many of them, no doubt, were imported from Rome with the invaders.   Having been provided by the Aberdovey surgeon with a golden master key to unlock the door, the Cardiff surgeon entered the inner sanctum of the old Welsh physicians to draw a clearer picture of their working-tools and methods.   In adopting the comparative approach, Mr. Griffiths not only placed the Myddfai doctors within the context of the period in which they flourished but also delved deeply in quest of the sources from which their inspiration sprang.   By the light he threw on the content of *Meddygon Myddfai* he rendered a signal service to Welsh medical historiography.   In the meantime P. Diverres, a French scholar, has made a very scholarly contribution to the textual study of the work.   It is, therefore, very much hoped that within the next few decades a competent medical historian will seek to build upon foundations which have already been so firmly laid.

We have already seen that our worthy began to take a great interest in the Cardiff Naturalists' Society almost as soon as he settled in Cardiff. Elected an ordinary member of the society in 1882 and to its council six years later he played a leading role in its development and progress right up to his death. On 8 March 1894 he addressed the members on the subject of "Welsh Weather-Proverbs",[24] the purpose of the paper being to draw attention to the wealth of material on this and kindred topics which lay within the scope and aims of the society. Having openly admitted that the chief problem in the preparation of the paper lay in providing an intelligible English version of the Welsh proverbs, he pointed out that some of the translations were crude and others written in doggerel verse. Despite the assistance of able friends he found the path from idiomatic Welsh to a free English translation perplexing. He suggested it would be instructive to compare the weather-lore of other European countries with that of Wales, but in view of the immensity of the task and the short time at his disposal, he decided to confine his discussion to Welsh and English proverbs connected with the months and seasons of the year. Taking each month in turn, he quoted several relevant examples of Welsh proverbs which he had translated into English. To provide added interest he cited proverbs of English origin and of similar meaning. He also gave a short list, translated from Welsh folk-lore, of proverbs relating to the seasons of the year. He added that he had collected many proverbs connected with weather, clouds, winds, fog and mist. Also of especial significance to him were old sayings based on observations of the habits of common domestic animals He concluded with these words:

> All over the country are scattered hundreds of proverbs. May I earnestly invite the co-operation of the members of this society in the important work of collecting them.
> The history of a country is incomplete without its mythology. We can all be collectors of facts.
> I am anxious that the scattered factors of our folk-lore should be collected, so that the Welsh Owen or Darwin, when he comes, may find at hand the materials for a complete and connected system of mythology.

[24] Cardiff Naturalists' Society, *Transactions*, vol. 26 (1895), part II, pp. 73-80.

In addition to ordinary membership of the Naturalists' Society and service on its council, Mr.Griffiths occupied a number of other roles. He acted for the years 1902-6 as honorary librarian. In 1904 he was elected president of the society in succession to T. W. Proger, F.Z.S., and at the inaugural meeting he addressed the members on the "Educational value of photography". Together with such enthusiasts as Dr. C. T. Vachell our worthy founded the photographic section, becoming its president in 1912-13. Having taken up the study of photography early in life, Mr. Griffiths freely placed his camera at the disposal of the society and its sections whenever the occasion demanded. A great lover of nature and a great walker, P. Rhys Griffiths, like his colleague, D. R. Paterson, knew every corner of Glamorgan intimately. We owe many photographic illustrations of its natural features and antiquities to his foresight. He realised how important this form of permanent record was in a county subjected to constant industrial changes and development. By the generous donation of a silver rose bowl which was to be competed for annually by members of the photographic section, he demonstrated a practical interest in a valuable aspect of artistic and scientific activity.

The redoubtable Paracelsus wrote that "the doctor must be a traveller because he must inquire of the world". In this respect the Cardiff surgeon followed the wise example of the Renaissance physician by travelling abroad as frequently as possible. A connoisseur of good food, Mr. Griffiths no doubt lost no opportunity at Continental restaurants of sampling a dish of roasted snails—a course which he regarded as the height of luxury. His wanderlust carried him far and wide, and the lectures which he delivered to the Naturalists' Society on his return were always well-illustrated by his own skilfully made slides. For example, on 14 October 1907 he "invited" the members to join him on a journey "To Moscow and Back", on 22 October 1910 he "transported" them "Through the Pillars of Hercules", and on 8 January 1914 he opened their eyes to the "Fascination of Venice". Unfortunately, these interesting addresses, although referred to in the *Transactions*, were never published. During the winter season 1905-6 the Cardiff City Library Committee arranged for a series of public lectures in four of their branch libraries. The new venture was received with such enthusiasm by the audiences that the committee decided to continue the series in future years. As one of the guest lecturers, our worthy spoke on such topics as a journey to Russia, life among the Arabs and a visit to the Western Mediterranean. He was evidently a popular public speaker. Earlier in his career, from 1887 to at least 1891, he had lectured on physiology and hygiene at the Science and Art Schools which were then held in the Central Library building.[25] By the early 1890's, if not before, he was a member of Cardiff Cymrodorion Society.

Although the motor-cycle did not become popular in any country until 1911-12, the prototypes of it were seen in France and Germany about 1885. A life-long cyclist, Mr. Griffiths had from time to time used an ordinary "push bike" in his daily work. Of a mechanical turn of mind, he realised as early as 1903[26] the advantages of the motor-cycle over the horse as a means of conveyance for medical men. Early that year, on the advice of some motor-cycling friends, he bought a $1\frac{3}{4}$ h.p. Werner machine which weighed about 100 lbs. and had a 22 inch frame. If in trouble from any cause, so low a frame permitted the feet of an average man to touch the ground with ease. Moreover, he was able to pedal the machine without difficulty provided he removed the drive-belt. Within a few months of purchase he had already ridden many hundreds of miles both in town and country, thus becoming a fairly efficient motor-cyclist. He had no difficulty in familiarising himself with the *modus operandi* of the machine, for its construction was simplicity itself. Needless to say, he experienced minor mechanical troubles but it seems he was quite competent in carrying out his own running repairs. By April 1903 he was able to dispense with the services of one horse, and in June of the same year he parted with a second. Caring little for cycling in wet weather, he still retained one beast for use in inclement conditions. He advised would-be cyclists to carry a spare belt and valve springs in addition to the ordinary riders' outfit. One drawback, he complained, was vibration, but this he reduced to a minimum by keeping the front tyre on the soft side and employing a large saddle. He derived infinite pleasure from motor-cycling and also found that he was able to do his work in a shorter time. More important still, his health improved in proportion to the exercise he took.

[25] See the syllabuses of the Schools for the period in question. Syllabuses for the post-1891 period, when the Schools were held in Dumfries Place at the present Students' Union building, are not available.
[26] See his contribution to the *British Medical Journal*, vol. II for 1903, pp. 119-20.

We now turn to the part played by our worthy as a leading South Wales medical man. In February 1895 he read before the South Wales and Monmouthshire branch of the British Medical Association a paper entitled "The remote effects of spinal injuries in miners". Later that year it was published in the Association's Journal.[27] Five years later he published in the same journal an article entitled "Perforating gastric ulcer, with notes on two successful cases after operation".[28] Another article on surgery "A case of resection of sternum for sarcomatous growth" appeared in 1902.[29] Not the least of Mr. Griffiths' other activities was his connection with the evolution and progress of the Medical School at Cardiff. One is, therefore, not surprised to find that the topic he chose as his presidential address to the Cardiff Medical Society in 1899 dealt with the work of the Society and the Medical School. Throughout his lifetime he toiled hard on behalf of and carried much influence with both these learned institutions. A study of the minutes of the Cardiff Medical Society is a revelation of the range, variety and complexity of the medical, surgical, and pathological problems which aroused his curiosity and interest and added to his professional repute. To record his contributions to that body would almost necessitate rewriting the minutes, a task beyond the scope of this essay. Suffice it to say that our surgeon was a tower of strength right up to his middle fifties when he must have been quite pleased to see younger medical men coming forward and taking an active part in the society's affairs.

P. Rhys Griffiths continued to act in the capacity of medical officer to outpatients at the Infirmary until 1895 when his resignation was followed by promotion to assistant surgeon. A further resignation in 1896 led to his appointment first as surgeon and later senior surgeon to the hospital. Few men did more for that charitable institution. His connection with it extended over a period of thirty-eight years, for thirty-four of which he served as member of the honorary medical staff. In addition to these voluntary professional obligations Mr. Griffiths gave much of his time to the administrative work of the institution. He was for a number of years chairman of the Medical Board and regularly attended the meetings of the Board

---

[27] Ibid., vol. I for 1895, pp. 967-8.
[28] Ibid., vol. I for 1900, pp. 572-3.
[29] *Lancet* , vol. II for 1902, pp. 991-2.

of Management and other committees. A kindly and genial personality, he was very popular with his colleagues, the hospital staff and patients. In 1903, together with Drs. Mitchell Stevens and H. C. Ensor, Mr. Griffiths was appointed to the staff of the Cottage Hospital, Mountain Ash, an institution which was reserved for obstetric cases after the new local General Hospital was opened in December 1924. There was no operating theatre at the Cottage Hospital until 1908—a state of affairs which must have been viewed with some concern by the team of visiting Cardiff specialists. In that year, however, matters were corrected when Lady Aberdare generously provided the necessary funds not only for a theatre but also for an extension to the building. During the First World War Mr. Griffiths rendered valuable services as a lieutenant-colonel on the staff of the Third Western General Hospital which not only had beds at the Infirmary but also in schools and other widely dispersed buildings in the city. His work contributed much to the high standard of efficiency attained by that military organisation through which large numbers of casualties passed. Exacting though these duties were he never relaxed his attention to the Cardiff (Royal) Infirmary which owed so much to his tireless, life-long service. In March 1919 on relinquishing his duties as honorary senior surgeon to the Infirmary and being appointed to the consulting staff, he reached the top rung of the ladder on which he had set his foot in 1882. He was not destined, however, to remain there for long.

On 12 October 1889 Evan Griffiths, junior, our worthy's father, died with tragic suddenness as he was walking from Ferndale to catch a train at Tylorstown. He was in his sixty-seventh year and had made a name for himself as an architect. As we have already stated, the British Schools, "The Poplars" (his own home) and Hen Dŷ Cwrdd were designed by him. Two chapels at Aberdare belonging to the Calvinistic Methodists, namely Bethania and Trinity, are also reckoned among his drawing board creations. He was still very active at the time of his death, and the same can be said of his only surviving son who died in his sixty-fourth year in much the same unexpected manner. On Tuesday morning, 13 July 1920, the latter had just entered a 1st class compartment on a Bristol bound train at the G.W.R. station, Cardiff, when he appeared to look faint. Realising the gravity of the situation some of the other passengers promptly drew the attention of the station officials to the surgeon's plight. The station master, having no doubts at all regarding Mr. Griffiths' fitness to travel, arranged his transfer to a nearby waiting room, where he expired almost immediately from a heart attack. A few days later his mortal remains were cremated in Golder's Green, London, at a private funeral service. Ironically enough, he had been for a period Consultant District Surgeon to the G.W.R. at Cardiff. Another appointment he had held was that of Medical Referee for No. 32 County Court Circuit.

It remains for us to give a brief account of Mr. Griffiths' family circle. He married the second daughter of Mr. S. W. Kelly, J.P. of Llandaff Road, Canton, and two daughters, Enid and Sylvia, were born to them. Enid married the eldest son of Sir Alfred Pearce Gould, the London surgeon, whilst Sylvia, who served as a V.A.D. nurse during the First World War, was still residing with her parents at their home in Newport Road when the father died. A brother of Mrs. Griffiths was His Honour Judge Hill Kelly, County Court Judge of the Cardiff district.

One of the most noteworthy facts about the family is that three of Mr. Griffiths' sisters married Unitarian ministers. The other two remained single and spent the whole of their life in the old family home at "The Poplars". About 1868 Hen Dŷ Cwrdd bought its first harmonium, and it is recorded that Anne and Mary Griffiths were the first to play that instrument and acted as organists for over ten years. Born in 1853, Anne not only taught in the Sunday School but also took a lively interest in social matters and public affairs. Among the first to support a Postal Mission to Wales, she stressed the duties and privileges of girls in *Yr Ymofynnydd*, *The Stepping Stone*, and other journals. She was treasurer to the Aberdare Women's Liberal Society and an officer of the local branch of the British Women's Temperance Society. On 7 July 1877 she married the Reverend Rees Jenkin Jones, a man we have more than once mentioned in connection with his ministry at Hen Dŷ Cwrdd and his headmastership of "Jones' School" or the Trecynon Seminary. Possessing great understanding and diligence in the execution of religious and social work coupled with an unselfish enthusiasm on behalf of all humane movements, she was a source of inspiration and encouragement to her husband at all times. In 1893 the Merthyr Board of Guardians made her a member of the Visiting Committee to the Poorhouse and six years later the Gadlys Ward elected her to the Board itself. When Aberdare Secondary School was opened in 1896, she was invited to act as a Governor and in accepting she became the only lady to sit on the Board at that time. When she died after a painful illness on 7 March 1899 at the age of forty-six, her remains were buried in the family vault at Trecynon cemetery. By her marriage to Rees Jenkin Jones she had five children, three girls and two sons. Their eldest son, Evan John Goronwy, decided to emulate his only maternal uncle and entered the medical profession. Educated at University College, Cardiff, and University College Hospital, London, Evan graduated M.B., B.S. in 1909 and M.D.(London) in 1913. During the First World War he was a lieutenant in the British Expeditionary Force. After the hostilities he became a practitioner in Swansea where he lived until his death on 2 February 1945.

We have already obtained several glimpses of Rees Jenkin Jones. Born on 17 September 1835 at Mount Pleasant Street, Trecynon, he was a scion on his mother's side of the Jones family of Llwyn-rhys, pioneers of nonconformity in Cardiganshire. In a period when Latin was considered essential to the cultivation of the mind, the boy was grounded in the language at an early age. Taking full advantage of his father's library, he is said to have read scores of learned books even when quite young. As he grew older, he was of immense help to his father in the classrooms at the Seminary, and that was probably the reason why he did not enter Carmarthen Presbyterian College until he was twenty. In 1859, his fourth and final year at the College, he won the Dr. Williams Scholarship which enabled him to enter Glasgow University. Among his teachers at the Scottish seat of learning was the great scientist, Professor Thomson (later Lord Kelvin), and it is interesting to note that the two men kept in contact with each other for the rest of their lives. At the end of his course at Glasgow in 1863 the Welsh student graduated M.A.

On the death of his ailing father on 19 December 1863, Rees Jenkin, as we have already seen, took his place in the pulpit of Hen Dŷ Cwrdd and also at the Seminary. A natural choice as successor to his father, the young graduate received a unanimous call from the congregation to become their spiritual and educational leader. Burning with energy and ideas, he proceeded to carry out his varied tasks with exemplary devotion and efficiency, but unfortunately the strain proved too much with the result that in 1872 he was forced to resign on the grounds of ill-health. He did not, however, remain idle, for ministerial and pedagogic work gave way to literary pursuits. A consistent and able contributor to *Yr Ymofynnydd* sincehis student days, he acted as editor of that monthly journal from 1873 until its cessation in 1879. When publication of the journal was resumed in 1881, he continued to be its editor for a further six years. The work not only involved routine editorial duties but necessitated the writing of many articles and columns on a wide variety of topics. In order to conceal his authorship, he signed the articles with all sorts of combinations of letters from the alphabet, the favourite initials being T.C.U., S.N.S., and M.G.P. In employing signatures of this kind he hoped that the readers would give credit for the article to writers other than himself. A philologist of international standing, he corresponded with Gaidoz (professor of Celtic in Paris) and Zimmern (professor of philology in Berlin). In 1876 he became a lecturer, acting as Principal, at Carmarthen Presbyterian College, where Watcyn Wyn, Ebenezer Griffith Jones and other able students attended his classes. Two years later he published a fine collection of hymns entitled *Emynau Mawl a Gweddi* and in 1895 another named *Emynau ac Odlau*. Long before the latter date R.J.J., as he was affectionately called, had become very well and widely known on account of his contributions to Welsh literary journals such as *Y Llenor, Yr Athraw, Cyfaill yr Aelwyd, Cymru*, and *Y Geninen*.

In 1879 he resumed his former duties as pastor of Hen Dŷ Cwrdd and head of the School. In the following year he was appointed as a delegate to two important conferences concerning Welsh education. Apart from his prowess in the pulpit—and this was considerable—he continued to write voluminously on bio-graphical, religious, and historical subjects in the local press and elsewhere. He was also responsible for many poetical and prose translations. Of interest to medical historians is his short letter published in *Cymru Fu*[30] a year after his marriage to Anne Griffiths. This letter, in which he sought information on books about Welsh medicine printed prior to the nineteenth century, appeared at a time when his brother-in-law, P. Rhys Griffiths, was contributing the results of his medical historical researches to the same journal. It

[30] Vol. I, p. 275.

would be interesting to know whether the two men ever discussed topics such as *Meddygon Myddfai* with each other. At this period R. J. Jones was honoured by an invitation to contribute articles to the *Dictionary of National Biography*. Among the fifty or so articles which appear above his name are those on Howel Harris, John Jones of Talsarn, Jack Glanygors, and Islwyn. He was the first president of Aberdare Cymrodorion Society. He almost reached his ninetieth year and upon his death on 15 October 1924 he was buried with other m members of his family at Trecynon cemetery. He will long be remembered as an outstanding professor, writer, hymnist, preacher and prophet—in fact, a veritable giant of the Unitarian cause.

We turn now to P. Rhys Griffiths' remaining sisters. In 1881 his sister Sarah married the Reverend George Evans, M.A., of Chester-field. Another sister, Mary, was a student at Bedford College, London, before entering the newly-founded University College at Cardiff in 1884. She married in 1893 the Reverend W. J. Phillips, M.A., the Unitarian minister at Nottage, Porthcawl. Their son, the Reverend Priestley Phillips, M.A., who became a Unitarian minister in various parts of England, is now living in retirement at Porthcawl. Of the two sisters who remained single, Jennie was for many years the French mistress at Aberdare County School. She died on 5 June 1938, while her sister Elizabeth Margaret, who kept house at "The Poplars", only survived her by a few years.

Grouped together on the tiled walls of the main corridor of the Cardiff Royal Infirmary are several impressive memorials to consultant physicians and surgeons who devoted a lifetime's skill to the welfare of the patients who entered that institution. There is, unfortunately, no such memorial to P. Rhys Griffiths, but as we walk through the building we cannot fail to sense the legacy which he bequeathed. He started life with no exceptional advantages save brain and will-power. Although his natural endowment was considerable, his success was mainly the result of incessant toil. The minutes of the Cardiff Medical Society are sufficient to show that he was an all-round clinician equally at home in the pathological laboratory as he was in the operating theatre. He was admired for his professional dependability and personal integrity. At the meetings of the Cardiff Medical and Naturalists' Societies he made valuable contributions on many subjects, but it is as a cultured Welshman whose interest in

Welsh medical lore led him to make so detailed a study of *Meddygon Myddfai* that we would choose above all else to remember him.

BIBLIOGRAPHICAL NOTE

The primary sources from which biographical information has been obtained are the obituary notices in the Cardiff newspapers, the *Transactions of Cardiff Naturalists' Society*, the *British Medical Journal*, and the *Lancet*. Mr. Griffiths's contributions to medical literature (most of which are mentioned in the text) together with the minutes and annual reports of the Societies and Institutions with which he was associated, i.e. Cardiff Royal Infirmary, Cardiff Medical Society, Cardiff Naturalists' Society, and Cardiff Public Libraries, have also yielded valuable information. The minute books of Cardiff Medical Society are deposited at the Glamorgan Record Office, County Hall, Cardiff, and a membership register of Cardiff Cymrodorion Society for the period 1890-5 is preserved at Cardiff Central Library.

Material on the religious and educational background of Aberdare and on Unitarianism has been drawn from *Gardd Aberdar* (1854); W. W. Price, *Park Schools Centenary (Canmlwyddiant Ysgol y Comin). Its history* (1948); D. Jacob Dafis, *Crefydd a gweriniaeth yn hanes yr Hen Dŷ Cwrdd, Aberdâr* (1951); *Yr Ymofynnydd* (monthly magazine of the Welsh Unitarians), various dates; R. J. Jones, "The origin and history of the Old Meeting House, Aberdare" in *Transactions of the Unitarian Historical Society*, vol. 1 (1916-8); and Roland Thomas, *Richard Price* (1924).

Turning to the medical side, we have made frequent recourse to D. Guthrie, *History of Medicine* (1945) and D. Mackenzie, *The Infancy of Medicine* (1927). All other sources have been cited either in the body of the article or the footnotes.

We are grateful to Mr. T. J. Hopkins of Cardiff Central Library for all the help he has given in the preparation of the article. We would also like to acknowledge the assistance willingly rendered by Mr. M. Williams, Hospital Secretary of the Aberdare Valley Sub-Group Hospitals, Miss E. Lumley-Jones, Librarian of the Welsh National School of Medicine, the Rev. T. J. Jones, Minister of West Grove Unitarian Church, Cardiff, and Mr. G. I. John, Librarian of Aberdare. Not the least of our debts is one to the late W. W. Price, the Aberdare historian, some of whose index cards, or rather copies of them kindly supplied by the National Library of Wales, guided us on our way in the initial stages of our work.

THE COAL MINING INDUSTRY IN
WEST GLAMORGAN

by

W. GERWYN THOMAS,

B.SC., PH.D., A.M.B.I.M., C.ENG., M.I.MIN.E.

THE earliest reference to coal mining in West Glamorgan occurs in about 1250 when Owen ap Alaythur granted to Margam Abbey all the "stone coal" on his land. The coal was worked near Margam, in the hill district of Penhydd, extending to the River Ffrwdwyllt,[1] and was intended for use at the Monks' Grange of Rossoulin and for the Abbey of Margam and its tenants. "Stone coal" refers to the hard anthracite coal of the area. Later, in 1281, John Giffard, Warden of Glamorgan for the Earl of Gloucester, in his accounts under "Manorium de Neath" includes the item "Issues of the Manor . . . from coals for the same time nothing, through lack of workmen there". The coal area referred to was probably at or near the Gnoll.[2]

The next earliest reference to coal mining occurs in 1306, when William de Breos, the Norman lord of Gower, granted a new charter to the borough and burgesses of Swansea.[3] One of the privileges granted was that the burgesses might have "pit coal in Byllywasta"[4] but only for their own consumption.

The coal industry was obviously still in its infancy at this time although there was a coal mine near Clyne and also one at Kilvey, to the east of the Tawe estuary. Coal was being produced in the lordship of Kilvey before 1340[5] and by the close of the century it was being worked on a considerable scale as seen from the accounts of the mine for the year 1399-1400.[6] The mine consisted of drifts into

[1] Rees, William, *Industry before the Industrial Revolution* (Cardiff, 1968), vol. I, p. 34.
[2] Phillips, D. Rhys, *History of the Vale of Neath* (Swansea, 1925), pp. 228-229.
[3] Jones, W. H., *History of the Port of Swansea* (Carmarthen, 1922), pp. 9-10.
[4] "Byllywasta" probably refers to Gelliwastad, above Morriston.
[5] Rees, William, op.cit., vol. I, pp. 79-80.
[6] South Wales and Monmouthshire Record Society Publications, No. 1, p. 180.

the hillside, a new adit being dug during that year, by piece work, for 60s. Water was drained from the mine by conduits, lighting was by candle and the coal was carried to the surface in barrows. Three hewers were employed at the coal face and there were thirty porters who not only carried the coal to the surface but also from the pithead to the waterside and on to the ships. The output of the colliery for the year amounted to about 4,000 tons and it was, therefore, a fairly large mine for those days.

In 1526, the Earl of Worcester, lord of Gower, leased to Sir Mathew Cradock of Swansea "all and all manner mines of coals . . ." within Gower and Kilvey.[7]

Reverting to Margam, in 1516 Abbot David of the Cistercian house of Margam granted a 70 year lease of lands in Dyffryn Ffrwdwyllt with the right to dig coal.[8]

Coal had also been worked on the Neath Abbey estate at Cadoxton from an early date, the last Abbot, Leyson Thomas receiving a yearly rent of 20s. from the coal at the time of the Dissolution. Afterwards, in 1541, Richard Cromwell the new owner of the estate continued the lease at the same rent.[9]

In addition to the early coal developments mentioned on the Abbey estates on the west side of the Neath river, lands belonging to the lord to the east and west of the river were also being worked for coal during the fourteenth and fifteenth centuries. Leland visited the Neath Valley about 1536-38 and noticed considerable activity in coal-works and shipping.[10]

The second half of the sixteenth century saw the beginning of an organised coal mining industry in Wales as distinct from the operations of the individual prospector and his few part time helpers. The chief coal mining centres in Wales during the sixteenth and seventeenth centuries were the Neath and Swansea areas. In these regions the sea gave direct access to the interior of the coalfield, facilitating the beginnings of an export trade in coal along the coast.

In the Vale of Neath at Cadoxton coal continued to be worked under lease during the sixteenth and seventeenth centuries and by about 1650 the coal works reverted to the owner, Edward Dodington, and later to David Evans of Eaglesbush. The pits were some distance

[7] Jones, W. H., op.cit., pp. 330-331.
[8] Rees, William, op.cit., vol. I, p. 81.
[9] Ibid.
[10] Phillips, D. Rhys, op.cit., p. 279.

from the river and connected to it by a waterway.[11]   Higher up the valley between the Rivers Nedd and Dulais there were two pits being worked before 1577 at the western end of the area.   Later, in 1632, developments took place at Bryndulais, near Seven Sisters.

In the borough of Neath towards the end of the sixteenth century, the lord of the manor, the Earl of Pembroke, proposed a scheme to the burgesses to increase the production of coal within the borough.[12]   They were to be allowed to produce coal for sale on payment of a royalty of 6d. a weigh (approximately five tons) for all coal sold overseas.   In the year 1597 a total of 221¼ weighs was exported from the "bank" of Neath.   Later, the burgesses were allowed to take coal both for their own use as of old and for sale on the common lands of the town in consideration of a yearly rental and a royalty of 6d. a weigh on coal sold or shipped out of the borough.   Later still one of the burgesses, David Evans, undertook the supply of coal to the burgesses for their own needs at favourable rates and to pay the royalty to the lord on coal sold outside the borough boundaries.   Trade overseas increased and the lease was renewed several times in the seventeenth century by David Evans's son Edward and by Herbert Evans (the Gnoll family).

Other exporters besides the Evans family were operating at or near Neath during the seventeenth century and dispatching coal from their mines, such as Richard Seys, Bussy Mansell, William Leyson and William Phillips.[13]

In 1686 Humphrey Mackworth by his marriage to the sole heiress of Sir Herbert Evans came into possession of the Gnoll estate and control of the Neath coal interests.   After 1695, Mackworth reorganised the working of the town pits, improving the ventilation and constructing a tramway from the pits to the town quay.   He introduced copper-smelting and silver refining at Neath, building copper furnaces (Melin Crythan) near the coal pits and made the coal-works at Neath the foremost in Wales at the time.   The site of Mackworth's three pits is marked on a plan drawn by M. O'Conner, about 1720 (*Plate* 1).   The pits are located on the plan by the letter E and referred to as "Ginn Houses for raising Coals" indicating that the coal winding arrangement was worked by a horse or horses. (*Plate* 2).

[11] Rees, William, op.cit., vol. I, p.85.
[12] Ibid., p. 86.
[13] Ibid., p. 88.

In a work by Waller on the copper and lead mines of Sir
Carbery Price, reference is made at length to Sir Humphrey
Mackworth's innovations at Neath.[14] He had a "new method of
coffering out the Water from his Shafts and Sinking Pits, and
thereby preventing the Charges of Water-engines" (water wheels);
"and his new Sailing Waggons, for cheap Carriage of his Coal to the
Water-side, Whereby one Horse does the Work of ten at all times;
but when any wind is stirring (which is seldom wanting near the
Sea) one Man and a small Sail does the work of Twenty . . .".

Under his town lease (granted by the burgesses for 31 years) in
1697 Mackworth had originally "attempted the recovery of the
coal works by the assistance of the colliers of that neighbourhood,
but failed of success, whereupon he travelled into other counties to
find skilful miners to assist him therein". He appears to have gone
to the North of England for he continues, "After great expense, and
by carrying on a level or wardway, commonly called a footrid or
waggon-way, after the manner used in Shropshire and Newcastle, he
recovered the said coal works, and at great expense, continued the
said waggon-way on wooden rails from the face of each wall of coal
—one thousand two hundred yards under-ground to the water side,
three quarters of a mile". The coal was apparently shipped to
Bridgwater among other parts at that time (1705).

According to Edward Lhuyd, writing towards the end of the
seventeenth century, "at Neath there are coal-mines up and down
everywhere, but the most considerable are near the Abbey where
many workmen are employed". The output from the Abbey pits
was most probably shipped not at the town quay, but at a quay on
the opposite side of the river near the Abbey, on the west bank of the
estuary.[15]

In 1627 we hear that the Lord of Glamorgan had "no manner
of mines" to the east of the lower reaches of the river Nedd outside
the borough of Neath. Sir Thomas Mansell, Hopkin Thomas and
Rice ap Evans of Llantwit are mentioned as working coal mines in
the area. Others, including the Evans family of the Gnoll, worked
leases of coal in the area before 1611 until 1667. Also in 1637,
Edward Evans, son of David, obtained the lease of other mineral
rights in Llantwit, which eventually passed to Walter Evans,

---

[14] Phillips, D. Rhys, op.cit., p. 234.
[15] Rees, William, op.cit., vol. I, p. 89.

Edward's son-in-law, of the Eaglesbush family. At the same time Walter Evans came into possession of Melin Crythan and Eaglesbush House on the outskirts of Neath.[16]

Coal had been worked in the Briton Ferry—Baglan area before 1502. The mines at Briton Ferry were worked during the sixteenth century by the Price family and afterwards, through marriage, by the Mansells. Bussy Mansell, as recorded earlier, was exporting coal from the town quay of Neath in 1663 and was mining in the Neath Abbey lands in 1670. His main interests, however, lay at Briton Ferry and Baglan. Bussy Mansell was succeeded on his death in 1699 by his grandson, Thomas Mansell of Briton Ferry. By the end of the century four pits had been opened up at Briton Ferry.[17]

The Baglan district was being rapidly opened up during the latter half of the seventeenth century and a valuable report on the Baglan coal mines for 1696-99 prepared by the agent of the pits, Anthony Thomas, is available to us through Edward Lhuyd. The pits lay in the low ground near the seashore, one containing "several veins to the number of forty at least". The veins here dip steeply to the north and underlay the church and churchyard of Baglan, the graves apparently being excavated in coal.

Turning again to the Swansea area, the coalmines of Kilvey to the west of the Nedd estuary were closely linked with the Briton Ferry mines, both forming part of the Mansell interests in the seventeenth century. As we have seen, Kilvey by the close of the fourteenth century had become the most important of the early coal-mining undertakings in Wales. By the sixteenth century, the coal at Kilvey was probably being worked by the Prices of Briton Ferry. In 1646, Walter Thomas of Swansea had coal pits at Kilvey and certain mines after 1640, probably those of the Price family, passed into the hands of Bussy Mansell and his partner Hopkin James. These may be the pits described as lying under the high road leading from Bonymaen to Llansamlet church associated in a survey of 1650 with the name Ffordd-y-glo (the coal way). A hundred years later, in 1750, Bussy, Lord Mansell of Margam, granted a lease of the pits in Llansamlet to Chauncy Townsend, to supply his copper works with coal, with power to construct a waggon-way.[18]

[16] Ibid., p. 91.
[17] Ibid., pp. 92-93.
[18] Ibid., vol. I, p. 94.

Coal was produced at Millwood (Llangyfelach) during the late sixteenth and seventeenth centuries, both under lease, by the Seys family of Rhyddin, and also by one of the Mansell family who owned the land.

In west Gower during the sixteenth century there were mines at Llanrhidian, Llandimore and Weobley; some belonged to Neath Abbey and others were under lay ownership. In the Loughor area in the opening years of the eighteenth century, Sir Humphrey Mackworth took up a lease at Penclawdd and on the glebe lands at Loughor. In 1730 Thomas Popkins of Forest had also taken a lease of coal mines in the parish of Loughor.

The west Gower lands under lay ownership belonged in 1530 to William, Earl of Pembroke, who leased them for coal working to William Herbert of Swansea. In 1626 the mines were in the hands of his nephew, William Herbert of Cogan.[19]

In 1667, Sir Richard Mansell came into possession of the manors of Llandimore, Weobley and Reynoldstown, as well as other lands in Gower. Mansell himself operated the pit at Y Wern in Llanrhidian at least until the year 1686-87 when 2,000 tons of coal were exported. Before 1730, coal mines were being developed under the salt marsh of Llanrhidian by Mathew Price, and in that year Mansell granted a lease to Robert Popkins to work coal in Llanrhidian parish. About the same time he granted a lease of the coalworks at Llanmorlais. The main operator was Gabriel Powell who also obtained from Mansell in 1749 a lease to enable him to use Salthouse Pill to export his coal.

In east Gower, at Clyne, coal had been mined during the middle ages, before 1319. In 1642, the lease of mines held there by Walter Thomas of Swansea was transferred to Richard Seys, who was still operating there in 1650. The mines were still in production at the end of the century. By the 1760's all Clyne forest coal was being worked under lease and at little profit by Messrs. Champion and Griffiths.

In a Gower Survey made for Oliver Cromwell (1650) when lord of the Seignory of Gower, a lease for mining coal at Morfa Lliw was reported to be held by John Williams for a royalty of four shillings a weigh.[20]

19 Ibid., vol. I, p. 97.
20 Ibid., vol. I, pp. 97-98.

Turning to Swansea itself we read[21] of the development of the harbour in the seventeenth century by the provision of "coale places" on the river side, and the imposition by the Corporation of dues for the laying of coal upon the places thus provided by the town (*Plate* 3). A long and detailed account submitted by William Jenkins to Sir Thomas Mansell, Bart., in 1707-8 shows the amounts of coal shipped in a month (17 January : 18 February) from the Great Pitt, Little Pitt, Middle Pitt, Pydew Pitt and Keven Pitt, at "White Rocke", "Middle Banke" and at "Upper Docke". The above coal, doubtless from Llansamlet or Birchgrove, formed a major source of supply for the export trade from Swansea at that time, as also did that from the pits at Millwood, Clyne and Kilvey. The Llansamlet pits referred to were, to some extent at any rate, the undertaking which was leased to Chauncy Townsend in 1750, by Bussy Mansell.

Turning to coal-working on the Swansea proper, or western side of the river, the Morris MS., quoting a letter of Robert Morris, says that the "coal trade began to flourish at Swansea in 1727". The local copper works, established in 1717, were supplied with coal at that time by only a few collieries. In 1727 it was obtained, though in insufficient quantities, from Popkin's Cwmbach and "Penivilia" pits. In 1728, Thomas Price of Penllergaer was supplying coal and a little later, Herbert Mackworth from Trewyddfa, at 17s. per weigh. The consumption at Thomas Lockwood & Company's Landore copper works was considerable, the payments to Popkin and Mackworth being about £111 monthly. In August 1728 Robert Morris, on behalf of Thomas Lockwood & Co., took over from Mackworth "the coal work he had at Treboth", which "was stiled Trwyddva". Mr. Mackworth was to receive half the profits. The intention was to sink a pit (for ventilation). The sinking cost £8 per fathom "in hard rock" and they "sunk a fathom a month", according to the Morris MS.

The lack of facilities at this time for the shipment of coal by sea prevented any great development. By 1799, however, although only six chaldrons (of 2,000 lbs.) went from Swansea to London, 139,486 chaldrons of bituminous and 13,319 of "stone coal" went to other ports. An interesting account of conditions at the end of the eighteenth century is supplied by the Rev. J. Evans in his letters written during a tour in South Wales and published in 1804. The

[21] Jones, W. H., op.cit., pp. 333-340.

river apparently was navigable for two miles above the bar, and there were "convenient quays, and slips for shipping and unshipping of goods" in what was termed the "Harbour of Swansea". *Plate* 4 shows an artist's impression of an early Welsh coal and shipping scene (location unknown). Also, the conveyance of goods for shipment was "facilitated by means of a canal on the western bank of the Tawey, accompanying it to Hennoyedd in Brecknockshire, and a shorter cut, private property, on the eastern bank, extending to Neath".

The Swansea canal was opened from Swansea to Godre'r-graig in 1796 and fully (to Hen-neuadd near Abercrave) in 1798.[22] Several factors led to its construction: the growth of collieries up the Tawe Valley; the possibility of enlarging the iron works at Ynyscedwyn and developing others; the growth of copper smelting that required transport of the copper ore to the works; the absence of a turnpike road up the valley; and the passing in 1791 of an Act to improve Swansea harbour.

The Swansea Canal incorporated at its lower end the Trewyddfa Canal, which consisted mainly of the original Morris's Canal. This was built about 1790, measured just over a mile in length, and ran parallel to the river from coal banks at Landore up to the Fforest Copper Works below Morriston. It was described in 1793 as belonging to Messrs. Lockwood & Cotton, Lord Eliot and John Morris. The canal referred to as being on the eastern bank was probably the Llansamlet (Smith's) Canal, built by John Smith, son-in-law of Chauncy Townsend, about 1784, replacing an earlier tramroad from Llansamlet down to the Tawe at Foxhole.

To quote from Rev. Evans's letters—"The largest colliery is at Pentre, the property of Mr. Morris of Clasmont. The whole hill is full of coal, and is obtained by what miners term open audits, i.e. horizontal shafts driven into the hill, which form levels for draining the work as well as ways for the delivery of the coal. There are within, some vertical shafts, beneath these levels, and whimsies[23] have given way to a more philosophical and expeditious machine, the improved steam engine of Boulton and Watt. One of these

---

[22] Hadfield, C., *The Canals of South Wales and the Border* (Cardiff, 1960), chapter III.

[23] Whimsey, a capstan or windlass, for raising coal by the weight of water, which descending in one bucket draws up another filled with coal. (Webster's Engineering Dictionary).

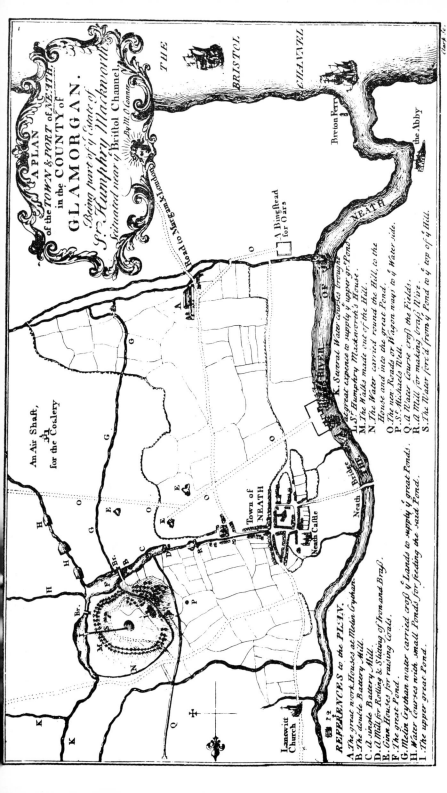

Plate 1 O'Conner's Plan of Neath, 1720

By permission of the British Museum

By permission of Cardiff Public Libraries

Plate 2 Gin Pit at Neath, c. 1787

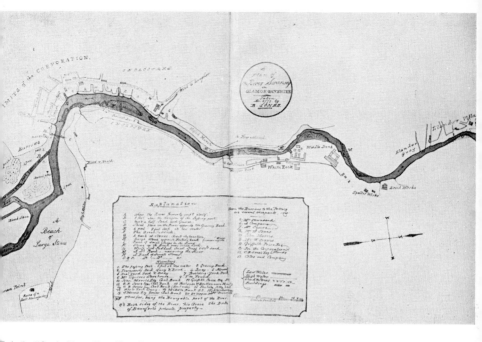

Plate 3   "Coale Places" on River Swansea, 1771   *Reproduced from W. H. Jones'* History of the Port of Swansea

Plate 4   Artist's impression of Welsh collieries and shipping arrangements in the late eighteenth and early nineteenth century

Plate 5 "Morris Castle" remains, Landore

By permission of the National Museum of Wales

Plate 6 Cornish Engine House, Scott's Pit, Llansamlet

audits, which we traced about a mile in length, admits low waggons, holding a chaldron each, which running on an iron railway, one horse with ease delivers at the quay (at Landore)".

The Morris MS.[24] gives details concerning the introduction of the tramways referred to above, and which indicate the enterprise of Lockwood, Morris & Co.—"Cast Iron Tram Plates—In Nov'r. 1776, I wrote to Messrs. Darby & Co. at Coal Brook Dale that I had sent them a pattern in wood about 4 ft. long and 5 in. wide, to cast Iron plates for wheeling Coal in my Collieries, each plate to weigh ab't 56 lbs.: that if they cou'd be supply'd at £8 p'ton I shou'd want immediately 100 Tons, and that the introduction of them wou'd occasion a vast consumption of metal never before us'd for such purpose".

Twelve years later, in 1778, we learn that there were about 240 tons of Cast Iron Tram plates underground at Landore colliery, i.e., $3\frac{3}{4}$ miles of tramway.

Further information about the early working of coal in the Swansea district from 1775 is provided in the manuscript notebook of Mr. (afterwards) Sir John Morris. He refers to the extension of Landore Colliery with new pits at Landore and on the Graig, and says that by July 1775 the collieries have a "prosperous app'ce". He also refers to rent from "Castle building"[25] (*Plate* 5). It is also clear from his notes that Lockwood, Morris & Co. appreciated the necessity for a larger pumping engine than the "Fire Eng'es" then at work, which would be capable of draining the whole of the extended colliery area. Copies of letters between John Morris (Lockwood, Morris & Co.) and Matthew Boulton and James Watt, from the end of 1778 until 1786, relating to the new pumping engine, are preserved in the Morris MS. Although the conclusion of the correspondence is not available, specifications were finally agreed and a large efficient pumping engine was introduced which successfully drained the whole of the extensive Landore colliery area.[26] It apparently cost £5,000 and pumped 100 gallons per stroke at twelve strokes per minute.

During and after the 1770's other pits were sunk in the lower

---

[24] Jones, W. H., op.cit., pp. 341-345.
[25] Refers to the experiment of building workmen's dwellings in the form of a block of tenements. Became known as Morris Castle and the remains may be seen today.
[26] Jones, W. H., op.cit., pp. 341-345.

Swansea Valley and further steam engines in the form of the beam engine of the Boulton & Watt or Cornish type were installed to cope with the ever-present water.   Such a pit was Scott's pit, Heol-las, Llansamlet, sunk in 1770 by Captain Scott.   He soon found himself in trouble from water and having no experience of dealing with it, abandoned the pit and returned to his old profession of building tramroads and completed one from Llansamlet to the riverside wharf at the Foxhole, Swansea.   A few years later he installed a Cornish pump and winding engine to complete the sinking of his pit.   The remains of the engine house may be seen today (*Plate* 6).   Unfortunately, Captain Scott's financial resources were by now so depleted that he had no money left to develop the colliery and sold it to his friend Charles Smith of Gwernllwynchwyth who operated it for its short working life from 1819 to 1838.[27]

"Squire" Smith, as he was known, was descended from Chauncy Townsend, who as we saw earlier, came into the lower Swansea Valley, with his son-in-law John Smith, and secured interests in various pits including the Church pit from the Morgan family of Gwernllwynchwyth.   John Smith developed the undertakings into a complex of pits,[28] and at his death in 1797, his sons Charles and Henry came into possession of the Llansamlet collieries.   From evidence given by Henry Smith before a committee of the House of Commons,[29] we gather that very deep pits were sunk at Llansamlet, that there were several very powerful fire-engines at work and that there were very expensive waggon-ways made with timber framework.   All this presumably before 1797.

Charles Smith, in addition to taking over Scott's pit also sank a pit which was named after him—Charles pit, and in 1839 he constructed a drift mine higher up the mountain side from Scott's pit which he named after his wife, Emily.   "Squire" Smith was an excellent geologist and a well liked personality by all accounts and his Charles pit and Emily colliery were very successful ventures.

"Squire" Smith was succeeded by his son, Charles Henry Smith, the last Smith of Llansamlet, who sold his colliery interests in about 1870 to the Foxhole Coal Company.

Another name, that of Vivian, is inextricably bound with the

---

[27] Gregory, H., Cuttings from *South Wales Evening Post* (Swansea, 1962-68), pp. 51-107.
[28] Hilton, K. J., *The Lower Swansea Valley Project* (London, 1967), p. 17.
[29] Wilkins, C., *The South Wales Coal Trade* (Cardiff, 1888), pp. 50-52.

development of industry in the Swansea area. John Vivian, originally of Truro, first came to Penclawdd about 1800 to represent the "Associated Miners of Cornwall" who had an idea that the value of their ores was not paid to them by the smelters. He operated the Penclawdd Copper Works on their joint account, charging a commission for smelting. John Vivian satisfied himself that copper smelting was a profitable occupation and sent his second son John Henry to study mining in Germany. He found a suitable site for new works, with an ample supply of coal of the proper quality and price, at Hafod on the Swansea river, and this was leased from the Duke of Beaufort and Lord Jersey, in 1810, in the names of Richard Hussey and John Henry Vivian.[30] Their enterprise prospered and expanded and the direction fell eventually upon H. Hussey Vivian (later Sir H. H. Vivian). In addition to copper and other works, the Vivians owned several collieries including Brynwyllach, Pentre, Brynhyfryd, Pentrefelen, Penfilia, Mynydd Newydd and Cathelyd in the Swansea area, and Morfa colliery, Port Talbot (1849).

Turning again to the Neath Valley, Sir Humphrey Mackworth died in 1727, and his son Herbert Evans Mackworth apparently concentrated on the development of the coal trade at the expense of his father's copper works. It was Herbert who largely developed the coal industry of Neath and sank numerous pits. From November 1743 to April 1744, 3,000 tons were shipped to sea, while the copper works used 700 tons. In 1744 Mackworth's pits included Greenway, New Greenway, Castle, Cole's, Bowen's, Little Greenway and Bassett. In 1751 there were in addition Gwainmorgan vein, Middle and South pits (Cimla), Gnoll or Mill pit, Tyn-y-wain and Cae-y-pandy. In 1753 there was a steam (or "fire") engine working at Gnoll.[31]

The next step in the Gnoll coal history occurred in 1801 with the end of the Mackworth era and the commissioning of Edward Martin of Morriston to report fully on the condition of the various pits etc. to C. Hanbury Leigh, who had recently married the widow of Sir Robert H. Mackworth.[32] The "Old Fire Engine Pit" is described as "stopped", but the Water Wheel Engine pit is said to be "now at work".

[30] Grant Francis, G., *Smelting of Copper in the Swansea District* (London, 1881), pp. 125-127.
[31] Taylor, Glen A., "The Mackworth Undertakings at Neath", *Transactions of the Neath Antiquarian Society*, vol. 7 (1937-39), pp. 69-70.
[32] Phillips, D. Rhys, op.cit., pp. 238-240.

Martin recommended some developments including the sinking of a new pit at the side of the Neath canal, on the grounds that the price of coal per weigh (five tons) had increased from 41s. in 1792 to 61s. in 1800 and that the expiry of the patent on Boulton and Watt's "Small Rotative Fire Engine" which raised baskets of 5 cwt., 100 fathoms, in a minute and a half, would save them £500 a year.

The coal operations of the Gnoll ceased almost entirely about 1809-10 and did not re-start until 1869-70, when Robert Parsons of Neath and others leased the property, surrendering it four years later in 1874 to the Hopkinson Co.—the Neath Collieries Co. Ltd. Afterwards Charles Evan Thomas of Gnoll worked the pits.

A change occurred towards the end of the eighteenth century culminating in the *Neath Canal Act* of 1791, which authorised the building of a canal from Glynneath for about 10½ miles to near Melincrythan pill, Neath.   The purpose of the canal was mainly to develop a coal export trade (from Neath Valley pits) and to bring iron ore down to the various iron works at Cwm Gwrach, Melin-y-Cwrt, Penrhiwtyn, Aberdulais and Neath Abbey.

The canal was completed about the end of 1795 and took boats carrying up to 25 tons.[33] An extension of 2½ miles from Melincrythan to Giant's Grave near Briton Ferry, where transhipment to coastal vessels would be easier, was completed in 1799.   Mention should be made of Mackworth's Canal which Sir Humphrey built between 1695 and 1700.   A short tidal cut (300 yards long) from a pill in the river Neath, it enabled small craft to navigate to within 400 ft. of the Melincrythan lead and copper works, about a mile below Neath. A tramroad joined the canal and the works.

The opening of the canal induced a number of new prospectors from England to lease coal areas in the valley and a comprehensive account[34] of this development along both banks of the Neath river makes fascinating reading.   From the head of the valley to the sea, on both banks, numerous coal mining operations were developed in the Vale of Neath in the nineteenth and early twentieth centuries. Space permits the mention of only a few of the more important undertakings starting from the top and working down the valley.

Herbert Mackworth worked coal at Banwen Pyrddin in 1743-44 and opened the Waen-Marchog colliery in 1791, after which John

---

[33] Hadfield, C., op.cit., pp. 62-66.
[34] Phillips, D. Rhys, op.cit., pp. 240-259.

Penrose took over in about 1816. It remained for years in his family and by 1873-4 a company had been formed known as Penrose & Starbuck. Sir D. R. Llewellyn developed the Rock colliery in the same neighbourhood in 1920.

Further down the valley on the right bank, at Aberpergwm, a coal lease was granted to Mary Williams, widow, in 1670. Aberpergwm colliery or "Gwaeth y Cwrt", as it was known, is first referred to under "Aberpergwm—1793—J. Foxes (ceased) 1805", and second, "Gwaeth Glo Aberpergwm—Geo. Williams". In 1808 Rees Williams entered a law suit to recover the Aberpergwm lease from Messrs. Cook & Co. of Birmingham who had secured it sometime after 1798 at a time when the Aberpergwm family were ignorant of the quality and value of the coal. He won the case and agreed to buy the defendant's interests in the colliery. In 1810 he acquired property at Giant's Grave for shipment of his coal.

From 1810 the Aberpergwm colliery remained a family concern until taken over by Sir D. R. Llewellyn (Vale of Neath Collieries Co. Ltd., Glyn Neath) in 1920. The undertaking had been considerably developed after 1900, with a branch railway, thus ending canal transport to Neath and Swansea. In 1928 Aberpergwm and three other Glynneath collieries of the Vale of Neath Collieries Co., viz. Maesgwyn, Pwllfaron, and Penstar drift, were absorbed into the Amalgamated Anthracite Collieries Ltd. combine, where they remained until nationalisation in 1947. Aberpergwm is still working today, producing high quality anthracite coal.

The "Ynysarwed Culm colliery" owned by Messrs. Morgan & Perkins was working in 1823-24. Subsequently other levels in the area were developed by various individuals. In 1904-5 the "Ynysarwed Colliery Co." (Messrs. Stephens, Lewis, Edwards and Howell) began large scale operations, opening a new level or a drift, with new sidings on the Vale of Neath Railway (which had opened at the end of 1851) and elaborate screens. The company operated successfully until 1918-1919, when the whole of the undertakings were purchased by Sir D. R. Llewellyn's "Ynisarwed Collieries Co. Ltd., Resolven". This company remained operative until 1947, when its collieries were vested in the National Coal Board.

Cadoxton collieries were owned in 1754 by Thomas of Cadoxton who shipped the coal from Neath bridge. In the first half of the nineteenth century a Mr. Wright worked coal in the area and the later, larger undertaking of David Bevan, of the Neath Brewery, dates from about 1854. He crossed the Rhydding Fault in 1866 and in 1870 opened out on that side. These operations ceased about 1881, when Bevan was developing the Seven Sisters pits in the Dulais Valley.

Reference was made earlier to coal working at Neath Abbey in the seventeenth century. The local Customs Records did not commence until 1709, but from that date onwards there are constant references to the shipping of coal from the river Nedd. Previous to 1793, the coal was worked by the landowners, the lords of the Abbey lands, and after this date Richard Parsons leased the Abbey estates minerals and took over the collieries. The coal is reported to have "very little cohesion", indicating that it lacked bituminous qualities, which is consistent with the general type of coal—mostly low volatile dry steam—found in the area from Neath westward to Swansea and for a few miles to the north, after which we enter the semi-anthracite belt and further north still the anthracite belt. In west Glamorgan, the latter extends eastwards from Gwaun-cae-gurwen and includes the upper Swansea Valley, Dulais Valley and most of the Neath Valley above Aberdulais.

One of the Abbey collieries was a drift and is featured in Donovan's sketch of Neath Abbey, 1805.[35] It shows a "ginn", that was used for winding coal out of the drift, and also shows a horse drawing a train of full trams from the colliery (*Plate* 7). Richard Parsons was succeeded by his son John, whose coal lease expired about 1850.

The first Quaker coal lease at Neath was taken out in 1806, when George Croker Fox, Peter Price and others, who had previously acquired the Neath Abbey Ironworks in 1792, leased the Dyffryn estate minerals. The Neath Abbey Coal Co. as it was known, operated until the death of Isaac Redwood in 1873 after which the property was sold to Messrs. Batters & Scott. It eventually went to the United Company which in time became the Main Colliery Co., and in 1898-9 they sank two new pits in the Skewen district.

In the Dyffryn Clydach area, the "Coalery at Warndee" is mentioned in 1772. In 1806 "Pwll Mawr", Bryncoch, was sunk for the Neath Abbey Coal Co., by William Kirkhouse, and was

---

[35] Donovan, E., *Excursions Through South Wales and Monmouthshire* (London, 1805), vol. II, p. 75.

reputed to be the deepest pit in the country at the time (200 yards).

Below Neath, towards the sea, in the old coal mining area of Coed Iarll, the Earlswood or Coed Iarll colliery was worked early in the first half of the nineteenth century at the time of the first Red Jacket copper works. Other nineteenth century collieries in the area were the Garnant, Cwrtybettws and Pant-y-Morfa. The latter sent coal by an incline from the Coed Iarll ridge to the Tennant canal which was constructed in 1824 to connect the Neath and Swansea canals.

The main colliery undertakings on the left bank of the river Neath start, at the top, with the British Iron Co. workings in 1825 at Cwm Gwrelych. There they had various coal and ironstone levels—there were apparently not less than sixteen known veins workable by levels into the mountain side. The lower veins, from three feet to ten feet in thickness, were anthracite, and the upper veins were bituminous coal which made good coke for iron manufacture.

Lower down the valley, on the hillside near Llyn Fach (opposite Glynneath), Fforchygrawn colliery was opened in 1860 and in 1871 it belonged to the Rhondda Mountain Colliery Co. The coal was let down over an incline plane to the railway sidings in the valley below, as was the case with many other collieries on the hillsides in the Vale of Neath and other valleys in South Wales. The remains of a rope drum and the course of its incline are still visible on the Llyn Fach site (*Plate* 8).

In the Cwmgwrach area, development in the early nineteenth century (about 1814) included opening out ancient levels. In 1816 a tramroad was constructed from Blaengwrach colliery to the Vale of Neath canal and a few years later Edward Protheroe's Cwmgwrach coal boats had the place of honour at the opening of Tennant's Neath-Swansea Junction Canal. The Dunraven and Adare Colliery was opened in 1871 and in 1903 the Empire colliery (C.&E.Collieries), the latter embracing most of Protheroe's old Fforch-goch under-taking. When the C. & E. Collieries were taken over by the National Coal Board in 1947, only the Cwmgwrach 1, 2 and 3 collieries were working. Blaengwrach colliery (together with other Glynneath and Resolven collieries) belonged to Cory Bros. & Co. Ltd., before being vested in the National Coal Board in 1947, and is still working today.

In the Resolven area at Cwmclydach, levels were opened in 1837 and in 1873 the Resolven collieries belonged to the Cardiff & Swansea Smokeless Steam Coal Co. whose directors included John Cory, Cardiff, and F. A. Yeo, Swansea. In time the firm took the name of Cory, Yeo & Co., and expanded with a series of levels and later on pits were sunk in Cwm Clydach, near Glyncastle. Two further levels were afterwards opened by the company. On vesting date, the Resolven collieries were owned by Cory Bros. & Co. Ltd., but only Glyncastle and Ffaldydre were then working, although as mentioned above, the Blaengwrach undertaking has since been reopened and reconstructed by the National Coal Board.

Mention must be made of the Melin-y-cwrt Valley near Resolven because Cefn Mawr at the head of the valley is considered by one authority[36] to be the coal area which Owen ap Alaythur leased to Margam Abbey about the year 1249, rather than Mynydd Penhydd a few miles to the south along the ridge. Mining was taking place here again in 1772 and in the late nineteenth century the Neath Merthyr Colliery Co. held the Cefn Mawr undertaking. In 1912 a new company had the colliery and during an exploration of the old workings they found an oak tram wheel, banded with iron, which was still in very good condition (*Plate* 9). Similarly, when the Blaen-y-Cwm seam was opened in 1880-6, just above Clun-Gwilym where coal had been worked in 1772 for the Melin-y-cwrt furnace, remains of old tools—mandrils of wood with iron points—were found.

The area from Melin-y-cwrt down to Tonna was worked extensively during the nineteenth and early twentieth centuries. The Ynysarwed Colliery Co. eventually took over the Melin-y-cwrt drift and developed others, as mentioned earlier, on the other side of the river at Abergarwed and Ynysbyllog, before being taken over by Sir D. R. Llewellyn. The new Ynysarwed Collieries Co. Ltd., in 1919-20 opened up a new coal area behind the Clun tinworks and reached the coal in 1923 in two drifts. The Wenallt colliery, Tonna, dates from about 1841 and was worked by Messrs. W. Llewellyn & Co. for their Aberdulais tinplate works.

There were still some small collieries operating in the Gnoll and Cymla areas in the mid-nineteenth century, such as Cefn Harla (north of the Gnoll) and Cymla colliery. Others in the area included Cefn Morfydd collieries, Cwm Cafan and Messrs. Weymouth & Green's Tonmawr colliery.

[36] Phillips, D. Rhys, op.cit., p. 257.

Plate 7 Donovan's Neath Abbey, 1805

Reproduced from Donovan's Excursions through South Wales and Mon., *vol. II, 1805*

Plate 8 Self-acting Incline near Llyn Fach   *Photograph by P. D. Howard*

Plate 9
Oak Tram Wheel, Cefn Mawr Colliery

*By permission of the
National Museum of Wales*

Plate 10   Miners' Underground Chapel, Mynydd Maen Colliery

By permission of Swansea Public Libraries

Plate 11 Winding Engine House, Mynydd Maen Colliery   *By permission of Swansea Public Libraries*

Plate 12   Bible used for miners' services at Mynydd Newydd Colliery

DEFNYDDIWYD Y BEIBL YMA MEWN CYFARFODYDD GWEDDI
A GYNHALIWYD BOB BORE LLUN O DAN Y DDAEAR
YNG NGLOFA MYNYDD NEWYDD ABERTAWE. FE'I DEFNYDDIWYD
YN GYNTAF YN Y FLWYDDYN 1871 AC YN GYSON HYD 1932
PAN GAUWYD Y LOFA.

THIS IS THE BIBLE USED AT PRAYER MEETINGS HELD
EVERY MONDAY MORNING BELOW GROUND AT THE OLD
MYNYDD NEWYDD COLLIERY SWANSEA. IT WAS CONTINUALLY
USED FROM 1871 UNTIL THE COLLIERY CLOSED IN 1932.

Plate 13 Double Beam Winding Engine, Broadoak Colliery, 1948   *By permission of the National Coal Board*

Plate 14 Clydach Merthyr Colliery, Clydach   *By permission of the National Museum of Wales*

We come then to Eaglesbush colliery in Cwmcrythan, where coal was being produced in 1802 according to the Gwyn MS., but this is probably a late date.   It appears that as early as 1803 Evans of Eaglesbush was in partnership there with Penrose and in 1833 George Penrose married Miss Evans and took up residence at Eaglesbush House.   In 1844 the company's title is given as Penrose & Evans.   In the early days the coal was brought by tramroad and incline to be shipped on the canal at Neath.   Later it was conveyed over a new tramroad to Briton Ferry where it was shipped at the river side.   The colliery was worked by a succession of companies and an entry for 1891 shows the colliery to be operated then by Eaglesbush Colliery Co. Ltd., Neath.[37]   An explosion occurred at the colliery in 1845-46 after which the first Struvé mechanical ventilator was installed there.[38]

Reference has been made to early coal working in the Briton Ferry-Baglan area.   Later efforts there include the Esgyn collieries, worked by Messrs. Penrose before the middle of the nineteenth century, the coal being conveyed by tramroad to a pill branching off the Vale of Neath canal, and thence to Giant's Grave for shipment.

At Baglan in 1778, Sir Herbert Mackworth wrote to the Board of Customs appealing for sanction to export the produce of his new Mackworth colliery as "culm" and so within the exemptions of the coal duty.   Later collieries in the area included Tor-y-Mynydd (Neath Abbey Co.—Foxes and Price), the Swan and Park collieries (finished in 1867) and the Baglan Swan Colliery Company's Baglan pit, sunk in 1862 and which apparently ceased working before 1880, although records show a Swan colliery, Baglan, abandoned about 1886.[39]   Returning to the right bank of the Neath river, to the west of Skewen, a number of levels including the Brithdir have been worked since the third quarter of the eighteenth century.   These levels followed the coal outcrops into the side of the Drumau mountain, a practice which, as we saw at the beginning of this chapter, was probably being carried out during the fourteenth and fifteenth centuries, on the eastern slopes, by various coal workers with leases from the lord of the manor of Cadoxton.

[37] H.M. Inspector of Mines, *List of Mines Worked in the Year 1891* (London, 1892), p. 212.
[38] Select Committee of the House of Lords, *Report on Accidents in Coal Mines*, (London, 1849).
[39] *List of Plans of Abandoned Mines, 1891* (London, 1892), p. 26.

Needless to say, the slopes of the mountain have since been riddled with coal mining operations. On the southern side, the Birchgrove undertakings of Chauncy Townsend and others and "Squire" Smith's Emily drift, were followed by the Birchgrove colliery (sunk in 1845) and the Sisters pit, Glais (sunk in 1873) on the eastern side. Also on this side, where the famous Graigola or Six Feet seam outcropped, was the Graigola colliery, Glais. The Graigola colliery was owned by John Parsons, who told Rhys Wm. Jones, the Children's Employment Commissioner in 1842[40] that the coal was brought up in the three levels by horses and at the two shafts by steam engines, which suggests quite a sizeable undertaking. It was apparently possible to walk underground from Bryncoch colliery on the other side of the Drumau mountain to Glais, via the Main, Cwmdu, Birchgrove, Sisters and Graigola collieries, emerging to the surface through one of the drifts at the latter, the whole distance of the underground journey being about ten miles.[41]

The impetus given to the coal industry by copper smelting, first at Neath (1584) and then Swansea (1717) led, as we have seen, to some thriving colliery undertakings around these two centres. The famous "Swansea Beds" containing in descending order the Swansea Four Feet, Five Feet, Six Feet, Three Feet and Two Feet seams, provided a supply of cheap, dry steam coal, suitable for smelting and the result was the establishment of collieries and smelting works as near to each other as possible to reduce transport costs to a minimum and so retain the advantage of cheap coal over outside competitors. Thus a thriving copper smelting industry grew up around Swansea, where thirteen works were established between 1717 and 1850, on the river banks in the lower Swansea Valley.[42]

The port of Swansea benefitted not only from the copper trade, with the import of ores and export of finished products, but also from the export of coal. From 1816 to 1818, 638,533 tons were shipped from Swansea. Cardiff on the other hand shipped only 864 tons;[43] the east Glamorgan coalfield had not yet got going as far as production of coal for sale was concerned.

[40] Ridd, T., "Pits and pit boys in the Swansea area." *Gower. Journal of the Gower Society, Swansea*, vol. 17, p. 44.
[41] Gregory, H., op.cit.
[42] Hilton, K. J., op.cit., p. 19.
[43] Forster Brown, T., "The South Wales Coalfield". *Trans. S. Wales Inst. Engrs.*, vol. 9, p. 62.

Among the coal undertakings which developed in the hinterland of Swansea in the dry steam belt was Vivian & Sons Ltd., with their Mynydd Newydd colliery. Sunk in 1843, the colliery suffered an explosion soon afterwards, as a result of which the men decided to establish a chapel underground in the Six Feet seam at a depth of 774 feet. A chamber was hewn out of the solid coal, sixteen yards long by six yards wide, and supported by timber along the sides and in rows across. The roof and sides were whitewashed and rough plank seats were placed between the rows of timbers. There, every Monday morning at 6.00 a.m., a service was held before the men proceeded to their working places. This practice continued for eighty years until 1924. The illustrations (*Plates* 10 and 11) are from an article written in 1899, when the miners' chapel was fifty years old.[44] The bible used for the services is shown in *Plate* 12.

Other undertakings included Thomas Williams (Llangennech) Ltd., who had three of his four pits in west Glamorgan, the fourth, Morlais colliery, being in Llangennech, Carmarthenshire. The three pits were Grovesend, Talyclun (both sunk in 1870) and Brynlliw (sunk in 1903-5) all near Pontardulais. Brynlliw closed in 1925, but was reopened in 1954 by the National Coal Board who carried out a major reorganisation and development scheme so that the colliery is today one of the West Wales Area's biggest producers of anthracite, the pit being just inside the anthracite belt.

In Gowerton the Berthlwyd and Cefngoleu collieries were separately owned by companies of that name, and worked the bituminous coal of the Gower peninsula. At Loughor were the Broadoak and Beili Glas collieries. Broadoak was sunk before 1870 and had a remarkable double beam steam winding engine, which worked there until the colliery closed in 1948 (*Plate* 13).

One of the best known colliery concerns in the Swansea area was Glasbrook Bros., Ltd. The founder, John Glasbrook, began his pursuit of coal in a small way with his brother-in-law at Rowan Hill colliery. Afterwards he became connected with collieries in the Aberdare Valley and only later commenced sinking at Gorseinon in the 1870's where he struck the Swansea Five Feet seam at a depth of 205 yards in the Garngoch No. 1 colliery. There followed the Garngoch No. 2 in the late 1880's and Garngoch No. 3 which was

[44] Moore, W. Walford, "A Chapel in the Fossil Woods". *Sunday Magazine* 1899.

sunk by the company in 1906-7.   Other Glasbrook collieries were the Cape pit and Cape slant sunk in 1899 and 1904 respectively at Gowerton.   The Glasbrook undertakings continued as such until 1947 when they were vested in the National Coal Board.

Caeduke colliery, Loughor, sunk in 1888, was operated for several years by the Loughor Colliery Co. (1910) Ltd., until it was taken over by Swansea Navigation Collieries Ltd. in 1939.   The Mountain colliery, Gorseinon, sunk in 1903-5 was owned by the Mountain Colliery Co. Ltd. until 1909, when it also was absorbed by the Swansea Navigation Collieries.   Of the two only Mountain colliery was working at vesting date and is still working today.

The Graigola Merthyr Co. Ltd., developed from an early colliery undertaking, founded by Frank Yeo and Thomas Cory, who in the early 1860's, in view of the difficulty of selling their small coal, went into the patent fuel business.   They developed at Swansea docks first one plant at the North Dock and later a very large plant at Kings Dock which had an output of 1,000,000 tons of patent fuel a year.[45]   The company also had collieries working a mineral area between Clydach and Pontardulais, mainly in the Graigola seam which is particularly suitable for fuel making.   The main ones appear to have been Birchrock, Pontardulais, opened in 1868 and closed sometime before 1914; Clydach Merthyr (1868) with Abergelli (1930) Slants, Clydach, and Graig Merthyr (1868) with Cefn Drim (1910) Slants, Pontardulais, both of which were taken over by the National Coal Board in 1947.   The Graig Merthyr undertaking is still operating today.

Clydach Merthyr was an interesting colliery in many ways. Underground it not only had the characteristically good roadways of Graigola seam workings (long lengths with sandstone roof requiring virtually no supports) but also a set of steam boilers and a blacksmith's forge.   The boilers and smithy were working up into the late 1940's at least, until the mine became "safety lamp" throughout.   The photograph (*Plate* 14) shows (centre) the boiler flue stack which was connected with the boilers underground; on the right is the Waddle ventilating fan and on the left is the colliery "slant" entrance.

A later company in the Clydach area was the Hendy Merthyr

---

45 The Graigola Merthyr Co. Ltd., *The South Wales Coalfield* (Cardiff, 1920-21), pp. 88, 93.

Colliery Co. Ltd., which transferred six collieries to the Coal Board at nationalisation. These were Hendy Merthyr, Nantycapel, Felinfran (originally Felinfran Colliery Co. Ltd.,), Guerets Slant, Tyladwyn and Maesmelyn. All except Guerets Slant were opened after 1930.

The Daren Colliery Co. Ltd., operated the Daren levels at Trebanos, Pontardawe, working the Hughes vein, at the base of the upper pennant measures. The levels were driven, slightly to the rise, into the hillside, and the coal was brought out under gravity by a tail-rope haulage system.

There were several other collieries and small companies operating in the Swansea hinterland, but the ones described are sufficient to show the development which went on to supply the demand of industry in the lower Swansea Valley, also elsewhere, e.g., Gowerton (tinplate), Penclawdd (copper) and Loughor (zinc).

The copper industry around Swansea reached its peak about 1860, but zinc smelting was already established and growing, particularly at Llansamlet and can be said to have "taken up the slack" very well, with the decline of copper. Zinc in its turn was succeeded by tinplate which started in Swansea in 1845 and reached its peak in 1890. The year 1869 was significant for Swansea, when the Landore Siemens Steel Company went into production to provide plenty of steel for tinplate and other requirements by the open-hearth process. A number of integrated steel and tinplate works were developed around Swansea resulting in an unusually heavy concentration of steel making capacity in one area.[46]

The result was a continuing growth of the coal industry in the Swansea hinterland (*Plate* 15), not only to supply the demands of industry, but, as has already been seen, to supply coal and patent fuel for export. In 1872 Swansea exported in the region of 750,000 tons, Neath over 300,000 tons (Cardiff over $2\frac{1}{2}$ million tons).

During the last three decades of the nineteenth century and up until the outbreak of the 1914-18 war, the coal industry in the Swansea Valley, in particular the upper part, and across to Gwaun-cae-gurwen, the Dulais Valley, and as has been seen, the upper Neath Valley, entered a period of intensive development. Swansea took most of the coal destined for export and the situation by 1913 is reflected in the figures[47] which show that in the peak output year

[46] Hilton, K. J., op.cit., pp. 27-30.
[47] *The South Wales Coal Annual*, 1915 (Cardiff).

of the South Wales coalfield, Swansea exported over 4½ million tons of coal and coke and over 920,000 tons of patent fuel. Of the total, 2,400,000 tons was anthracite—the chief customers for anthracite being France (1 million tons), Italy (580,000 tons), Germany (195,000 tons) and Sweden (111,000 tons).

It is evident therefore that the last quarter or so of the nineteenth century saw the rapid recognition of the excellence and usefulness of anthracite, particularly for closed stoves both at home and abroad. This was in addition to its recognised suitability as a fuel for malting, horticulture and in limekilns. The production of anthracite also received an impetus following its successful application for iron-making at Ynyscedwyn in 1837.

Although anthracite coal was worked in Gwaun-cae-Gurwen, the most westerly point of Glamorganshire, in the early seventeenth century, the first pit was sunk in 1837 by Charles Morgan. He was succeeded by his son, Richard Morgan, who in 1874 sold the Gwaun-cae-Gurwen colliery to a number of Yorkshire men (Messrs. Cleeves, Hargreaves, Sails, Bartholomew and Sellars) who formed the G.C.G. Colliery Co. The original winding pit, afterwards known as the Old Pit, was provided with a beam winding engine and flat rope drums until 1886. There is no doubt that the original G.C.G. Colliery Co. were pioneers in establishing the anthracite trade. The company had sunk the Maerdy pit by 1886, 240 yards deep to the Big Vein. In 1910 the property was further developed when the East pit was sunk to a depth of 355 yards, through the Big Vein to the Peacock; a cross measures drift was later driven down to the Middle Vein. Coal winding was done by electricity—one of the earliest installations in the country. In 1916 the undertaking was acquired by Lord Rhondda and his associates including D. R. Llewellyn, and subsequently in 1921-22 the shareholding passed into the hands of Messrs. Guest, Keen & Nettlefolds Ltd., but the concern continued to operate as a separate company, with Sir D. R. Llewellyn as chairman and Lord Buckland, vice-chairman.[48] The reorganised company extended operations further by sinking the Steer pit, 18 feet diameter, from banking level, 354 yards to the Lower Vein; the coal winding level was, however, from the Middle Vein at 340 yards. Sinking was started on 11 March 1924 and completed on 17 December of the same year (*Plate* 16).

[48] Gwaun-cae-Gurwen Colliery Co. Ltd., commemorative booklet, October 1927.

In 1927 the G.C.G. Colliery Company Ltd., were in the first stages of sinking another down-cast pit at Cwmgorse, to a depth of 600 yards, to be known as the Buckland pit. The output of the collieries prior to the development of the Steer pit averaged 300,000 tons per annum. It was hoped to increase this substantially with the Steer and Buckland pits. In 1928 the company was taken over by the Amalgamated Anthracite Collieries Ltd. and the Buckland pit was never developed.

A mile or so to the south of Gwaun-cae-Gurwen at Cwmgorse, on the road to Pontardawe, the Cwmgorse colliery was opened in 1888. Known as the Cwmgorse Colliery Co. Ltd., they worked the Red Vein, 4 ft. 6 in. thick, which occurs above the Big Vein, access to which was by a pair of drifts which eventually extended in for well over a mile. The colliery became the New Cwmgorse Colliery Company Ltd., and then from 1925-30 it belonged to Cleeves Western Valley Anthracite Collieries Ltd. before being taken over by the Amalgamated Anthracite Collieries Ltd. In 1948, as in the case of other A.A.C. collieries, it was vested in the National Coal Board.

Halfway between Gwaun-cae-Gurwen and Pontardulais is the new Abernant anthracite colliery. This major development is intended to work large reserves of anthracite which lie at an average depth of 800 yards over an area of seven square miles. The colliery is laid out on the most modern lines (*Plate* 17) and is progressing steadily in spite of severe initial geological difficulties, so that in due course it will provide as much anthracite as several of the previous mines in the locality and at a much higher output per manshift.

Before proceeding to the upper Swansea Valley, above Pontardawe, it is necessary to look once more at the Dyffryn Clydach area, between Pontardawe and Neath. Reference was made earlier to the "Coalery at Warndee" (1772) and the Bryncoch colliery of 1806. By the early 1920's[49] there was a New Wernddu slant operating at Alltwen, working the Graigola seam; the Main Colliery Co. (Neath Abbey) was operating Court Herbert (Neath), Nos. 1 and 6 Main (Bryncoch) and Nos. 3, 4 and 7 Main colliery at Skewen. The New Marchowell Colliery Co. was operating also at Bryncoch at this time with the Marchowell level. Birchgrove colliery was still working (the Graigola seam) and so was the Copper pit, Morriston, working the Swansea two feet and three feet seams. All the above were closed, however, before 1938.

We re-enter the anthracite belt, on proceeding up the Swansea Valley, at Tareni colliery Nos. 1 and 2, opposite Godre'rgraig. Sunk in 1902-3, the colliery belonged in 1914 to the South Wales Primrose Coal Co. Ltd., and was working the Red, Big and Brass (Peacock) Veins. The company also owned New Primrose (Pontardawe, 1880) Cwmnantllwyd, Gwyn's drift and Wainycoed—all in Cilybebyll—and dating from 1897, 1910 and 1890 respectively. The above collieries were taken over by the Tareni Colliery Company Ltd. in 1928, who operated them until 1947 when the undertaking was nationalised. Only the Tareni colliery was then working.

Above Godre'rgraig, in the Upper Tawe and Cwm Twrch region, there were a number of collieries, working mainly anthracite, whose development makes a fascinating story on its own. Briefly, one of the earliest collieries was opened in 1758 above Tarren Gwyddon opposite Ystalyfera and the coal was sent down to Llansamlet on horseback. In 1794 the Cyfyng level was started just where construction work on the Swansea canal had exposed a coal seam, a little below Ystalyfera. In 1797 Edward Martin of Morriston came to Cwmtwrch and investigated a seam on the north east side of the valley. Clay ironstone had also been worked in this area before this to supply the furnaces at Ynyscedwyn. After the opening of the canal in 1798, Martin constructed a tramroad from his collieries, down the valley of the Twrch to the canal at Gurnos. From then on numerous collieries were opened in the upper Swansea Valley and a number of adventurers came to try their luck. One of these was Daniel Harper who in 1801 took over a number of workings at Ystalyfera and developed other new seams; his first new level, just above the Ystalyfera iron works, was known as "Lefel Harper" which he opened in 1805. Another was opened in 1812 off the side of the road above Craigarw, which became known later as Pwllbach. This level was later bought by Thomas Walters of Swansea, who also developed the Ynysceinon pit lower down the Swansea valley. The pit closed in 1861 due to numerous faults and disturbances.

In 1854 Walters sank the Crimea pit on the Allt y Grug side of the valley from Ynysceinon. He was unlucky here again for the same reason and the pit closed in 1862.

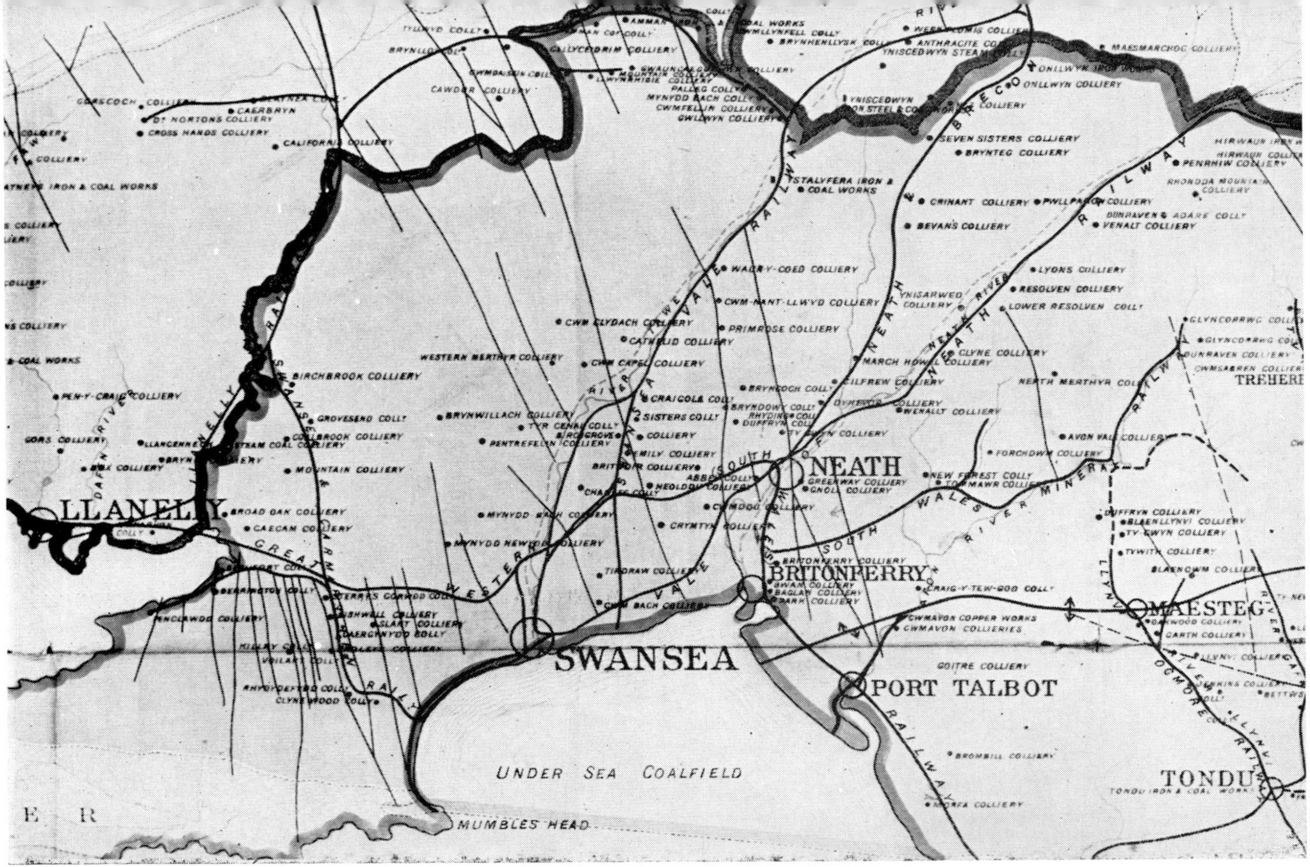

Plate 15 West Glamorgan Collieries in 1875 (after T. Forster Brown) *Trans. S. Wales Inst. Engrs.*, vol. 9, plate 9

Reproduced by permission of the South Wales Institute of Engineers

Plate 16 Steer Pit, Gwaun-cae-Gurwen, 1952

By permission of the National Coal Board

Plate 17   Abernant Colliery, Pontardawe

By permission of the National Coal Board

Plate 18   Seven Sisters Colliery, Dulais Valley, 1967

By permission of the National Museum of Wales

Plate 19 Onllwyn No. 1 Colliery, prior to 1900

By permission of the National Coal Board

Working back up the valley and on the hillside we have the Cambrian Mercantile colliery, owned by a syndicate of that name. There, the Ynysarwed Vein (of the upper coal measures) outcropped and was worked.[50] At Ystalyfera, on the opposite side of the valley, from Ystalyfera and Pwllbach collieries were the New Varteg and Yniscu collieries which worked the Red Vein.

In 1827 the company of Treacher and James sank a pit about a quarter of a mile above the Ystalyfera iron works which proved very successful. In 1831 they sold it to James Palmer Budd who developed other mines in the area and later took over the iron furnaces erected in 1837 by Treacher and James at Ystalyfera.

Budd proceeded to develop the patches as well as his collieries to obtain coal and ironstone for his works. His biggest mine was Wern Plymis which supplied his works with 2,000 tons of coal and 900 tons of ironstone per month and which was started in 1845. Another mine worked by the Ystalyfera Iron Co. was the Gilwen drift, opened in 1860.

A more recent slant at Ystalyfera colliery was developed in 1914, which is shown in the early 1920's to be operated by Ystalyfera Collieries Ltd. Also early twentieth century is the new Pwllbach slant, operated by the Pwllbach Colliery Co. Tirbach colliery, again at Ystalyfera, dates from 1899 and was operated, with Pwllbach, by the same company until they were taken over by Henderson's Welsh Anthracite Company in 1930. The Ystalyfera Collieries Ltd. went over to the Welsh Anthracite Collieries for a short period before the latter was also taken over by Henderson's. A fourth west Glamorgan colliery operated by the firm from 1930 was the Cwmllynfell colliery. These collieries remained with Henderson's until nationalisation.

Cwmllynfell pit was sunk in 1820 by Reynolds and Aubrey (later James & Aubrey) and was one of the local collieries developed to satisfy the increase in demand following the advent of the Swansea canal. The first winding arrangement was a water balance gear which used water to counter balance the coal load. The water was returned to the surface at Cwmllynfell by the use of a big waterwheel alongside the shaft which operated a beam pumping arrangement with pump rods going down the shaft. This arrangement was used until 1879 when the pit was drowned. The colliery was reopened

[50] Davies, J. H., *History of Pontardawe and District* (Llandybie, 1967), p. 69.

some years later and was operated from 1924 to 1930 by the Cwmllynfell Anthracite Collieries Ltd.

The Swansea Vale Railway reached Ystalyfera in 1859 and Brynaman in 1864[51] and there was no longer the limit on production that had existed when the collieries had to depend on the canal. From then onwards the upper Swansea region was able to make its full contribution to the development of the anthracite coal trade.

Similarly, in the Dulais Valley, when the mineral railway opened from Neath to Onllwyn in 1864 (later named the Neath and Brecon, with its extension to Brecon), the development of the local anthracite seams was pursued energetically and without delay.

Within a few years a coal pit was sunk by David Bevan on Nant Melyn farm. This was unsuccessful due to a disturbance and he started another lower down on Bryncae fields. The first sod for this was cut in March 1872 by one of his seven daughters, Miss Isabella Bevan, using a silver spade. Apparently some wanted to call the pit Bryncae, others Isabella, but the owner's son, Evan Evans Bevan, maintained that since he had seven sisters, no preference should be shown to any one of them and so the pit was named the Seven Sisters colliery[52] (*Plate* 18). The sinking was completed in 1875 when the Nine Feet seam was struck at 630 feet depth.

In addition to the Seven Sisters pits, at this period Evans and Bevan also had the Brynteg colliery. Others in the valley before 1891 were Crynant colliery (Crynant Colliery Co. Ltd.), Maesymarchog and Onllwyn (Griffith Thomas, Swansea). The latter two eventually became the Onllwyn No. 3 and No. 1 respectively and were taken over by Evans and Bevan in the early 1900's (*Plate* 19). The Dilwyn colliery in Seven Sisters belonged to the company of that name, the first slant dated from 1884. It was taken over by Evans and Bevan in the 1930's, as also was the Crynant colliery (Crynant Colliery Co.) some time later, before 1945. Other concerns besides Evans and Bevan in the Dulais Valley were the Blaenant Colliery Co. Ltd., Crynant (the Blaenant level dates from 1875); the Llwynon levels 1 and 2, and Cefncoed colliery, Crynant. Both the latter belonged to the Llwynon Colliery Co., the level dating from 1901 and the Cefncoed pits from 1926. Llwynon

[51] Bowen, R. E., "Some notes on railway development in the Swansea and Neath areas". *The Journal of the South East Wales Industrial Archaeology Society*, vol. 1, no. 2 (Cardiff, 1966), pp. 34-43.
[52] Evans, Chris. *The industrial and social history of Seven Sisters* (Cardiff, 1964).

worked the No. 2 Rhondda seam, a bituminous coal in the upper measures, whereas Cefncoed, like most of the other Dulais Valley collieries mentioned worked the anthracite coal of the middle and lower measures. The Llwynon Company was taken over by the Amalgamated Anthracite Collieries Ltd. in 1928 and in 1947 all the above Dulais Valley Companies were vested in the National Coal Board.

During the period of its heyday the Dulais Valley sent millions of tons of high quality anthracite for export, mainly from Swansea. (The coal went by the Neath and Brecon line to Neath junction and then by agreement with the Vale of Neath railway over their mixed gauge track to Swansea).

A recent development in the Dulais Valley is the Treforgan colliery, a drift mine, exploiting Red Vein anthracite coal and doing so very economically with full mechanisation.

ACKNOWLEDGEMENT

The author wishes to acknowledge the ready co-operation and valuable assistance he has received in the course of his researches from the Director and his staff, National Coal Board, West Wales area, Tondu.

WIL HOPCYN AND THE MAID OF CEFN YDFA

by

EMERITUS PROFESSOR G. J. WILLIAMS, M.A.

IN spite of all the efforts made in Wales during the last forty years[1] to discover the truth about many aspects of the history of Welsh literature, people who ought to know better are still publishing theories and relating tales which have been definitely proved to be unreliable and groundless. If one refers to the opinion of research workers, it is suggested that there is no unanimity on the point or that there is a difference of opinion among scholars, as if those who cling to the old ideas had themselves done no end of research. Is there any other country, I wonder, where men who have not spent as much as five minutes in careful study of any point in the history of their literature are able to strut about as authorities and experts? Very often the refuge of these quacks is the Gorsedd of Bards. In the year 1896 Sir John Morris-Jones published a series of articles in the magazine *Cymru* on that institution, proving that it was something completely recent and that the pronouncements made on the Logan Stone were nothing but the fruit of superstition and ignorance. But despite all this, people continued to speak of the antiquity of the Gorsedd for many years afterwards, no notice being taken of the new light available in Sir John Morris-Jones' articles.

It is through reading a recently published book, *Souvenir of the Wil Hopcyn Memorial*,[2] that I have been moved to write the above paragraph. For, although it was published in the year 1927, the

---

[1] [As pointed out in the introduction to this volume, the original Welsh version of this article consisted of two contributions to the Welsh periodical *Y Llenor*. They were published in vol. VI (1927), no. 4 and vol. VII (1928), no. 1. In this translation, the space on page 238 indicates where the first contribution ended and the second began. Welsh quotations retained in the text of the article are translated in the footnotes, and all footnotes enclosed within square brackets are editorial additions].

[2] [Edited by William Edwards and published at Llangynwyd in 1927 by the Wil Hopcyn Memorial Committee].

authors are strong in the faith when they mention Rhys Goch ap Rhiccert and his poetry, and Ieuan Fawr ap y Diwlith.[3] They refer to the "Chair of Glamorgan" as an ancient institution, and one can suspect that they still believe in the School of Glamorgan as it is found in *Cyfrinach Beirdd Ynys Prydain*.[4] The authors have a firm and simple faith, and it has never dawned upon them, I should think, that what is chronicled by them as authentic history is nothing but unfounded tradition or recent fabrication. It is clear that they belong to the school of Ab Ithel and Myfyr Morganwg.[5] But it is a little disheartening for those who wish to promote scholarly research in Wales to see responsible men publishing such a book as this in the year 1927, and ignoring all the new light which has been cast upon the above mentioned points during the last forty years.

The introduction says that the aim of the book is to give "the authentic story of the Maid of Cefn Ydfa and Wil Hopcyn" and to augment a fund "for the purpose of erecting a memorial stone over the grave of Wil Hopcyn". One might think therefore that they would have made a special effort to discover the truth and carefully read what had already been published on the subject. But as far as I can perceive, they have done nothing except reiterate what the late T. C. Evans (Cadrawd) says in his *History of Llangynwyd Parish* (1887), as if the whole of its contents resulted from diligent research. No notice is taken of Dafydd Morganwg's article in *Cymru*[6] on "Wil Hopcyn a'r Ferch o Gefn Ydfa", where he seeks to prove that the tale is "a groundless and incredible legend". The points which Dafydd Morganwg raised have not received much attention, and the tale is therefore told in the year 1927 as an "authentic story".

My aim in this article is to try and trace the history of Wil Hopcyn, and to determine how much truth there is in the story told by Cadrawd about Wil's connection with "the Maid of Cefn Ydfa". We know very little of his history. The registers of the parish of Llangynwyd show that he was born in the month of November 1700,

---

[3] [Two outstanding literary figures "created" by Iolo Morganwg].
[4] [A Bardic Grammar which Iolo claimed to have "discovered". In 1829, three years after his death, it was published by his son Taliesin].
[5] [Myfyr Morganwg and ab Ithel accepted and developed Iolo's theories on Bardism and Druidism. See the articles in *The Dictionary of Welsh Biography* and Roy Denning's "Druidism at Pontypridd" in *Glamorgan Historian*, vol. I.]
[6] Vol. X (1896), pp. 307-13.

and that his father's name was Hopkin Thomas. Dr. L. J. Hopkin-James saw two references to him in the Margam manuscripts.[7] This is the first:

> Counterpart of a successive Lease by the Rt. Ho. Thomas, Lord Mansel, Baron of Margam, to Diana Thomas, of Langonoyd, co. Glam., widow, William Hopkin and Jenkin Hopkin of the same her sons, of meadow land called Gwayne-y-llan, 8 acr—in Langonoyd, and a house and land near the Church there . . .

This was dated 25 March 1722. The other reference shows that "William Hopkin" was a tax collector in 1723. He is also referred to in *Y Fel Gafod* (1813)—the work of Lewys Hopcyn, the poet of Llandyfodwg, collected by his son-in-law, John Miles of Pencoed. Mention is made of him as a poet who created some disturbance in an Eisteddfod held at Cymmer in 1735. Lewys Hopcyn composed *englynion* to Wil Hopcyn "about his satirical poem to the Poets at the Cymmer Eisteddfod on St. David's Day, 1735".[8] This is the first:

> Daeth Will Hopkin flin aflonydd—i'n mysg,
> Er mysgu'n llawenydd;
> Gŵr oedd ddig, nid gwar i'w ddydd,
> Yn ei galon mae'n g'wilydd.[9]

And again:

> Yn nhre, tuai ble, tew blin—yn glynu,
> Glanach bod Will Hopkin,
> Na dod a'i naws draws i drin,
> Gwyr o addysg o'u gwreiddin.[10]

In the writings of Iolo Morganwg there are references to other Eisteddfodau said to have been held at this period. In the Llanover MSS.[11] it is stated that the poets had met in Pyle about 1740, and that "Wiliam Hopkin of Llangynwyd" was one of them. He composed a satirical *englyn* in this Eisteddfod too, for Iolo states that

---

[7] *Hopkiniaid Morganwg*, p. 68.
[8] Ibid., p. 292.
[9] The tiresome, restless Will Hopkin came into our midst with the intention of destroying our joy. He was an angry man, and at no time during his life was he gentle; his heart is a disgrace.
[10] It is more seemly for Will Hopkin to remain in the town, as he persists in his obtuse and troublesome disputing, than to come here, with his quarrelsome nature, to chide men of learning and to disturb their peace.
[11] C2, p. 360.

he addressed a brother bard, Nicolas Rhys, of Newcastle, Bridgend, with these words:

Nicolas, ŵr diflas ei dôn—anhynod
Yn hanes prydyddion,
'Y nglanas yw d'englynion,
Y clwt sych, clyw, taw â sôn.[12]

Other references to him occur in Iolo's manuscripts. He is named as one of the bards who had sung in the traditional manner of Glamorgan, i.e. had sung light and high-spirited love songs in the manner of Rhys Goch ap Rhiccert.[13] Iolo refers to Wil Hopcyn and Dafydd Nicolas of Aberpergwm as two bards who had kept the tradition alive in the eighteenth century. And to affirm this he attributes very many beautiful poems (probably of his own composition) to Dafydd Nicolas. He only attributes a few to Wil Hopcyn, although he says that he had seen "more than twenty of the poems of Wil Hopcyn, the poet from Llangynwyd" in a manuscript which belonged to Dafydd Rhisiart of Llandocheu (Llandough), near Cowbridge. "I took a transcript of two or three of them, but no more". These poems will be mentioned later.

Iolo also copied the inscription on Wil's gravestone and records, on the authority of Siôn Bradford, that he belonged to the family of Hopcyniaid Morgannwg, and was descended from Hopcyn Twm Philip of Gelli Fid, a bard who flourished in the last half of the sixteenth century. This note was published by ab Ithel in *Taliesin*, and everyone who has written about Wil Hopcyn from that day to this talks of him as one of the Hopcyniaid. But I have not found proof that Iolo had any ground for this assertion, no more than for many of his other assertions.

The literary men of Wales at the beginning of the last century knew little about Wil Hopcyn. It is true that William Owen [–Pughe] includes him in *The Cambrian Biography* (1803), but all that is said about him is that he was one of the bards of the Glamorgan Gorsedd and that he died about 1780. William Owen probably saw these facts in a list which was in Iolo's possession and was called "Bardic Pedigree". Indeed, he had already published it in his *Heroic Elegies of Llywarch Hen* (1792).[14] There it is said that William

[12] Nicholas, man of unpleasant voice, unknown in the record of poets, your stanzas are a great affliction to me; listen, you dry rag, cease your prattle.
[13] Llanover MS. C63, p. 170.
[14] p. lxiii.

Hopkin was an "awenydd"[15] in the Glamorgan Gorsedd in 1760. I don't know how Iolo came to make a mistake in his dates, unless he compiled the list before he saw that Wil had died in 1741. However, the compilers of biographical dictionaries in the last century knew nothing about Wil Hopcyn apart from what was in *The Cambrian Biography*. That is what is found in Robert Williams's *Eminent Welshmen* (1852), Josiah Thomas Jones's *Geiriadur Bywgraffyddol* (1870), and Isaac Foulkes's *Enwogion Cymru* (1870). And stranger still, that is all that Edward Williams (Bardd Glas Morganwg) gives in the *Cyneirlyfr* (1826). Remembering that Edward Williams—or Iolo Fardd Glas, as he called himself—lived in Glamorgan and associated with the poets of the county throughout his life, one might well suppose that he would know far more about Wil Hopcyn. But all he does is repeat the words of William Owen and state that Wil Hopcyn died about 1780. It is thus clear that the literary men of Wales knew nothing about the latter until his name was connected about the middle of the last century with the romance of "The Maid of Cefn Ydfa".

In the year 1838 a prize was offered at Abergavenny Eisteddfod for the best collection of original unpublished Welsh airs, with the words as sung by the peasantry of Wales. Miss M. J. Williams of Aberpergwm won the prize, and in the year 1844 she published her collection and gave it the title *Ancient National Airs of Gwent and Morganwg*. Among them there occurs an air which she calls "Bugeila'r Gwenith Gwyn", together with the four verses which by today are so well known. This is the note which Miss Williams has about the song.[16]

> Sung in all parts of Glamorganshire with many different sets of words. The measure is easy and popular.

Where did Miss Williams obtain the four verses? Writing about the song "Cerais ferch", she says:[17]

> Taken down from the singing of the celebrated bard, Edward Williams (Iolo Morganwg) before mentioned, who sang it with other words, which the collector cannot remember.

---

[15] [Bardic disciple, i.e. the fourth order in the Bardic System as reconstructed by William Owen and Iolo].

[16] *Ancient National Airs*, p. 82. [The four verses together with an English translation are printed in an appendix to this article].

[17] Ibid.

As will be seen later, Iolo had a copy of the words, so it is not impossible that she obtained them from that source. Iolo's manuscripts were in the possession of his son, ab Iolo, in Merthyr at the time, and we know that she saw some of them.[18] But one thing is difficult to explain. If she had obtained the words from Iolo himself or from his manuscripts, it is strange that she did not mention that Wil Hopcyn was the author, because Iolo ascribed the song to him. Yet some words in it, such as *gwarineb*, suggest that Iolo's copy was in front of her. I shall return to this point later. The only two things I must notice now are that Miss Williams probably did not know who the author of the four verses was, and that many other words were being sung to this air in Glamorgan.

In the meantime ab Iolo had seen references to Wil Hopcyn in his father's manuscripts and noticed that the four verses of "Bugeilio'r Gwenith Gwyn" were attributed to him. He tried to collect the poet's work and asked the Vicar of Llangynwyd and his wife, Mr. and Mrs. R. Pendril Llewelyn,[19] for their help. He had evidently told them that Wil Hopcyn was the author of the song "Bugeilio'r Gwenith Gwyn" which had been published by Miss M. J. Williams. That was the commencement of collecting tales, traditions and *tribannau* and of weaving a romance around Wil Hopcyn.

R. Pendril Llewelyn was instituted to the vicarage of Llangynwyd in 1841, and there he remained until 1891. It is said that Mrs. Llewelyn was an able woman and that she took an exceptional interest in the folk-lore and traditions of Llangynwyd and the neighbourhood. In the article referred to previously Dafydd Morganwg states:

> As far as I have found after fairly close study, Mrs. Penderel (sic) Llewelyn started the story in its tragic form.

She copied the "Song of Maescadlawr" which was attributed at Llangynwyd to Wil Hopcyn and sent it to *The Cambrian*. In the number dated 30 August 1845 there is a translation of that song, and it is said:

> Some further communication on this subject, and traditionary tales respecting William Hopkin, will be sent again.

[18] Ibid., p. 84.
[19] See *The Cambrian*, 23 August, 1845. [Further information on Mr. and Mrs. Pendril Llewelyn will be found on pages 245-6].

Then in the number dated 10 October 1845 Mr. and Mrs. Llewelyn give the history of Wil Hopcyn, and since this was the first time for the story of the Cefn Ydfa tragedy to appear in black and white, some quotations from it are given below:

> William Hopkin, who wrote the Song of Maescadlawr was by trade a tiler and plasterer.[20]   Though his calling was humble—not so his poetic genius.

There follows the inscription which is said to be cut on his tombstone together with the records of his baptism and burial in the Llangynwyd parish registers.   Then the story of the Maid of Cefn Ydfa is narrated:

> He unfortunately fell in love with a lady, far his superior in rank, a daughter of the Thomas's, of Ceven Ydfa.   She returned his love; and being compelled to marry another she lost her reason.   Tales, teeming with romance, are related by the hill folk of the attachment of this lady and her humble lover.   The love songs of William Hopkin to "the maid of Ceven Ydfa" are excessively beautiful, and it is a subject of regret that many of them are now nearly lost.   In the collection of the ancient national airs of Gwent and Morganwg, by Miss Jane Williams, of Aberpergwm, page 38-9, appears an amatory poem, universally attributed among his native hills to William Hopkin, in honour of "the lady of Ceven Ydfa".

After this there appears an English translation of the song "Bugeilio'r Gwenith Gwyn".   In the year 1846 Mrs. Llewelyn published the air together with the Welsh words and the English translation, and for the first time the song was called "The Maid of Ceven Ydva".   So the story spread, and undoubtedly it became a very popular tale. Additions were made to it, and verses and *tribannau* handed down by oral tradition in the neighbourhood of Llangynwyd were connected with the affair of Wil Hopcyn and the Maid of Cefn Ydfa.   The song was published as a ballad, and it was certainly sung in fairs throughout South and North Wales.   Sometimes a summary of the story was printed above the song.[21]   At another time the ballad singer himself would compose an extra verse at the end such as:

---

[20] This was probably the only authority that Ceiriog and Llyfnwy and Cadrawd had for saying that Wil was a tiler by trade.

[21] See a collection of ballads at Cardiff Central Library (W7.162), p. 70.

Tydi yw'r mab a garaf mwy,
　　Ti roddaist glwy'n fy nwyfron,
A'r serch tuag atat sy'n mawrhau
　　O fewn i giliau'r galon;
Awn i Langynwyd gyda'r dydd
　　Er profi'm ffydd cadarna',
Cei roddi'r fodrwy'n sel o'th serch
　　I'r ferch o Gefn—Udfa.[22]

In 1864 the poet Ceiriog published the story of the courtship of
the maid of Cefn Ydfa in *Y Bardd a'r Cerddor: gyda Hen Ystraeon
am danynt*.[23] I am not certain as to where he obtained the details.
He may have seen the ballad which included a summary of the story,
and perhaps the details had appeared in some form or other in a
newspaper or magazine.　But Ceiriog's story is very different from
the one narrated later by Llyfnwy and Cadrawd.　Ceiriog gives the
young lady's name as Catrin Madog, and her father, H. Madog, a
lawyer by profession, as being alive at the time when she was in love
with Wil.　He suggests at the end that the story of the "roof top
courtship" which he includes is the fruit of his own imagination.　He
tells the tale of her writing letters to Wil, and using blood—from the
cat's ear, he says—as ink, and putting the letters in a hollow tree.
He states that she was forced to marry against her will, but he does
not give any details.　But the strangest thing in Ceiriog's account is
that he claims to have in his possession a manuscript containing a
number of love poems composed by Wil Hopcyn.　He quotes the
song "Bugeilio'r Gwenith Gwyn" and another piece in which the
bard greets "Citi fach" (little Kitty).　He refers to another which
contains, he says, sixteen verses on "Y Tro Cyntaf y gwelodd Catrin"
(The First Time he saw Catrin). I have not seen any further reference
to these songs in any book or manuscript.　One must remember
that Ceiriog says that he was polishing up the old tales, "since old
folk traditions were like old coats,—some without sleeves, others
without buttons, others without tails, and all of them full of holes".
"I told the narrator"[24] he says "that he had the liberty to polish up
and patch as much as he liked, but not to *make* an old coat".

[22] You are the youth whom I shall henceforth love; you have wounded me in my
breast, and love for you continues to increase within the recesses of my heart.
Let us go to Llangynwyd at the break of day to prove my very strong faith.
You can give the ring to the maid of Cefn Ydfa as a proof of your love for her.

[23] [A title meaning "The Bard and the Musician: with Old Stories about them"].

[24] [The stories are narrated by a character named Sir Meurig Grynswth].

Therefore much of what was afterwards related as fact probably emanated from Ceiriog's fancy and imagination.

By such means the story became famous throughout Wales. "The Maid of Cefn Ydfa" was the subject of the *Rhieingerdd*[25] at Neath Eisteddfod in 1866. Mynyddog[26] was the winner, and his poem is founded on Ceiriog's story. In the year 1869 Thomas Morgan (Llyfnwy) of Llangynwyd published a booklet, *The Cupid*, giving the story of Wil Hopcyn and the maid of Cefn Ydfa, and this little work has an important place in the history of the tale's development. The history of the Cefn Ydfa family and that of Anthony Maddocks of Cwm Risga was investigated. It was found that the maid's name was Ann and that her father had died in 1706. Many traditional old verses and poems were collected together to provide a fully developed version of the story. We must also remember that Mr. and Mrs. Pendril Llewelyn assisted Llyfnwy when he was collecting the material.

In the year 1887 Cadrawd related the story in its finished form in his *History of Llangynwyd Parish*. He realised, though, that everything could not be accepted as authentic history. He saw a copy of the will of Ann Thomas's father and observed that there was no foundation for one of the story's chief points, namely that Anthony Maddocks of Cwm Risga was one of Ann Thomas's guardians and that he had influenced and forced her to marry his son. "Whatever part Mr. Maddocks took in bringing about a marriage between his son and heir and Ann Thomas, it cannot be said that any such authority had been accorded him by the father".[27] Cadrawd got hold of the marriage settlement of "Mrs. Ann Thomas of Kefngnydfa" and "Anthony Maddocks" and quoted extensively from it.[28] As I have previously stated, it is just as Cadrawd told the story that it is narrated in the *Souvenir of the Wil Hopcyn Memorial*.

This is the story to which credence is generally given today, and so fascinating is it that hundreds of people come annually, it is said, to visit the grave of "the Maid of Cefn Ydfa" in Llangynwyd. Our task now is to find out whether there is any foundation to the story.

[25] [In the Middle Ages the *Rhieingerdd* was a formal poem in praise of an aristocratic lady. By the 19th century it had come to signify nothing more than a love poem].

[26] [Richard Davies (1833-77), an eminent Montgomeryshire poet].

[27] *History of Llangynwyd parish*, p. 92.

[28] [The document is now preserved among the Baglan MSS. at Cardiff Central Library].

We have seen that Dafydd Morganwg (1830-1905) maintained that it was a "groundless and incredible legend", but he does not doubt that Wil Hopcyn composed the traditional verses that were published by Mrs. Pendril Llewelyn and Llyfmwy. But these verses show, he insists, that Wil was an idler and a red-nosed drunkard, and that it was very improbable that the maid of Cefn Ydfa would be courting such a person. Besides, he says, there is nothing in the song "Bugeilio'r Gwenith Gwyn" suggesting that he composed it when the mother had forbidden him to come near the house, as Cadrawd stated.[29] "Wil" Dafydd Morganwg continues "seems to be on his knees begging the young lady to listen to him and to have mercy on him. The end of the poem is sufficient proof that she had complete freedom but was refusing to listen to him". He also maintains that the tale about her being forced to marry Anthony Maddocks against her will is untrue. She was baptised on 8 May 1704 and married on 5 May 1725. "If she was a week old when she was baptised (and it is very probable that she was more), then she was over 21 when she married". She could therefore have pleased herself and have married Wil Hopcyn if she wished to do so.

In my opinion one fact seems perfectly clear, viz. that it was in the last century that the name of the Maid of Cefn Ydfa was associated with the song "Bugeilio'r Gwenith Gwyn". The earliest copy is in the hand of Iolo Morganwg.[30] Above it appears the note "Can o waith Wil Hopkin, Eos Morganwg", and underneath it "Wil Hopkin ai Cant cylch 1740". He gives four verses, although the one beginning "Tra fo dŵr yn y môr hallt" is not there but another instead:

> Haws tynnu'r llong i benn y brynn
> Ai llanw yn dynn a cherrig
> Haws ffrwyno'r mor sy'n chwyrn ei daith
> Ai donnau maith chwyddedig
> Haws cwnnu bys a bwrw i lawr
> Gadernyd mawr y mynydd
> Na chwnnu'r serch o nghalon i
> Sydd arnat ti'n dragywydd.[31]

[29] Op. cit., p. 95.
[30] Llanover MS. C12. [The words above the copy mean "A Song by Wil Hopkin, Nightingale of Glamorgan" and those beneath "Wil Hopkin composed it *circa* 1740"].
[31] It is easier to haul a ship fully loaded with stones to the top of a hill, to harness the quick with its endless high waves, to cast down the mountains, in all their great might, by the mere raising of a finger, than to remove the unceasing love for you which fills my heart.

There is another copy in Iolo's handwriting in one of the manuscripts of Edward Jones (Bardd y Brenin)[32] at Aberystwyth. If I remember correctly, it has three verses. Can we believe Iolo's assertion that Wil Hopcyn composed them? By now it is known that Iolo composed poems and attributed them to the old poets of Glamorgan. Indeed, there are many instances of the practice in the manuscript we have just cited. But I would not want to state that he composed this poem, although there is no doubt that he altered it. It is almost certain that the line "a serchus iaith gwarineb" is his work. I therefore suggest that he copied an old country song and after alterations (and perhaps additions) attributed it to one of the Glamorgan poets. He is known to have dealt with other poems in this manner. We have noticed that Miss Williams of Aberpergwm does not say who the author was, although she names the authors of many other songs contained in her book. We should not therefore attach much importance to Mrs. Pendril Llewelyn's assertion that the song was "universally attributed among his native hills to William Hopkin".

The point being dealt with in this article, however, is the link between the song and the Maid of Cefn Ydfa. Iolo does not refer to the story. Indeed, he says the song was composed "about 1740", and thus within thirteen years after the maid's death. Miss Williams of Aberpergwm does not mention Cefn Ydfa. The first to do this, as far as is known, was Mrs. Pendril Llewelyn in her letter to *The Cambrian* in October 1845. The link afterwards developed into an essential part of the tale.

Reference has already been made to one very strange thing in connection with Wil. In the "Bardic pedigree" which Iolo maintained he copied from Siôn Bradford's manuscript it is said that "William Hopkins" was an "awenydd" in the "Gorsedd" of Glamorgan in 1760. Among the names of the "awenyddion" in that "Gorsedd" is Edward Williams, and in all probability that person was Iolo himself, although he was only thirteen years of age. He compiled this list sometime about 1790, because it was published

---

[32] [No such copy can be found in Edward Jones's MSS. at the National Library of Wales. Mr. Daniel Huws, a member of the staff, points out that the version in Llanover MS. C65, p. 293, contains three verses only].

in *The Heroic Elegies of Llywarch Hen* (1792). At that time, therefore, Iolo must have believed that William Hopcyn died after 1760.
Later on he went to Llangynwyd, saw the gravestone of a certain
"William Hopkin" who had been buried in 1741, and maintained
that this man was the poet. I do not know how he sought to
reconcile this with the date he had given in the "Bardic pedigree".

Searching through the parish registers of Llangynwyd one comes
across three men bearing the name "William Hopkin" in the
eighteenth century. The first died in 1741, the second in 1769, and
the third in 1802. Which of them was the poet? It seems that at
first Iolo thought it was the second, and Iolo Fardd Glas, a poet
born in Glamorgan about 1770, maintained in his *Cyneirlyfr* (1826)
that Wil Hopcyn died about 1780. But if this was the poet, the story
related by Llyfnwy and Cadrawd cannot be true. He was a married
man, and children were born to him and his wife, Elizabeth Thomas,
in 1742 and 1745. The date of his birth is not certain, but if he was
the "Gulielmus", son of Hopkin Evan, who was baptised in 1718,
then he was a seven year old boy when Anthony Maddocks and Ann
Thomas of Cefn Ydfa were married.

But it is generally believed that the poet was the person who
died in 1741. Have we sufficient reason for believing that this is
correct? I think that everybody relies on Iolo's judgement. Did
the old inhabitants of Llangynwyd tell him that the gravestone
which he had seen in the cemetery was that of Wil Hopcyn the poet?
This is possible, but when we remember the way in which he
mutilated the literary history of Glamorgan, it behoves us to be
very wary before we accept his evidence. We have already stated
that ab Iolo was collecting Wil Hopcyn's poems about 1845, when
Mr. and Mrs. Pendril Llewelyn began to publish the history of Wil
in *The Cambrian*, and he probably told them about the reference to
the gravestone in his father's manuscripts. They searched the parish
registers and found that this man had been born in 1700 and died in
1741. From that time onwards he has been regarded as the poet
who composed love songs in the eighteenth century.

But is there sufficient proof of this? If he composed the "Song
of Maescadlawr", he must have been of age as a poet between 1730
and 1738. In *The Cambrian* in 1845 Mr. and Mrs. Llewelyn showed
that it was composed before 1738. There is a reference in it to
Nancy Hutton, a maid who was born in 1717, and therefore it was

probably not composed until about 1730.[33] This does not seem to prove anything, because it is not impossible that he was the man whose children were baptised in 1742 and 1745 and who died in 1769. But granting that the one who died in 1741 was the poet, are the facts known about him consistent with the traditions that Mrs. Llewelyn, Cadrawd and Llyfnwy collected about his connection with the Maid of Cefn Ydfa? There is one interesting entry in the Llangynwyd parish registers in the year 1723-24, "Anne ye daughter of Will: Hopkin and Jennett Jenkin was baptised ye 8th of 7ber".[34] Was this the Wil Hopcyn we are concerned with now? He was born in 1700, and he could therefore have been married by 1723. I have searched the Llangynwyd registers without seeing a reference to any other man bearing the name during that period. The name of a certain "William Thomas Hopkin" who married in 1717 and died in 1736 occurs, but his wife's name was Magdalen David. One difficulty remains. Who was Jennett Jenkin, a wife or a mistress? The marriage is not entered, but they could possibly have married in another parish. The name Jennette Jenkin occurs in 1709 as the wife of Leolinus David, and in 1715 a child of Evan Thomas and Jennette Jenkin was baptised. This does not seem to prove anything except that the Wil Hopcyn who lived in 1723 had begot a child either by his wife or his mistress, and this two years before Ann Thomas of Cefn Ydfa married Anthony Maddocks.[35]

One other point should be considered, namely the gravestone mentioned by Iolo. Much has been made of this stone in order to show that Wil Hopcyn was greatly respected in Llangynwyd. In the month of February 1894 Cadrawd read before Newport Cymrodorion Society a paper replying to the attack made by Dafydd Morganwg on Wil and on the story of the Maid of Cefn Ydfa in lecturing to Cardiff Cymrodorion Society the previous season. Dafydd sought

[33] It is uncertain whether we can depend on the references given in *Y Fel Gafod* to the Eisteddfod which is supposed to have been held at Cymmer in 1735. (See above, p. 230.) Lewys Hopcyn's work was collected by his son-in-law, John Miles of Pencoed, in 1813, and Iolo supplied him with a few poems. One of Iolo's favourite recreations was to compose the history of Eisteddfodau which, he claimed, were held by the poets of Glamorgan. Therefore it is possible that the account given in *Y Fel Gafod* is merely the product of his own imagination.

[34] The quotation is from the Bishop's Transcripts [now in the National Library of Wales].

[35] It is possible to add one fact, namely that a certain "Gennet Hopkin" was buried at Llangynwyd in 1784.

to prove that Wil was an idler and a drunkard, but Cadrawd
insisted that he was highly respected in Llangynwyd because the
parishioners insisted on placing a beautiful stone on his grave, poor
man as he was. Indeed, if Cadrawd had searched the transcripts
of the Llangynwyd register, he would have seen that the record of
Wil's burial in 1741 calls him a "pauper". This would have
strengthened his argument. But one thing was forgotten. According to Iolo's copy, the stone was originally one above Wil's father's
grave, and his father died at least twenty years before him. Diana
Thomas, his mother, is called a widow in 1722.[36] It is therefore
evident that the stone is not one placed there by the people of
Llangynwyd as a mark of their respect for Wil Hopcyn. Another
William Hopkin who was buried in 1802 has been mentioned, but it
is impossible to connect him with the story.

Let us now consider whether the known facts about Ann
Thomas, Cefn Ydfa, agree with the tale which is related by Llyfnwy
and Cadrawd. Dafydd Morganwg maintained that she was probably
over twenty-one years of age when she married Anthony Maddocks.
She was baptised on 8 May 1704 and married on 4 May 1725.[37] If
therefore she was only a week old when she was baptised, she would
have been over twenty-one years of age and able to do as she pleased.
Those who believe so firmly that the story is genuine cannot explain
why she agreed to conform to the wishes of her mother and uncle
except by supposing that she did so at a time of weakness! According to the traditions which Llyfnwy collected it was said that
Anthony Maddocks, father of the bridegroom, was one of Ann
Thomas's guardians, and that he used his influence in every way to
force the maid to accept his son. After searching the will of Ann
Thomas's father in the probate registry at Llandaff, that statement
was found to be completely erroneous and Cadrawd and others had
to dispense with that part of the story. Indeed, as more facts came
to light, they of necessity changed the story very often. At this
period Cadrawd was obtaining much help from David Jones, a
Glamorgan man who lived in Wallington, Surrey. There are very
many of his letters among Cadrawd's papers in Cardiff Central
Library, and some of them reveal that newly discovered facts made

---

[36] See *Hopkiniaid Morganwg*, p. 68.
[37] If Cadrawd and his successors had paid proper attention to the parish registers,
they would have seen that the marriage was on the fourth of May, not the
fifth.

him very dubious about the story. In a letter[38] which he sent to Cadrawd on 15 September 1883 he says:

> With regard to my version of the story I fear that it w^d not bear looking at beside the . . . facts now made manifest. When I looked over it last, viz. just before sending you the rest of the MS. I saw that it w^d have to be re-cast and of course re-written to make it harmonious with the more exact information wch has in the interval been picked up at Llangynwyd, and now here is new matter wch still further disturbs the combinations previously made. I think you had better try your own hand at putting the material into shape.

It is evident from this that they were rewriting the story to make it agree with the new facts which were discovered from time to time.

There are variations to the story about the death of the Maid. Some say that she died before Wil reached her bedside, and others that she died in his arms. Cadrawd says one other thing: "one daughter was the only issue of this marriage, who was buried a little before her ill-fated mother".[39] Was there a tradition in Llangynwyd that she died after giving birth to a child? There is nothing in the parish registers to confirm this. It is stated that "Catherine the daughter of Anthony Madocks and Ann Madocks" was buried 28 May 1727, i.e. three weeks before Ann Thomas. But this Ann was the daughter of the old Anthony Maddocks, and a sister to the Anthony Maddocks who married the maid of Cefn Ydfa. Did this entry mislead Llyfnwy and Cadrawd? The men who relate the "authentic story" have made no attempt at all to explain this point.

Even if we grant that Wil Hopcyn composed the song "Bugeilio'r Gwenith Gwyn", there is nothing in it that can be connected with the story. This is what the *Souvenir of the Wil Hopcyn Memorial* says about the song:

> There is a legend that during her imprisonment Ann wrote a letter to her lover on a dried sycamore leaf with blood drawn from her own veins. In all probability it was at this time also that Wil Hopcyn composed what is, perhaps, the most poignant love-song in the Welsh language—"Bugeilio'r Gwenith Gwyn".

Have the men who wrote these words read the song? I hope they have, but their words, indeed, bring considerable doubt into my

[38] [Cardiff MS. 1.194, vol. 6, item 1].
[39] Cadrawd does nothing but repeat Llyfnwy's words. See *The Cupid*, p. 8.

mind.   There is nothing in the song except an element which is
quite common in all the love poetry of Wales, namely a gentleman
begging his lady friend to take pity on him:

> Paham na ddeui ar fy ôl
> Ryw ddydd ar ôl ei gilydd?
> Er mwyn y Gŵr a wnaeth dy wedd,
> Dod im drugaredd bellach.
> O cwyd fy mhen o'r galar maith
> A serchus iaith gwarineb.[40]

Is it the picture of a youth singing to a maid who is closely imprisoned
and using her blood to write to him that is presented in these words?
It is strange to find responsible men repeating such nonsense in
1927, i.e. some thirty years after Dafydd Morganwg made the matter
perfectly clear in 1896.[41]

We can see now that the story which is related by Llyfnwy and
Cadrawd is inconsistent with the facts which we know about the
Wil Hopcyn who died in 1741 and about Ann Thomas of Cefn Ydfa.
But granting that the traditions which were collected and weaved
into a story in the last century contain many unfounded fancies, one
can ask whether Mrs. Pendril Llewelyn had any foundation for the
story that she published in *The Cambrian* in 1845.   I have previously
said that there is no mention of the story anywhere before that time.
Iolo does not refer to the tale in his manuscripts although he
mentions Wil Hopcyn a few times.   If the tale goes back to the
eighteenth century, it is strange that some poet did not write a ballad
giving the story of the courtship.   It would have been a subject of
delight to the ballad writers of the period.

It must be remembered that similar traditions, namely a rich
lady, a poor lover and cruel parents, are common enough.   There
are English and Welsh ballads relating tales of the kind, although the
couple usually marry in the end.   This is what the late Principal
J. H. Davies says concerning such poems:

[40] Mrs. Pendril Llewelyn's translation is printed in the appendix.
[41] The same is true of the other traditional stanzas which have been ascribed to
   Wil Hopcyn.   For instance, it is claimed that the following stanza refers to the
   maiden dying in Wil's arms:
   I imagined that I embraced my fair loved one, and that I pressed her to me
   three times in succession without uttering a word; she placed a sweet, a very
   sweet, kiss on my lips, without my urging her to do so, and this was a
   hundred times sweeter than wine".
He who searches diligently enough for something is sure to find it.

Another class of ballads of which there are many instances in the catalogue are those which may be called Romantic Ballads, most of which are concerned with sweethearts and cruel parents or guardians . . . Many of these ballads no doubt have their counterparts in English and other languages, but it is curious that in all the fifteen ballads which may be classified under this head in the Bibliography, the parties concerned are of unequal birth, either the maiden is of humble birth and the swain of noble blood or *vice versa*.[42]

A similar story is related in the Teifi Valley about a man by the name of Morgan Jones of Dolau Gwyrddion, not far from Lampeter. The version given in D. Stanley Jones's book, *Myfyrion ar Fin Afonydd* (1904),[43] is as follows: Morgan Jones was enamoured of Elen, daughter of a certain Sir Watkin Wynne of Dyffryn Llynod, Llandysul. He failed to get permission of the parents, as the maid was descended from the gentry of the district. Both were faithful to each other for ten years, although Elen had been sent three times to France. The young man heard that she was seriously ill with small pox. He visited her during the middle of the night, with the result that he caught the disease. They both died during the same week. It is said that the popular ballad, *Morgan Jones o'r Dolau*, was printed by Siôn Rhydderch, and therefore before 1728.[44]

Popular in Llangynwyd was a tradition about another maid who was forced to marry a man of greater status than the one she loved, namely the second daughter of Gelli Lenor. Her name was Catherine James, and she was in love with a poor man by the name of Siôn Bivan. Her parents wanted her to marry Robert Jenkins, a widower from Ewenny. Bivan had to join the army, and when he was on active service, Catherine's father arranged for another boy from Llangynwyd who was in the army to write a letter to Gelli Lenor with the information that Siôn Bivan had been killed. Then the young girl was persuaded to marry Robert Jenkins, and when they were coming out from the church they met Siôn Bivan. The young lady, however, did not die this time but lived to become the mother of twenty-one children.

---

[42] See *A Bibliography of Welsh Ballads* (London, 1908), p. xii.
[43] pp. 54-55.
[44] 1728 is thought to be the date when Siôn Rhydderch or John Roderick, one of the best known early Welsh printers, ceased printing at Shrewsbury.

A poem Siôn Bivan is said to have composed occurs in one of Cadrawd's manuscripts at Cardiff Central Library:

> Ffarwel fo i Gelli Lenor
> Lle rhoes i droion maith
> I garu'n ôl fy ffansi
> Swrneion lawr gwaith.[45]

Notice the third line. Was this story confused with the Cefn Ydfa one? Ceiriog calls the maid of Cefn Ydfa Catrin (Catherine), and he possessed a poem in which Wil Hopcyn, he said, addressed "Citi fach" (little Kitty). He also referred to another poem on "Y tro cyntaf y gwelodd Catrin". Had Ceiriog got hold of some form of the tale which confuses the Maid of Cefn Ydfa with the Maid of Gelli Lenor? Or is the story of the Maid of Gelli Lenor the origin of the whole thing?

It is evident that a love affair between a poor suitor and a wealthy maid was a common subject in Wales as in other countries. Such stories were popular in Llangynwyd. But why was Wil Hopcyn's name connected with a story of the kind? It is clear that Wil was famous in the parish as an author of love songs. When mentioning a manuscript which contained more than a score of Wil's lyrics Iolo says that he was the author of the sweetest love poems that had ever been composed in Wales. If this was so, it would have been natural to connect his name with such traditional tales, for it is a very common practice in the literary history of every country to devise tales in order to explain the works of a poet. We need only mention the stories which in Wales have been woven around Dafydd ap Gwilym in order to explain his *cywyddau*.[46]

In the year 1841 Mrs. Pendril Llewelyn came to Llangynwyd. She took a great interest in the traditional lore of the parish, and like so many gifted ladies of the time, she was exceptionally fond of romantic stories.[47] Indeed, her own life was a romance. She came of a wealthy family and was well educated.[48] Her parents wanted

---

[45] Farewell to Gelli Lenor, where I made many journeys, over a long period, to make love to the girl of my choice.

[46] See William Owen[-Pughe]'s introduction to *Barddoniaeth Dafydd ap Gwilym* (London, 1789).

[47] Her son, Dr. J. P. Llewelyn of London, was kind enough to tell me that this was true. I would like to thank him for the valuable material he has supplied for this article.

[48] [She was the daughter of Thomas Rhys, headmaster of the Eagle School at Cowbridge and owner of landed property in the same area].

her to marry a gentleman from Scotland, but she chose to follow her
own inclination and marry a poor curate. Thus it is not surprising
that she took an interest in tales of romance. Undoubtedly it was
she who completed the work of connecting the traditional lore of the
parish with Wil Hopcyn, its love poet. She and her husband
searched the local registers to obtain the poet's history and noticed
the entry recording the marriage of the maid of Cefn Ydfa to
Anthony Maddocks. Then the tale began to take its final form. The
next step was to collect as much of Wil Hopcyn's work as local people
could remember, and incorporate it into the tale. An example is a
triban about Ann Llewelyn:

> Mae Ann Llewelyn felen
> Yn fy marnu drach fy nghefen,
> Ond ni all wella'm gwedd a'm gwaith
> Y neidr fraith anniben.[49]

This Ann Llewelyn became the maid "who betrayed his sweet and
stolen interviews with his mistress". I cannot for the life of me
understand how the second line of the *triban* proves that the girl
betrayed the secret. The worst example of all is the verse which is
said to refer to the maid dying in Wil's arms.[50]

Every historian knows that it is extremely dangerous to base the
history of a poet on verses which are attributed to him in his own
neighbourhood. An excellent example of this are the verses recited
in Anglesey at the beginning of the last century in connection with
Goronwy Owen. O. Prydderch Williams (Eryr Mon) says in his
book *Yr Hen Feirdd* (1865)[51] that Ellis Wynne of Glasynys came to
visit Goronwy Owen and seeing his home asked:

> Goronwy'r gwyneb graenus
> Teneu dy law, tyna dy lys?[52]

Goronwy replied:

> Ellis Wynne o Lasynys
> A'i groen yn wynnach na'i grys.[53]

Goronwy Owen was born in 1723, and Ellis Wynne died in 1734.

[49] The yellow-skinned Ann Llywelyn criticises me behind my back; but she, the
motley, untidy snake, cannot improve my appearance or my work.
[50] See footnote 41 above.
[51] p. 32.
[52] Goronwy, man of fine countenance and of slim hands, behold your court?
[53] Ellis Wynn of Glasynys, (a man) whose skin is whiter than his shirt.

The story therefore is completely unfounded. This proves that one cannot depend on traditional poems and tales, and by today biographers of Welsh literary men take care not to depend on such sources. It is, however, exactly what the authors of the *Souvenir of the Wil Hopcyn Memorial*, in telling the story of Wil Hopcyn, are still doing. They quote old *tribannau* and base the poet's history on them, just as men like Eryr Mon did in dealing with Goronwy Owen. It is not surprising to find such methods used in the nineteenth century, but one would expect better and more reliable work in 1927.

After Mrs. Pendril Llewelyn related the story in 1845, all the elements found in such romantic tales were soon added, i.e. cruel parents, confining the maid to her room, sending messages by a servant to her lover, hiding letters in a hollow tree, using blood instead of ink, and the maid languishing after being forced to marry a wealthy man against her will. As previously mentioned, it was Ceiriog's fancy that added many of the details given by Llyfnwy in 1869 and included by Cadrawd in his *History of Llangynwyd Parish*.

But the authors of the *Souvenir* state that the inhabitants of Llangynwyd believe the story. They obtained it, they say, from their ancestors, and they point out places connected with it. All this does not prove anything. Romantic tales are easily spread, and once the romantic writers of Llangynwyd referred to some place in connection with the story, the inhabitants would straightaway be showing it to visitors in order to preserve memory of the Maid's adversity. The cellar where she is said to have been confined is an interesting example of this. In the year 1883 one of the American Welsh came to Llangynwyd and visited Cefn Ydfa. The cellar "in which the maid was imprisoned by her mother so as to prevent her meeting with the young poet"[54] was shown to him. Cadrawd wrote a letter to the *Western Mail* of 22 August 1863 saying that the story of the cellar was all nonsense and that it was Craigfryn Hughes, in his novel *Y Ferch o Gefn Ydfa* (1881), who was the first to mention it. He continued:

> I never heard of the maid being imprisoned in a cellar before I read it in that distorted story.

[54] See the *Western Mail*, 16 August 1883, when Morien quotes from an article which the American wrote in *Y Drych*.

But despite all this the inhabitants showed the cellar to the American in 1883! And Mr. Frederick Evans, Cadrawd's son, says in *Tir Iarll* (1912):

> Some say that in order to break her spirit she was incarcerated in the cellar, which may still be seen at Cefn Ydfa.

Further on there is a picture of the cellar! This is ample proof of how much reliance can be placed on what is related and shown by local inhabitants.

Examples of similar things are found in other places. The story of Gelert, Llywelyn's dog, is one. Mr. D. E. Jenkins in his book on Beddgelert[55] states that it is only in recent times that the story of the man who killed his dog has been connected with Beddgelert. It is a story which, like the one about the poor lover and the wealthy maid, is common in the folk lore of every country. Who, then, connected this story with Beddgelert? Mr. D. E. Jenkins's answer is as follows:

> It was David Prichard, the first landlord of the Royal Goat Hotel, who came into the parish about the year 1793, and hailed from South Wales. He was a man of superior intelligence, and very fond of hearing and relating stories . . . The tale of "The Man who killed his Greyhound" was well known in South Wales, and he soon began to colour it to the village of his adoption.[56]

Then he proceeded to mark the spot where the dog was buried:

> It was he (i.e., David Prichard) along with William Prichard, the parish clerk, and Richard Edwards of Pen y Bont Fach, who raised the stone that is exhibited today on the spot that was afterwards called "The Dog's Grave".[57]

Before long this legend was accepted as part of the old traditions of the district, and if anyone dared to doubt its genuineness, the newspapers would probably state that there was "a difference of opinion among scholars". Hundreds of credulous English and Welsh people come every year to visit the dog's grave, just as they flock to Llangynwyd to weep upon the grave of the maid of Cefn Ydfa.

But doubt about the truth of the Cefn Ydfa story is not something recent. Dr. I. P. Llewelyn, son of Mrs. Pendril Llewelyn, was

---

[55] *Bedd Gelert, its facts, fairies and folk-lore* (Portmadoc, 1899).
[56] Ibid., p. 67.
[57] Ibid., p. 69.

born and bred in Llangynwyd. After I published the first part of this article, he kindly wrote to me and said that the story was nothing but idle nonsense. "I have never believed it," he said. We know what was the opinion of Dafydd Morganwg, a man who knew more about the history of his county than almost any one else of his day. I have already mentioned that Morien had written an article on the point to the *Western Mail* of 16 August 1883, quoting from an article an American had written in *Y Drych*. The following day the leading article of the *Western Mail* dealt with the story, and here are some quotations from it:

> That was a very pretty story our correspondent *Morien* told us yesterday of the pilgrimage recently made by the editor of an American paper to the grave of the "Maid of Cefn Ydfa". A very pretty story, and prettily introduced. The pity is there is so little truth in it . . . So much of the story of the "Maid of Cefn Ydfa" is apocryphal that we might be pardoned if we said that we did not believe a word of it. And the wonder is a "cute Yankee" like the pilgrim who has been recently retailing it should not have found it worth his while to inquire a little into the facts . . . A very slight acquaintance with history is sufficient to make one suspicious of all such legends . . . The case of the "Maid of Cefn Ydfa" is no exception to the general rule. Her parents might reasonably have objected to her marriage with the not over savoury or sober "Wil Hopkin", but she herself married of her own free will another man, who made her an excellent husband. The story of the imprisonment, the blood-writing, and the rest of it is all moonshine.

I have made these quotations in order to show how men of Glamorgan looked upon the story forty-five years ago. It is safe to say that Dafydd Morganwg and the writer of the article in the *Western Mail* represented the opinion of those who had a greater attachment to the truth than to romantic stories.

APPENDIX

CAN Y "GWENITH GWYN"

Myfi sydd fachgen ifanc ffol,
    Yn caru'n ol fy ffansi;
Mi yn bugeilio'r gwenith gwyn,
    Ac arall yn ei fedi:
O p'am na ddeui ar fy ol,
    Rhyw ddydd ar ol ei gilydd,
Gwaeth 'rwy'n dy wel'd, y feinir fach,
    O glanach, lanach, beunydd.

O glanach, lanach, wyt bob dydd,
    Neu fi sy'm ffydd yn ffolach;
Er mwyn y Gwr a wnaeth dy wedd,
    Gwna i'm drugaredd bellach:
O cwyd dy ben, gwel oco draw,
    Rho i mi'th law, Wen dirion,
Gwaeth yn dy fynwes berth ei thro,
    Mae allwedd clo fy nghalon.

Mi godais heddyw gyda'r wawr,
    Gan frysio'n fawr fy'm lludded,
Fel cawn gusanu llun dy droed,
    Fu'r hyd y coed yn cerdded:
O cwyd fy mhen o'r galar maith,
    A serchus iaith gwarineb,
Gwaeth mwy na'r byd i'r neb a'th gar,
    Yw golwg ar dy wyneb.

Tra b'o dw'r y môr yn hallt,
    A thra bo 'ngwallt yn tyfu,
A thra b'o calon dan fy mron,
    Mi fydda'n ffyddlon i ti:
O dywed i mi'r gwir dan gêl,
    A rho dan sêl atebion,
P'un ai myfi, neu arall, Wen,
    Sydd oreu gan dy galon?

WATCHING THE BLOOMING WHEAT

Translated by Mrs. Pendril Llewelyn

A simple youthful swain am I,
　　Who loves at fancy's pleasure;
I fondly watch the blooming wheat,
　　And other reaps the treasure:
Oh! wherefore still despise my suit,
　　Why pining keep thy lover?
For some new charm, thou matchless fair,
　　I day by day discover.

Each day reveals some new-born grace,
　　Or does fond faith deceive me?
In love to Him who formed thy face,
　　With pity now receive me.
Oh! raise thine eyes—one look bestow,
　　Yield, yield thine hand, my fairest;
For in thy bosom, witching maid,
　　My heart's sole key thou bearest.

In deepest woe this day I rose,
　　And sped at morning's gloaming
To kiss each spot where thy fair foot
　　Had in yon grove been roaming.
Oh! raise my head bowed down with grief,
　　With kindest accents speaking,
Than worlds more dear is thy one glance
　　To him whose heart is breaking.

While hair adorns my aching brow,
　　This heart will beat sincerely,
Whilst ocean rolls its briny flow,
　　So long I'll love thee dearly:
Oh! tell the truth, in secret tell,
　　And under seal discover,
If it be I—or who is blest,
　　As thy pure heart's best lover.

Both versions are printed as they appear in Cadrawd's *History of Llangynwyd parish.*

SWANSEA AND MUMBLES RAILWAY:

A BRIEF HISTORY

SOMETIME in the year 1800, Sir John Morris of Clasemont began discussing with other influential Swansea citizens the idea of constructing a railway between Swansea Canal and Oystermouth. Probably in secret and with some trepidation. For railroads which were then appearing in other parts of the country were looked upon with a certain amount of suspicion and distaste.

But the Swansea pioneers were undaunted. In 1803 they committed their plan to paper. A year later they promoted a Parliamentary Bill which became law on 29 June of that year.

The Act read:

> Whereas the making and maintaining of a Railway or Tramroad for the passage of Wagons and other Carriages to communicate with the Swansea Canal near a certain place called The Brewery Bank, within the Town of Swansea in the County of Glamorgan to, or near to, a certain field called Castle Hill, in the Parish of Oystermouth in the said County of Glamorgan and also the making and maintaining of a Branch of such Railway or Tramroad, to communicate therewith, from a certain place near the Mount in the said Town of Swansea, in the County aforesaid, to, or nearly to, Swansea Pier; and likewise the making and maintaining of another Branch of such Railway or Tramroad to communicate therewith from a certain place near Blackpill, to or nearly to a certain place called Ynys in the Parish of Swansea in the said County of Glamorgan.

A point of particular interest about this Act is that the "haling or drawing" of the wagons or other carriages was to be done by "men, horses or otherwise", powers which were sufficient to cover the introduction of steam locomotives nearly three-quarters of a century later. There can be little doubt that it was the earliest Act to be framed in this manner.

At that time, Swansea was a gay resort of fashion with its castle looking down upon peaceful green fields and stretches of golden sand,

and one can well imagine that the idea of laying down miles of iron-work for the purpose of drawing noisy, clanking trucks heavily laden with limestone, coal and iron ore adjacent to the citizens' playground, was not allowed to pass without some opposition.

Within a week of the bill becoming law, on 4 July 1804, the first meeting of the "Oystermouth Railway or Tramroad Company" was held in the *Bush Inn*, Swansea. Sir John Morris announced the list of shareholders (each share being worth £100): the most Noble Henry Charles, Duke of Beaufort . . . five shares; Sir John Morris, of Clasemont, Baronet . . . five shares; John Edmund, of Swansea, Ironmonger . . . two shares; Edward Martin, of Morriston, Gentle-man . . . five shares; Benjamin French of the same, Gentleman . . . four shares; John Jeffreys, of Swansea, Esquire . . . three shares; The Burgesses of the Borough of Swansea . . . five shares.

The original line began in Swansea at a point near the bottom of the Cwm, ran down the Strand to the site of the Royal Institution and thence down Burrows Road to Bond Street, from there it passed along the beach to Gorse Lane and then between the sandbank and Singleton Park to Blackpill at which point it again went along the beach to the Dunns (Mumbles), and then along the road to quarries at the back of the *Ship and Castle* hotel. There was also the branch from Blackpill up Clyne Valley to a spot called Ynys.

Orginally it was not intended to work the line for passenger traffic, but merely for the purpose of developing the iron mines and limestone quarries. Early documents, however, reveal that passen-ger traffic first started on 25 March 1807. This service was provided by a contractor who offered the company a fixed sum "for permission to run a wagon or wagons on the Tramroad for a year . . . for the conveyance of passengers". This was an outstanding event, for it was the first public passenger service by rail in this country, indeed in the world. The distinction of providing this is often credited to the Stockton and Darlington Railway, but this was anticipated by nearly twenty years by the Mumbles line. Evidently the Oystermouth passenger traffic was a profitable venture, for the next year the same contractor and two others jointly offered a greater sum for the renewal of the contract.

In August 1808 Miss Elizabeth Isabella Spence, writer of "novels and accounts of travel", wrote to her friend the Dowager Countess of Winterton:

I never spent an afternoon with more delight than in exploring the romantic scenery of Oystermouth. I was conveyed there in a carriage of a singular construction, built for the conveniency of parties, who go hence to Oystermouth to spend the day. This car contains twelve persons and is constructed chiefly of iron, its four wheels run on an iron railway by the aid of one horse, and is an easy and light vehicle.

But there were other views. Mr. Richard Ayton, in *A Voyage Round Great Britain Undertaken in 1813*, wrote:

We made an excursion to Oystermouth, a village near the western extremity of Swansea Bay, in the tram car, a singular kind of vehicle established for the accommodation of visitors to this place. It is a very long carriage, supported on four low iron wheels, carries sixteen persons, exclusive of the driver, is drawn by one horse, and rolls along over an iron rail-road at the rate of five miles an hour, and with the noise of twenty sledge hammers in full play. The passage is only four miles, but it is quite sufficient to make one reel from the car at the journey's end, in a state of dizziness and confusion of the senses that it is well if he recovers from in a week.

Horses served as the motive power for the first seventy years of the railway's existence. *The Cambrian* of 18 April 1807, however, reported an attempt to drive the tram by wind:

An experiment of a novel kind was made on the Oystermouth Tram-road yesterday, to ascertain the practicability of a carriage proceeding to the Mumbles without horse, by the aid of the wind alone. Some jolly Sons of Neptune rigged a wagon with a lug-sail, and the wind blowing strong and as fair as could be wished, set out from our quay, and after clearing the houses dropped anchor at the end of the tramroad in less than three-quarters of an hour, having come a distance of about 4½ miles.

For some years the line prospered. Then in 1826, a road was made between Swansea and Oystermouth. Passengers flocked to the road's horse buses. The railway went out of service for passengers, and for nearly thirty years the line lay almost derelict, accommodating only a small quantity of goods traffic. For a time passengers had to rely on road transport between Swansea and Mumbles which was provided by James Williams' Royal Mail omnibuses. The first evidence of passenger service being resumed by the Railway Company was in the year 1860.

The passenger railway owed its salvation to George Byng Morris who had owned the railway since 1840 under a mortgage foreclosure. He initiated important developments. In 1855 the line was relaid with edge rails and by 1860 a service was opened between Swansea and Oystermouth.

Then for nearly thirty years the affairs of the railway were turbulent. A veritable "tug-of-war" as to ownership and running rights developed. Even the melodrama of a burglary was reported at the residence of Mr. G. B. Morris. *The Cambrian* of 17 August 1860 said, "a tin case containing some deeds belonging to the Oystermouth Railway Company was found on the adjoining green". This tantalising brief notice may have referred to an event of not great importance, but the reference to the railway deeds might indicate that some rival railway promoter was anxious to know the extent of the documentary evidence of title possessed by Morris.

In 1861, competition was looming up; an Act was passed authorising the Llanelly Railway to provide a railway to run parallel to the Oystermouth Railway from Blackpill to Swansea. By the *Llanelly Railway (Extension to Mumbles) Act* of 1865, this railway company was authorised to build a line which would have competed with the Oystermouth Railway throughout its length. This extension never materialised however.

In 1864, while the Blackpill to Swansea section of the Llanelly Railway was under construction, an agreement was reached to sell the Oystermouth Railway for £20,000 to John Dickson, a railway contractor who was interested in extending the Neath and Brecon Railway to the Mumbles. Dickson was unable, however, to pay the amount by the due date. He was adjudicated bankrupt and the Oystermouth Railway remained in the hands of George Byng Morris. Later, there were to be repercussions over this deal which was to involve the Swansea Improvements and Tramways Company in costly and bitter litigation over a period of many years.

Little had been done in the shape of improvements to the railway system and horses were still being used as motive power. It was not until 1877, when the Swansea Improvements and Tramways Company (established in the year 1873) came to an agreement with Morris to work the Oystermouth undertaking and to pay him an annual rental of £1,600, that things really began to happen. Within six weeks of entering into formal possession, steam traction was introduced.

It should be noted now how the far seeing Act of 1804 with its clause "haling or drawing of wagons to be done by men, horses or otherwise" greatly facilitated the introduction of steam traction, for no further authorisation by Parliament was necessary.

Like many other important advances, this change met with determined resistance. Among those who offered strenuous opposition to the displacement of the horses were such progressive townsmen as Lord Swansea (then Mr. Henry Hussey Vivian), Mr. Lewis Llewellyn, M.P., and the then Mayor of Swansea, Dr. James Rogers. Their main objection was that the engines would frighten the horses, which would bolt and cause danger to life and limb. The company's manager, Mr. Abbott, went to pains to explain that the steam engine it was proposed to use was of a type that, "could be worked without showing any steam, is practically noiseless and shows no smoke because coke is used as fuel. Moreover it is covered in, similarly to an ordinary car and consequently does not frighten horses more than ordinary cars do". Abbott was referring to the famous tramway locomotive brought out by Henry Hughes.

A trial trip was made on 16 August 1877. Hughes' engine, *The Pioneer*, was attached to two large cars containing over eighty passengers and ran at the specified speed of 8 m.p.h. The opponents of steam locomotion on the line subjected the engine to various tests to see its effect on horses using the adjacent road. Dr. James Rogers, the Mayor, who had voiced his abhorrence of steam railway engines, brought the head of his spirited horse to within a couple of yards of the locomotive. The animal never turned a hair and the doctor frankly acknowledged himself satisfied! Regular steam traction began the next day, 17 August.

Alas, the triumph was short lived. John Dickson, through his trustee in bankruptcy, re-appeared on the scene. In order to wind up his affairs, the trustee claimed the right to pay the agreed purchase money to George Byng Morris for the freehold of the Oystermouth Railway. The court accepted this right and in consequence the Railway had to be put up for auction. It was ultimately sold for £31,000 and it transpired that the purchasers were friends of John Dickson. They turned the railway into a limited company called the Swansea and Mumbles Railway Company Limited and put Dickson in charge again. Little time was lost in repudiating the tenancy of the Tramways Company. Legal wrangles ensued resulting in the

Picture of a coach on the Oystermouth Railway, painted by J. Ashford, 1819. This is the only drawing extant of the type of rail vehicle used for passengers in the early part of the nineteenth century

Horse-drawn passenger coach on the Oystermouth Railway *c.* 1865

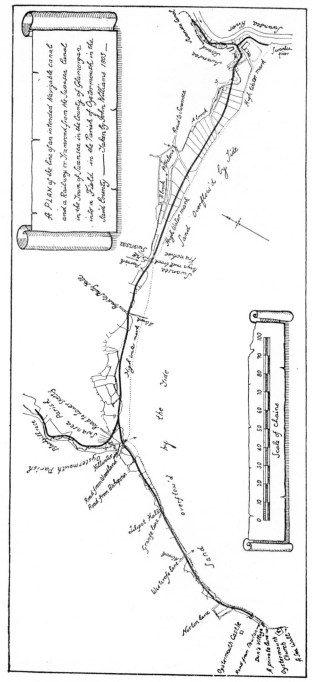

A PLAN of the line of an intended Navigable canal and a Railway or Tramroad from the Swansea Canal in the Town of Swansea in the County of Glamorgan into a Field in the Parish of Oystermouth in the said County. —— Taken by John Williams 1803 —

Scale of chains

0 10 20 30 40 50 60 70 80 90 100

Reduced reproduction of an original plan drawn to scale of 8 chains or 176 yards to the inch

Swansea October, 1804

Oystermouth Tram Road D^r

To Benjⁿ French trõ fwᵈ ... 9. 12. —

Labourers work Cont^d

J Bowen ... 1/4 day ...	2. 6.	
D Evan ... 1 3/4 do ...	3. 6	
W Powell ... 2 1/4 do ...	4. 6	
J Jones ... 4 1/4 do ...	8. 6	
Hen^y Bevan ... 3 do ...	6. —	
Job Morgan ... 4 do ...	8. —	
Evan Jenkin ... 2 1/2 do ...	5. —	
John Jenkin ... 2 1/2 1/6 ...	3. 9	
Williams ... 3 ... 2/ ...	6. —	11.19.9
Enoch Rees making Culvert 3 1/2 @ 3/ ...	10. 6	
Hack & Stone for A & E Williams 4 days 7/	1. 8. —	1.18.6

Moving Gravel for Job

J Rody 230 y^{ds} ... @ 2 1/2 p y^d	2. 18. 4	
do allowed for Extra whd^g 1/2 p do ...	11. 8	
J Lewis 324 yds ... @ 2 1/2	3. 7. 6	
W Roberts 240 do ... @ 2 1/2	2. 10. —	9.7.6

Blocks & Stone for Build^g

Wm Jenkins for 494 Pair Blocks		
trõ from Eyeluck and delid at foot of	24. 14. —	
Canal ... @ 12 p p^r		
W Lewis for 497 pair Stones delivered		
on the Quay ... 12	24. 17. —	
do 40 Perch Stone for Foxhole @ 2/	4. —	
J Walker for Barg^e hire 7 loads @ 2/6	17. 6	54. 8. 6
Enoch Rees for 22 Yards Culvert @ 3/		3. 6. —

Paid Sundry Labourers &c levelling
and marking out the line of the then intended
Canals heretofore in the Sum of 1803 to 1804 } 3. 19. —

Carried forward ... 84. 19. 3

A page from the first cash book in operation on the railway. Benjamin French, mentioned thereon, besides being a shareholder was not only responsible for a considerable amount of construction work, but also it was he who first conceived the idea of carrying passengers on the railway. This idea became fact on 25 March 1807—the earliest known date of the regular conveyance of passengers by rail

An interior view of the decorated coach used by King Edward VI

and Queen Alexandra on a visit to Swansea in July 1904

A train on the Swansea and Mumbles Railway in 1877, headed by Hughes's patent steam locomotive *The Pioneer*. It was as a result of the introduction of this engine that objections to steam working (on the grounds that horses would be frightened) were withdrawn

The decorated coach used by King Edward VII and Queen Alexandra in July 1904

This picture was taken in 1906. The caption said: "Mumbles train nearly full"

The coaches used here were known locally as "The Cattle Trucks". They were of wood, with seats running down the sides and the centre, which were also back to back. They were used as 3rd class travel and for children's outings as can be seen by this photograph.

Accumulator car first used in 1902. It stored its own current, but this method of locomotion proved unsuccessful

Arriving at Mumbles Pier. On the right can be seen the old Winter Gardens where popular concerts were held

Photographs by kind permission of South Wales Transport Co. Ltd.

Swansea Improvements and Tramways Company losing their right to operate steam traction, but allowing them to work horse-drawn vehicles immediately behind the Swansea and Mumbles Railway steam trains.

The position changed again towards the end of 1884. Sir John Jones Jenkins and Robert Capper obtained a lease of the railway, and again the Swansea Improvements and Tramways Company was invited to work the line by steam, for a period of six-and-a-half years. On the expiration of this arrangement, Sir John Jenkins took the working into his own hands. Legal battles ensued, which resulted in the Tramways Company having to work horse cars behind the steam train for a second time.

After costly wrangling the Swansea Improvements and Tramways Company, for a measure of yearly compensation, withdrew the horse-drawn service on the last day of March 1896. That was the last appearance of the horse on the railway.

Meanwhile an important development had taken place. In 1889 the Mumbles Railway and Pier Company was formed to lay a line from the Mumbles Head to Oystermouth and to construct a pier at Mumbles. The railway was opened from Oystermouth to Southend in 1893, and the remainder of the line, together with the pier, was finished in 1898.

The following year a new era opened when negotiations were initiated between the two railway undertakings and the tramways company, in which a controlling interest had by then been acquired by the British Electric Traction Company Limited, at that time pioneering electric tramways in many parts of the country. The result was that the railway and pier were leased to the Swansea Improvements and Tramways Company for 999 years. This placed the tramways company for all practical purposes in the position of owner.

The turn of the century saw the hey-day of the Mumbles Railway. Affectionately known as the "Puffing Billy", it was great fun to undertake the hazardous and adventurous journey to the Mumbles, especially on Bank Holidays. The fact that one could get off and walk alongside it for long portions of the journey only added to the gaiety of the occasion. Many a child earned plenty of coppers by turning "cartwheels" and performing other acrobatic feats alongside the train as it was puffing its majestic way to the Mumbles. The cry "halfpenny o'a penny oh" invited passengers to throw out their money. The train was so full those days that passengers could be seen clinging like limpets to any hand hold—outside the carriages— and even pleased to be able to do so.

During the next few years many changes were made to the railway and the pier and traffic between Swansea and the Mumbles greatly increased. In fact, the pier became one of the most popular resorts in the locality. Attractions provided by the Company were all that a pleasure-seeker could wish for. Concerts, bands, competitions, were held throughout the season, with sacred concerts on Sunday afternoons and evenings.

As all this was going on, the beginning of another chapter in the railway's history was shaping. Research and experiments into other methods and modes of transport were being made. The horse trams in Swansea had given place to an electrified system. An unsuccessful experiment was made to operate specially built battery cars on the railway. When their Majesties King Edward VII and Queen Alexandra came by yacht to Swansea to cut the first sod of the King's Dock, they travelled to the dockside in one of these cars which had had its electrical equipment removed and had now been adapted for use with the steam train.

There was another royal visit to the railway on 19 July 1920 when King George V and Queen Mary opened the Queen's Dock, Swansea.

The ultimate electrification of the railway did not take place until 1929. It is probable that such a step would have been taken many years before, but for the 1914-18 war and its aftermath.

Application was made in July 1924 to the Ministry of Transport, under the *Railways* (*Electrical Power*) *Act*, 1903, as the result of which the Minister made the following order in May 1925:

> The Oystermouth Railway or Tramroad and Mumbles Railway (Electrical Power) Order, 1925, an order made under the above-named Act to facilitate the introduction of electrical power on certain railways or tramroads worked by the Swansea Improvements and Tramways Company.

The Tramways Company did not avail themselves of the powers given by this Act and in 1927 they assigned the lease of the Railway and Pier to the South Wales Transport Company Limited with the object of securing the co-ordination of all Swansea–Mumbles road and rail services and so avoiding unnecessary and uneconomical

competition between the two forms of transport. The South Wales
Transport Company immediately took in hand the electrification of
the line. Many not very apparent difficulties had to be overcome in
carrying out the work of electrification but the sympathetic support
received from the Swansea Corporation greatly facilitated it. In
March 1929 the last steam trains ran over the Mumbles Railway and
electrified services began. Thirteen double-decked cars were in use,
each seating 106 passengers; 48 on the lower saloon and 58 on the
upper deck. They were easily the biggest electrically-driven tram-
way-type cars built for service in this country. There was an entrance
platform and staircase at each end, both entrances being on the land-
ward side. A train might be composed of one or two of these
coaches, so that a maximum of 212 seats could be available for any
journey.

There is no record of any signalling or other safety devices having
been used prior to the electrification of the line, but in order to overcome severe speed restrictions which would have been imposed by the
Ministry of Transport something had to be done. Eventually an
automatic block signal system was installed, the signals being set by
the car's pantograph touching a contact-maker which energised the
signalling circuit. At the same time other light signals were brought
into use, to indicate whether the points at passing loops were securely
locked. It is believed that the introduction of this type of signalling
was unique to a light railway.

In the subsequent years, the railway rendered yeoman service;
it probably reached its peak during the war years of 1939-45 when
petrol rationing made it almost impossible for cars to be used and 'bus
services had to be reduced. With the easing of restrictions and their
ultimate abandonment came the decline of passengers using the
railway. More and more car owners meant fewer and fewer train
passengers and naturally a subsequent loss of earnings. Not only
did the traffic fall but costs increased alarmingly. The railway began
to lose money. It had to be subsidised by the rest of the South
Wales Transport undertaking; in effect, the bus passenger. So just
as steam had ousted the horse, just as electricity had ousted steam, the
internal combustion engine was ousting electricity. The 1950's saw
marked developments in the motor bus. It got bigger and better.

Meanwhile, on the Mumbles Railway there was first a gradual
and then a steep fall in traffic. This, allied to a rapid increase in

operating costs caused the directors of the South Wales Transport Company to order a thorough investigation of the railway. Arising from this it was found that to keep the trains going, no less a sum than £350,000 would be needed. The fact had to be faced, the Mumbles Railway could not earn its keep, and with great reluctance the directors decided to close the undertaking and supplant it with services of modern, well-equipped motor buses. The last day of operation by the railway undertaking was 5 January 1960.

We have recorded briefly in cold facts the important stages in the development of the Mumbles Railway, but coupled with that history was a warm and human relationship between the Railway and the residents of Swansea and Mumbles. Possibly because it was to many a symbol of happiness by the seaside. Not surprisingly then, when its ultimate fate was announced, there was a distinct feeling of personal loss. In its passing it laid down the mantle of the "Oldest Surviving Passenger Railway in the World" but no one can take from it the proud title of being the "First Passenger Railway in the World".

ACKNOWLEDGEMENT

Thanks are extended to the South Wales Transport Co. Ltd., Swansea, through whose kindness this article and the illustrations which accompany it are reproduced.

INDEX